The Vistas of American Military History 1800-1898

A team of leading American military historians here investigate the factors that shaped the United States Army in the nineteenth century.

Throwing new light on its history, this deeply researched book explores a multiplicity of themes. These include the social structure, command system and relationship with civil power, which are all important in assessing its efficiency and behaviour in war. Also considered is the way the army is depicted in military literature and cinema, which affects its social portrait.

Deliberately exploring neglected themes, this key work includes discussion on:
- the roles of the many volunteer colonels in the Mexican War, 1846-48
- Robert Wettemann and the alleged 'isolation' of the US Army in the nineteenth century
- John Ford's famous 'cavalry trilogy' of motion pictures.

Containing so much food for thought for students of US history and military history, this is an entertaining as well as instructional book.

This book was previously published as a special issue of *American Nineteenth Century History*.

Brian Holden Reid is Professor in the Department of War Studies, King's College, UCL, London, UK

Joseph G. Dawson III is Professor of History at Texas A&M University, College Station, Texas.

The Vistas of American Military History 1800-1898

Edited by Brian Holden Reid & Joseph G. Dawson III

LONDON AND NEW YORK

Published 2007 by Routledge
2 Park Square, Milton Park, Abingdon, Oxon OX14 4RN
52 Vanderbilt Avenue, New York, NY 10017

First issued in paperback 2018

Routledge is an imprint of the Taylor & Francis Group, an informa business

Copyright © 2007 Taylor & Francis

All rights reserved. No part of this book may be reprinted or reproduced or utilised in any form or by any electronic, mechanical, or other means, now known or hereafter invented, including photocopying and recording, or in any information storage or retrieval system, without permission in writing from the publishers.

Notice:
Product or corporate names may be trademarks or registered trademarks, and are used only for identification and explanation without intent to infringe.

British Library Cataloguing in Publication Data
A catalogue record for this book is available from the British Library

Library of Congress Cataloging in Publication Data
A catalog record for this book has been requested

Typeset in Minion by Genesis Typesetting Ltd, Rochester, Kent

ISBN 13: 978-1-138-88199-0 (pbk)
ISBN 13: 978-0-415-37319-7 (hbk)

CONTENTS

Introduction
The Vistas of American Military History
Brian Holden Reid   1

1 **Part 1: General Themes**
The Commanding Generals and the Question of Civil Control in the Antebellum U.S. Army
William B. Skelton   15

2 John M. Schofield and the 'Multipurpose' Army
Robert Wooster   35

3 A Part or Apart: The Alleged Isolation of Antebellum U.S. Army Officers
Robert P. Wettemann, Jr.   55

4 **Part 2: Special Subjects**
How the Army Became Accepted: West Point Socialization, Military Accountability, and the Nation-State During the Jacksonian Era
Samuel J. Watson   81

5 Leaders for Manifest Destiny: American Volunteer Colonels Serving in the U.S.-Mexican War
Joseph G. Dawson III   115

6 Soldiers of the Pen: The Literary Careers of Richard Taylor, John Bell Hood, and W. H. Tunnard
Glenn Robins   143

7 'Romantic isn't it, Miss Dandridge?': Sources and Meanings of John Ford's Cavalry Trilogy
Frank J. Wetta and Martin A. Novelli   161

Notes on Contributors   185

Index   187

INTRODUCTION

The Vistas of American Military History
Brian Holden Reid

The following collection of essays on American military history, or more accurately, on the interpenetration of the military in American life more generally, has been aimed at scholars of US history who are not military historians. This group might include those who are interested in military affairs but would not regard themselves as specialists, those who have no great interest in the subject, and indeed those who would not regard themselves as interested in the matter at all (at any rate until they open these pages, it is hoped). Even a cursory glance at this book should reveal how the study of the military dimension has an impact upon the study of the perennial and urgent issues that engage historians of the United States in the nineteenth century.[1]

Military historians in the US are not alone in thinking themselves an unappreciated and even shunned minority whose work is at best under-valued, at worst treated as if it should be distributed in the proverbial plain, brown paper wrappings. Younger American military historians sometimes express envy at the high public profile of such scholars in Britain, and the honors lauded on figures like Michael Howard and John Keegan. They also feel that new directions in the subject tend to be pioneered in Britain. Strong grounds exist for believing that such a defensive outlook is unnecessary (and it is absent from the work that appears here). Two of the most distinguished American historians, James M. McPherson and David Hackett Fischer, write excellent military history within a social, political, economic and cultural context; they both lack formal training in the subject but are attracted to military affairs because of their intrinsic importance.[2]

The authors of these studies are a blend of the senior and established with younger, rising figures who are sure to make a profound impact on the subject. It is perhaps as well to clarify at the outset what they are *not* writing about. There are no essays on defense policy or strategy or their correlation with foreign policy. This is an area that has attracted political scientists who explore the relationship between federal institutions and the American propensity either to make war or to desist from it.[3] Indeed, there is virtually nothing on operational military history, the battles and campaigns in which Americans were engaged during this period (including the momentous actions of the Civil War). The last two contributions, however, do reflect upon the way in which the experience of war has been recorded, embellished and represented in both written and visual form. Operational military history is, of course, a perfectly legitimate area of study: we cannot hope to understand either military men (and increasingly women, too) or their institutions unless we study, analyze and assess their conduct of warfare – after all, their *raison d'être* in the first place. Indeed, straightforward operational military history, spearheaded by the final works of the late Russell F. Weigley, has undergone a major revival in recent years.

The approach adopted here is more concerned with delineating the significance of the military dimension for American society. Thirty years ago or more such an approach would have been branded a contribution to the 'new' military history, that which seeks to explore the relationship between 'war and society.' The label 'new' is immediately appealing, suggestive of not just novelty but innovation, resulting, it is assumed, in sharper perception and understanding. But such a label is also transient, for the approach is no longer new but has garnered some luscious fruits; also historians should hesitate before assuming that it is the only way to explore the American military past. Certainly, no such claims are made here. One essay, for instance, continues to reflect the strong biographical tradition that has so characterized the study of military history.

This Introduction has not merely sought to summarize the contents of each contribution, but also attempts to establish the links between them and explore the issues they raise, and offers a signpost that will direct attention towards areas of historical controversy (especially those areas where the contributions are likely to disagree). It thus aims to review the subject area generally and offer thoughts on subjects that still require research or reappraisal.

In seeking to establish and clarify the links between the military and American society, the contributors (all of whom are American except for one of the editors) are reflecting some deep currents in American thought. The philosopher, William James, wrote an influential essay before World War I entitled, 'A Moral Equivalent of War,' in which he argued that the moral virtues associated with waging armed conflict were an adhesive that bound disparate societies together. He thought that they should be introduced to invigorate the arts of peace – not least the challenges posed by irrigation and land reclamation, the construction of roads, and all the measures that improve what historian Merle Curti terms 'our essentially unplanned culture.'[4] But the Introduction will attempt to explore these matters in a comparative way, not simply because the comparative approach assists in the development of broader perspectives, but also because the central features of the American military tradition were inherited from Great Britain. Consequently, the comparison with the British Army is the most instructive.[5]

The first, if not the central theme of this collection is that the nature of American civil–military relations has largely determined not just its military institutions but its social life. The majority of contributors return repeatedly to the widespread fear (inherited from Britain but accentuated by the experience of the American Revolution, 1775–83) of standing armies and the hostility towards military professionalism this generated throughout the nineteenth century. The US and Britain have been remarkably immune to the ambitions of 'the man on horseback.' Oliver Cromwell, the Lord General and later Lord Protector (1649–58) exercised a measure (of comparatively mild) military dictatorship, although he continually sought to restore Parliamentary sovereignty. Nonetheless, this type of rule came as such a shock to Anglo-American political culture that Cromwell (not, after all, a regular but a volunteer officer), and the standing and highly proficient army became a model henceforth for all progressive societies to avoid. In both Britain and the US the marked hostility to military professionalism as the possible harbinger of military dictatorship – evinced, for instance, by the Duke of Wellington (Prime Minister, 1828–30) in his defense of the purchase of commissions – did not prevent its inculcation in the two armies in the years 1830–50 especially.[6]

Any discussion of the threat of a military *coup* should also take into account the experience of newer, emerging states. In the 1960s and 1970s the new states (especially those of Africa) had very few highly educated or well-trained members of professions save those in the ex-colonial armed forces (in some ways this problem has worsened over the last 40 years). Almost the only Africans who had any experience of complex bureaucratic structures were civil servants, and former non-commissioned officers and their troops. After independence these former NCOs became officers, and thus had the self-confidence (unlike the civil servants) to challenge professional politicians when the economies of the new states began to totter and then crumble. The American case was one of far more widely diffused education and incomparably higher levels of organizational experience in commerce, agriculture, law, and governance, over longer periods of time. It is argued below that the United States Military Academy at West Point developed as the basis for an informal, national administrative cadre.[7]

Nonetheless, the political controversy that resulted from the rise in the US Army's professional stature threatened not just to reduce it to the margins of the policy debate but to damage its central institutions. William Skelton makes abundantly clear in his magisterial analysis of the troubled role of the commanding general that ferocious disputes touched the very highest levels. He (and other contributors) stress that the most important figure who attempted to give the US Army durable institutions was John C. Calhoun, the Secretary of War in the administration of James Monroe (1817–25). Calhoun's biographers have failed to give this chapter in his life the attention it deserves. Calhoun, one of the few able, innovating secretaries of war before Jefferson Davis (1853–57), unwittingly introduced the most aggravating issue in American civil–military relations at the highest level when, in 1821, he rather casually ordered Major General Jacob Brown to take command of the Army after the reductions of that year.

Calhoun had previously created a series of staff bureaus – the adjutant and inspector general, quartermaster, engineering, medical, subsistence and pay – which were based in Washington DC and provided the Army's logistical sinews. Its command and administration became separated, and Calhoun hoped that a commanding general would bring unity to the system and act on behalf of the civil power. This vision could never be realized because the chiefs of the bureaus tended to by-pass the general-in-chief and report directly to the Secretary of War. Calhoun's successors were happy to encourage this practice because it increased their power over the Army.

The serious disputes that developed subsequently reflect on a whole range of matters that were thrown up by emerging military professionalism. What should the commanding general actually do? His role remained curiously undefined. His duties were never detailed, and the position is not mentioned in the 1821 General Regulations (ironically drafted by Brigadier General Winfield Scott who held the position for two terms before 1861); moreover, it figures in neither legislation nor the constitution. Commanding generals were wont to emphasize their role as head of the regular army by imploring their officers to steer well clear of politics. Yet commanding generals Winfield Scott and Ulysses S. Grant were presidential candidates in 1852 and 1868 and 1872 respectively. A third, William T. Sherman, had a nomination for the taking but lacked a thirst for the office, while a fourth, Nelson A. Miles hankered for it too openly for political comfort.[8]

The failed candidate, Scott, had to endure the indignity of having to work for the administration of a victorious candidate, Franklin Pierce, who had served without distinction under his command in the Mexican War, and who had gone on to defeat him in the presidential election of 1852. His sulkiness doubtless contributed to the sour atmosphere and heated disputes that erupted after the appointment of Jefferson Davis, a close confident of the president, as Secretary of War. The American Army, like the British, is prone to claim that it is uninterested in political activity while remaining politically engaged.[9]

Both these countries came very late to the general staff revolution of the last half of the nineteenth century. The role of the general-in-chief (or general commanding, then after 1887 commander-in-chief in Britain, a position that remained in the hands of a member of the royal family, 1856–95) rather obscured the significance of these developments. The Prussian general staff system fused command and administration of great armies. In the US confusion over the duties of the commanding general marked the Civil War. Should he behave like a superior field commander, as Grant did in 1864–65, or should he administer as Henry W. Halleck did (to much opprobrium in 1862–64)? In 1864 Halleck even received the title Chief of Staff, but did not preside over any cohesive general staff. The head of the bureaus reported (temporarily) to Grant, not to him. These complex matters are in urgent need of reassessment.[10]

A case study of one of the most politically astute yet neglected commanding generals, Robert Wooster's attractively written and cogently argued reappraisal of John M Schofield, reveals the degree to which the challenge of the Civil War did not solve the structural problems that continued to haunt the US Army. Schofield actually served for two months as Secretary of War at the end of Andrew Johnson's term long before his appointment as commanding general in 1888. After Grant's election to the presidency in 1868, Schofield ordered the heads of the bureaus to report to Grant's successor as commanding general, Sherman; but his orders were hurriedly withdrawn by Grant's nominee as Secretary of War, John A Rawlins, who served briefly before his premature death in 1869. Thus the contest between Scott and Davis was renewed between Sherman and Rawlins' successor, William W. Belknap.[11]

These disputes had one other striking legacy. The post-1865 Frontier Army's main priorities were focused on duties that were often far from martial, mainly involvement in building projects, such as roads, canals, and the improvements to rivers, or serving as the standard bearer for American values in unruly, violent country. It served primarily as a frontier constabulary, regulating the relations between the Indian tribes and the expanding frontier population, and sometimes between feuding groups of settlers whose interests were in conflict. Periodically it sought the forced removal of Indians to reservations. Combined with the important police duties it carried out during the military occupation of the former Confederate states, 1865–77, this experience produced the type of army that showed itself capable of meeting a wide variety of challenges – a 'multipurpose' force, to use Wooster's apt term. The term is a good one, first proposed several years ago by another historian, Michael Tate, and then widely adopted by others, including Wooster in his piece. Such a force did not face the likelihood of waging foreign war, at any rate, against a foe of the first rank, and thus became preoccupied with the minor tactics of small unit actions. Here again the comparison with the British Army is revealing: a small force appropriately preoccupied with 'small wars' before the outbreak of the South African War in 1899.

Neither the US nor British armies were faced with the relatively uncluttered priority of preparing for a great war of mass involvement against France, as the Prussian general staff dedicated itself in the years 1880–1914. And both armies, too, were able to avoid facing up to the implications of the general staff system until the organizational humiliations inflicted on them in the Spanish-American War of 1898, and in the early phase of the South African War a year later. Later reforms required the abolition of the positions of commanding general and commander in chief in 1903 and 1906 respectively (although the reform faced greater opposition in the US than in Britain).[12]

Wooster's argument concerning the 'multipurpose' US Army fits neatly into discussion of its degree of alienation, intellectual and social isolation as well as physical isolation, from the mainstream of American life and expanding economy in the nineteenth century. Robert Wettemann deals imaginatively with a sorely neglected subject considering its socio-economic implications. Both Wettemann and Wooster are agreed on the essentials. They both argue that the US Army was not isolated from its parent society. This is a basic question about the American military experience that has revived in importance since the millennium. Contemporary commentators have become anxious that the US Army has become dominated by evangelicals since the Vietnam War, and appears to hold in contempt the values of contemporary urban America, supposedly liberal, materialistic, relativist and hedonistic.[13] With its contemporary resonance, discussions of this theme are likely to be regarded as offering important insights into the historical experience of the US Army. Both Wooster and Wettemann acknowledge the importance of an influential article written by John M. Gates in the Journal of the US Army War College.[14]

Gates completed his research for this article while on a sabbatical year with the Department of War Studies, King's College London, and first offered his findings in

1978 to the Military History Seminar at the Institute of Historical Research, University of London. Gates challenged the conventional wisdom of a gloomy, introverted, and quite disillusioned US Army that had become the standard fare of broad, synoptic histories.[15] Wettemann believes that Gates' (and Wooster's) argument can be extended back in time and further developed. Once again John C. Calhoun can be identified as a signal influence on the Army's fortunes. Wettemann identifies the passage of the General Survey Act (1824) as the prime stimulus for the constructive engagement that he identifies. The Act empowered the president to appoint officers to carry out civil internal improvements. The United States Military Academy at West Point provided the only pool of scientifically equipped engineers in America.

Jacksonian Democracy directed its ire at elites and intellectuals, and West Point graduates offered inviting targets as they personified both. In his Maysville veto Andrew Jackson attacked not only internal improvements but the army officers who worked on them. They were ordered to return to their regiments by the Secretary of War, Lewis Cass. In 1836 Franklin Pierce, who had always interested himself in military affairs, argued that any system that permitted a significant number of graduates to leave for jobs in civil life must be inefficient and need reform. Actually, the number of West Pointers who left shortly after graduating is much smaller than is commonly believed. But despite the savage denunciation they faced, army officers continued to work on a significant number of national building projects and did so throughout Jackson's presidency. It was left to Martin Van Buren in 1838 to prevent any serving officer from offering their services to incorporated companies to aid in the completion of internal improvements.

The contributors to this Special Issue have not always agreed on the dimensions and degree of isolation that the US Army experienced during the first half of the nineteenth century. Those disagreements are not evident here (although they can be identified in the footnotes). Samuel J. Watson's essay is wholly consonant with the approach of Robert Wettemann. His is an important essay, a careful and scholarly exegesis based not just on a wealth of knowledge of the military dimension but on an impressive grasp of the historiography of the early Republic. Watson explores the nature of professionalism by reference to the concept of 'socialization.' Towards the end of the essay he discusses in detail the ethos of the United States Military Academy at West Point. Throughout he argues that the US Army had become generally accepted in American political culture before 1846. This overarching thesis permits him to develop a subsidiary argument, namely that such assurance was dependent on civilian tolerance of the military's own view of its professional status.

Watson does not ignore the critics of West Point. They frequently turned its virtues on their head and called them vices. West Point encouraged meticulousness and painstaking attention to detail. The latter could be regarded under the pressure of a great war as a self-defeating obsession with trivia at the expense of the great questions of the hour. In 1862 northern congressional critics of West Point alleged that West Point graduates failed to display the breadth of imagination and flashes of intuition required to bring the Civil War to a rapid, victorious conclusion. Watson argues (quite rightly) that a more convincing explanation than their education as cadets, is the utter inexperience of generals such as George B. McClellan and Don Carlos Buell in conducting large-scale operations. These demanded such a great psychological leap in the dark that it is not surprising that both sought escape in the contemplation of logistical detail.[16]

Watson emphasizes that the Radical Republicans were really suspicious of the political attitudes (and ambitions) of West Pointers. The Radicals were frequently former anti-slavery Whigs, such as Benjamin F. Wade, but in their attacks on West Point they showed themselves the spiritual heirs of Jacksonian Democracy. Watson's careful analysis shows that the charge that West Point created an 'aristocratic' elite was not baseless. The great majority of cadets sprang from upper middle class, professional or office-holding backgrounds. Some cadets came from families whose status had dropped to that of genteel poverty – here Robert E. Lee is a good example, whose mother made the most of political and social connections in Washington DC to further her son's fortunes.[17]

The savage anti-elitism and anti-intellectualism of West Point's critics and their preference for the 'school of experience' forms an American variation on the British radical assault on the Army at the same period. Members of the aristocracy and gentry, by definition, could not be accomplished professionals but only inert fops and wastrels. The comparison is not exact since in the American case Radical critics came close to arguing that specialized military education was useless: it generated stupidity and pedantry, whereas in Britain the critics argued for more military education, not less, as a means of advancing merit; in the US the argument was made that military study blocked merit because West Point graduates laid claim to a monopoly of military sagacity. But the source of the suspicion is identical, namely the prejudice that the 'aristocrat,' however defined, is incapable of manly, good, and timely judgment, but must be an effete, feeble dunderhead. As one critic of West Pointers wrote vehemently, 'Their caution is educated until it is hardly distinguishable from cowardice.'[18]

Watson argues that such tensions were the result of a half-formed democracy. Congress had the opportunity to amend the West Point appointment process should it have seen fit to do so but it left the system alone. It lay exclusively in the hands of the Secretary of War, but from the mid-1820s congressmen were increasingly consulted. Watson suggests that one measure of the Army's accountability during the 1830s (a measure of increased professionalism) lay in its ability to respond to congressional audit. Just as in our own day, officers then spent far more time compiling statistics and filling out forms justifying expenditure than they did with their troops. Watson reminds us that in terms of corporate structure (despite its small size) the purchasing power of the US Army was greater that that of any other American institution before 1846.

Joseph G. Dawson III's contribution represents the obverse side of the coin from Watson's. He examines the background of the volunteer colonels who served during the Mexican War (1846–48). His approach is influenced by the model provided by his mentor, T. Harry Williams, *Hayes of the Twenty-Third* (1965), a study of a Civil War colonel, Rutherford B. Hayes, the later president.[19] Dawson thus offers a valuable case study of the 'interpenetration' of the military in American political and social life. The Whig Party, of course, opposed the Mexican War, but 14 out of a total of 64 of the colonels were Whigs. The Whig Party dominated the colonelcies of Virginia, North Carolina, and Kentucky. The colonels represented three broad types: those who had previously served in the regular army, those who had a distinct party allegiance, and those who had previously held political office. They included eight sitting or previous members of the House of Representatives, two former state governors, and one lieutenant governor.

Regimental command offered numerous attractions to professional politicians, not least the chance to display courage and leadership that would advance their causes in future elections and add to their names a glamour that is acquired from a whiff of gunpowder. Dawson deals judiciously with the varying levels of military skill that the colonels brought to their duties. Even if their troops derived little benefit from their presence, there can be no doubt that their political careers prospered from the martial connection. Of the 58 surviving colonels, no less that 30 sought election or a political appointment in the years 1848–65. Fifteen of them would later serve as general officers in the Civil War (nine for the Confederacy, six for the Union). Dawson has made an important contribution to our knowledge of middle ranking officers by opening up a neglected topic for further research – especially on the Union side in the Civil War.

The last two essays consider the way in which American military experience has been evoked in both print and motion pictures. Glenn Robins offers an absorbing study of intellectual history in delineating the philosophical and intellectual framework utilized by writers dedicated to the Lost Cause. This is a style of writing that has had and doubtless will continue to have an important influence on the writing of Confederate history. Historian Mark Grimsley believes that its associated network of mythology meets a deep-seated need in the human (and not just American) psyche, particularly the desire to admire a valiant underdog who puts up a stout fight before being overwhelmed by a mighty power; but the pluck and skill of the loser is such that it holds out the prospect that defeat is not inevitable. Hence the appealing sense of tragedy and unfulfilled achievement that is an important component of the Lost Cause canon.[20]

Robins explores its nature by reference to three works, Richard Taylor's *Destruction and Reconstruction* (1879), John B. Hood's *Advance and Retreat* (1880), and W. H. Tunnard, *A Southern Record: The History of the Third Regiment Louisiana Infantry* (1866). Robins argues that the Lost Cause is not simply an outpouring of sentimentality based on various degrees of overt racism. He suggests that it is a compound of Reason and Romanticism. These elements are not contradictory, Robins maintains, because the first provides the basis for a useable past for Southerners, and the second facilitates the use of dynamic, self-conscious, and striking images. One immediately thinks of Charles Marshall's description of Robert E. Lee at the climactic moment of the Battle of Chancellorsville as 'having ascended to the dignity of the gods.'[21] Such pictures in words, especially once Confederate victories turned to defeats, convey a sense of noble suffering for ideals that characterizes Lost Cause writing.

Robins' choice of writers ensures that his focus is not exclusively on the Eastern theatre. He notes the influence of the works of Thomas Carlyle on Richard Taylor's treatment of the great figures of the Civil War. He appropriated Carlyle's concept of 'sincerity' as the distinguishing mark of a hero. This attribute is exploited to settle old scores (that go back to his father's presidency, 1849–50) with the Confederacy's vice president, Alexander H. Stephens. Stephens is found very deficient in the quality, but Lee, Stonewall Jackson, and General George B. McClellan have it in abundance. Taylor also places himself in the same spiritual category as the first heroes of the Confederacy by depicting his defiance of the Northern material and technological superiority on the Mississippi River and elsewhere. He thus links himself with those Confederates who displayed superior generalship but claimed to have been defeated by superior resources alone – an equation that the Lost Cause assumed as a given.[22]

Robins' choice of a writer that exemplified the Enlightenment is an odd one – John B. Hood – not a general often identified with cerebral dexterity. Hood's *Advance and Retreat* is a thinly disguised diatribe against the violence done, not to the enemy, but to the integrity of the historical record by Joseph E Johnston in his *Narrative of Military Operations* (1874). Hood had a great deal to conceal as well, but Robins focuses on his exchange with Sherman after the latter's expulsion of the civilian population from Atlanta in the autumn of 1864. Hood refers to various Enlightenment authors: Grotius and Vattel (as well as Sir William Napier and Henry W. Halleck). Vattel's concept of the limitations that war required fitted with Hood's notion of how wars should be fought honorably.

W. H. Tunnard is the least known but in many ways the most interesting of the authors selected. He was highly educated and refined but never held a rank higher than sergeant. He thus serves as a splendid counterpart to the two generals. Tunnard explores the harsh reality of war without sentimentality. He, too, elevates sincerity and honor as the hallmarks by which the Confederacy's actions should be judged. He reveals no disillusionment with the cause he has chosen to champion. He could never be Wilfred Owen or Siegfried Sassoon, but then he was a much more typical Confederate soldier than either of these two poets were typical of the average 'Tommy' in 1917–18.

Robins has undoubtedly identified a major question worthy of much greater attention than it has hitherto received. Why, despite a proportionately greater sacrifice in life than the British endured during the World War I, did the US not experience a period of 'disenchantment' with the Civil War – perhaps after 1877? – as the British did after 1929? Robins shows that the values of the Lost Cause transcended and survived the rise of a New South. Taylor, Hood, and Tunnard argue that Confederate leaders were worthy of admiration and emulation. The New South continued to hail Confederate heroes. Though defeated they continued to receive plaudits rather than the denigration heaped upon victorious British leaders of 1914–18 that continues to this day.[23]

In this volume, post-1865 military history – the 'twilight of the Old Army' or rather, how it has been represented much later – is covered by a study in film history by Frank Wetta and Martin Novelli. They offer a fascinating and evocative discussion of John Ford's famous 'cavalry trilogy' of motion pictures. George Macdonald Fraser, who has robust and sensible views on how warfare is depicted by later generations, has described the cinema as 'the illustrator of the story of mankind.' It is in this spirit that Wetta and Novelli assess the sources of the films, including Remington's paintings. They also compare and contrast the films with the sparser and sharper stories by James Warner

Bellah on which they are based. Ford added the 'love interest' and cloying sentimentality that made them more palatable for a cinema audience.

Yet despite the vein of saccharine, the three films – *Fort Apache* (1948), *She Wore a Yellow Ribbon* (1949), and *Rio Grande* (1950) – are certainly not romanticizations of war let alone of casual violence, despite the frequency of comic (and rather staged) brawls that punctuate the plots, usually involving the non-commissioned officers. While reading Wetta and Novelli's careful discussion of the trilogy's strengths and weaknesses, one cannot turn the page without becoming aware of the incomprehension and ignorance of most film critics when dealing with life in the US (or any other) Army. Several seem to get carried away with their own misguided cleverness – seeming at one point to endorse genocide.

Wetta and Novelli make explicit the Anglo-American comparison underlying this Introduction by explaining that in the 1870s the US cavalry on the Great Plains played a similar role as the British Army in Africa during the Ashanti War (1873–74), against the Zulus (1879), and (most topically since 2001) in Afghanistan (1878–80). At Little Big Horn (1876) and Isandlwana (1879) they both proved capable of making mistakes (not least underestimating their enemy).

The films dwell on failures as well as successes, and taken as a whole they present a beguiling myth of the frontier. Yet it is important to recall, and here the connection with Robins' reassessment of Lost Cause writings is most evident, that a myth is not necessarily an untruth or invention. Ford's three films undoubtedly embroider the past and heighten its colors. However, any scholar with the slightest acquaintance with the British or American Armies will quickly realize that the trilogy offers the best and most authentic depiction of regular soldiering in the 1870s. It succeeds in capturing its elusive 'atmosphere', and this is a major achievement.

How do these contributions influence the way we examine the US Army as a fighting force? What effects did the 'interpenetration' of American society have, with civilian life influencing the military and vice versa? The standard interpretation of American military policy and strategy is Russell F. Weigley's *The American Way of War* (1973). This book was written during the Cold War. It shows the effects of the nuclear arms race between the United States and the Soviet Union, and of a world view shaped by World War II and the Korean War; the Vietnam War had yet to be concluded when it appeared. Weigley saw the American approach to war being influenced by scale, firepower, and a passion for closing with the enemy by employing a strategy of annihilation that sought his complete destruction.[24]

We now live in a very different world, where armies are more likely to be conducting counter-insurgency operations, peacekeeping or the relief and protection of refugees. Any drastic revision of Weigley's approach will doubtless be influenced by this environment. It is obviously the task of an individual scholar rather than a group. Still, the evidence furnished by these studies seems to support the view that Weigley's interpretation does need urgent readjustment. The US Army's heavy involvement in civilian activities during the nineteenth century produced a force that neglected its higher military tasks – strategy and operations – because it was so small and those tasks were not a high priority. Its tasks, moreover, were varied and complex, and consequently the US Army excelled at small operations demanding flexible tactics and high levels of improvisation and initiative. Its most impressive feature was an ability to overcome structural constraints and a lack of preparedness for war in short periods of time. US commanders adjusted to circumstances in short order, although they made mistakes – the Civil War is littered with them. The lack of a standing army had fashioned that defensive caste of mind that many civilians in 1862 found so frustrating.

The stress on such factors represents a very different approach to the subject than Weigley's. It confirms also the relevance of the comparison with the British Army. Both armies during the twentieth century struggled to overcome their inheritance from the nineteenth. Both have displayed what Brian M. Linn has accurately described as 'a great deal of seat-of-the-pants improvisation.' The contributors of this group of studies have illuminated the sources of that particular gift.[25]

Notes

[1] The concept of 'interpenetration' is taken from Watt, *Succeeding John Bull*, 98.
[2] This is a medley of views given as a reaction to a talk, Brian Holden Reid, 'The State of Military History in Britain' to the UNC/Duke Graduate Students' Seminar, University of North Carolina Chapel Hill, 1 March 2005. I do not necessarily agree with this flattering view of British military history, but cite it as evidence of a feeling among American research students of being beleaguered.
[3] An example of the genre is Scott A. Silverstone, *Divided Union*.
[4] James, *Memories and Studies*, 287–91; Curti, *Roots of American Loyalty*. For the influence of James' essay on military thought, see Holden Reid *J. F. C. Fuller: Military Thinker*, 71–2.
[5] Vann Woodward, ed. *The Comparative Approach to American History* still remains the essential starting point for such an enterprise. On the British connection, see Marcus Cunliffe, 'The American Military Tradition', in *British Essays on American History*, edited by Allen and Hills, 210–11; Holden Reid, 'America and War', in *A New Introduction to American Studies*, edited by Temperley and Bigsby, 302–25.
[6] Cromwell had no military experience at all before 1643 (when he was 43 years old). See the essays by Austin Woolrych, 'Cromwell the Soldier', and Derek Hirst, 'The Lord Protector 1653–1658', in *Oliver Cromwell and the English Revolution*, edited by Morrill, 93, 119–24, 138; Hill, *God's Englishman*, 143–5, 175–7; Howard, *Studies in War and Peace*, 61–4; Strachan, *Wellington's Legacy*, 117, 121–2, 130–32, 139–41.
[7] Gutteridge, *Military Regimes in Africa*, 58–9.
[8] Schlesinger and Israel, eds. *History of American Presidential Elections*, III, 944–6, 1250–51, for Scott and Grant's reaction to their nominations. In 1884 Sherman declared unequivocally in responding to warning of an imminent nomination: 'I will not accept if nominated and will not serve if elected.' Twenty years earlier he had observed sardonically, 'If forced to choose between the penitentiary and the White House... I would say the penitentiary, thank you.' Lewis, *Sherman: Fighting Prophet*, 411, 631. On Miles' efforts to gain a presidential nomination in 1904, see DeMontravel, *A Hero to his Fighting Men*, 361–2.
[9] See Strachan, *The Politics of the British Army*, 18–19.
[10] See Holden Reid, 'Command and Leadership in the Civil War, 1861–65', in *The American Civil War*, edited by Grant and Holden Reid, 163–4.
[11] Marszalek, *Sherman: A Soldier's Passion for Order*, 385–9; on the hierarchical confusion, see Holden Reid, 'Civil Military Relations and the Legacy of the Civil War', in *Legacy of Disunion*, edited by Grant and Parish, 157–8.

[12] Jamieson, *Crossing the Deadly Ground*, 4, 121; Wooster, *Nelson A. Miles and the Twilight of the Frontier Army*, 104; Halik Kochansky, 'Planning for War in the Final Years of *Pax Britannica*, 1889–1903' in French and Holden Reid, eds. *The British General Staff: Reform and Innovation*, 12–13.
[13] Loveland, *American Evangelicals and the US Military, 1942–1993*.
[14] Gates, 'The Alleged Isolation of US Army Officers in the Late 19th Century', 32–45. For the historiographical context, see Dawson, *The Late 19th Century US Army, 1865–1898*, 6–7.
[15] For instance, Weigley, *History of the United States Army*, 265, 272–3.
[16] Holden Reid, 'Command and Leadership in the Civil War', 145–6, 151–2.
[17] Holden Reid, *Robert E. Lee*, 47–8.
[18] Williams, 'The Attack Upon West Point during the Civil War,' 498–9; Strachan, *Politics of the British Army*, 14. Strachan also points out the British assumption that 'somehow the British army, but no other army, is saddled [with such people].'
[19] Williams, *Hayes of the Twenty-Third*.
[20] Grimsley, *And Keep Moving On*, 238–9.
[21] Quoted by many biographers of Lee. See, for instance, Dowdey, *Lee*, 354.
[22] Holden Reid, *Lee*, 30, 32, 37–9.
[23] Montague's book, *Disenchantment* was published in the forefront of the 'goodly literature of disappointment' (1) that became a cascade after 1929. On the question of the limited extent to which Owen and Sassoon reflected the views of other officers let alone the rank and file of the British Army on the Western Front, see Bond, *The Unquiet Western Front*, 27–8, 81. For a reaction to the stream of denigration, see Terraine's (1989) Introduction to the reissue of *Douglas Haig: The Educated Soldier*, xiii–xviii.
[24] Weigley, *The American Way of War*.
[25] Brian M. Linn, 'The American Way of War Revisited,' 502–3, 506–7.

References

Allen, H. C. and C. P. Hill, eds. *British Essays on American History*. London: Edward Arnold, 1957.
Bigsby, Christopher and Howard Temperley, eds. *America and War*. 5th ed. London: Pearson, 2006.
Bond, Brian. *The Unquiet Western Front: Britain's Role in History and Literature*. Cambridge University Press, 2002.
Curti, Merle. *The Roots of American Loyalty*. New York: Columbia University Press, 1946.
Dawson III, Joseph G. *The Late 19th Century US Army, 1865–1898: A Research Guide*. New York: Greenwood Press, 1990.
DeMontravel, Peter R. *A Hero to his Fighting Men: Nelson A. Miles, 1839–1925*. Kent State University Press, 1998.
Dowdey, Clifford. *Lee: A Biography*. London: Gollanz, 1970.
French, David, and Brian Holden Reid, eds. *The British General Staff: Reform and Innovation*. London: Frank Cass, 2002.
Gates, John M. 'The Alleged Isolation of US Army Officers in the Late 19th Century.' *Parameters* 10 (1980): 32–45.
Grant, Susan-Mary, and Brian Holden Reid, eds. *The American Civil War: Explanations and Reconsiderations*. London: Longman, 2000.
Grant, Susan-Mary, and Peter J. Parish, eds. *Legacy of Disunion: The Enduring Significance of the American Civil War*. Baton Rouge: Louisiana State University Press, 2003.
Grimsley, Mark. *And Keep Moving On*. Lincoln NE: University of Nebraska Press, 2002.
Gutteridge, William F. *Military Regimes in Africa*. London: Methuen, 1975.
Hill, Christopher. *God's Englishman*. London: Weidenfeld & Nicolson, 1970.
Holden Reid, Brian. *J. F.C. Fuller: Military Thinker*. London: Macmillan, 1987, 1990.
Holden Reid, Brian. *Robert E. Lee: Icon for a Nation*. London: Weidenfeld & Nicolson, 2005.

Howard, Michael. *Studies in War and Peace.* London: Temple Smith, 1970.

James, William. *Memories and Studies.* London: Longman Green, 1911.

Jamieson, Perry D. *Crossing the Deadly Ground: United States Army Tactics, 1865–18.* Tuscaloosa: University of Alabama Press, 1994.

Lewis, Lloyd. *Sherman: Fighting Prophet.* New York: Harcourt Brace, 1932.

Linn, Brian M. 'The American Way of War Revisited'. *Journal of Military History* 66 (2002).

Loveland, Anne C. *American Evangelicals and the US Military, 1942–1993.* Baton Rouge: Louisiana State University Press, 1996.

Marszalek, John. *Sherman: A Soldier's Passion for Order.* New York: Free Press, 1993.

Montague, C. E. *Disenchantment.* London: Chatto & Windus, 1924.

Morrill, John, ed. *Oliver Cromwell and the English Revolution.* London: Longman, 1990.

Schlesinger, Arthur M., and Fred L. Israel, eds. *History of American Presidential Elections.* New York: Chelsea House, 1985.

Silverstone, Scott A. *Divided Union: The Politics of War in the Early American Republic.* Ithaca: Cornell University Press, 2004.

Strachan, Hew. *Wellington's Legacy: The Reform of the British Army.* Manchester University Press, 1984.

———. *The Politics of the British Army.* Cambridge University Press, 1997.

Temperley, Howard, and Christopher Bigsby, eds. *A New Introduction to American Studies.* 5th ed. London: Pearson, 2006.

Terraine, John. *Douglas Haig: The Educated Soldier.* London: Leo Cooper, 1963/1990.

Vann Woodward, C., ed. *The Comparative Approach to American History.* New York: Oxford University Press, 1968/1997.

Watt, Donald Cameron. *Succeeding John Bull: America in Britain's Place.* Cambridge University Press, 1984.

Weigley, Russell F. *The American Way of War: A History of United States Military Strategy and Policy.* Bloomington: Indiana University Press, 1973, reprint 1977.

———. *History of the United States Army.* New York: Macmillan, 1967.

Williams, T. Harry. 'The Attack Upon West Point during the Civil War.' *The Mississippi Valley Historical Review* 25 (March 1939).

———. *Hayes of the Twenty-Third.* New York: Alfred A. Knopf, 1965.

Wooster, Robert. *Nelson A. Miles and the Twilight of the Frontier Army.* Lincoln NE: University of Nebraska Press, 1993.

PART 1: GENERAL THEMES

The Commanding Generals and the Question of Civil Control in the Antebellum U.S. Army

William B. Skelton

One of the least discussed but most important of America's political traditions is civilian control of the military.[1] In contrast with many European nations and the majority of nations in developing regions of the world, the United States has never experienced a military coup d'etat, and direct military challenges to civilian authority have been infrequent and of limited consequence. The most serious exception to this pattern was the so-called Newburgh conspiracy in the closing stages of the Revolutionary War, when a faction within the officer corps of George Washington's Continental Army threatened military intervention in order to win concessions from Congress on pensions and other post-service benefits. However, this was an ambiguous affair, manipulated by civilian politicians as a means to pressure the states into strengthening national authority and eventually quashed within the army itself. Its failure left the tissue of civil supremacy intact.[2] Moreover, the adoption of the Constitution soon afterwards, with its careful division of authority over the armed forces between president and Congress and over the militia between the states and federal government, went far toward permanently institutionalizing the civil-military nexus.

Nevertheless, the very existence of the Constitution cannot fully explain the long-term success of civil control in the United States. Armies in other nations have shown little reluctance to override written constitutions and impose their will when they have perceived the need and opportunity. Surely more important than formal constitutional constraints have been deeper conditions of American society and political culture. One of these was the long-standing Anglo-American distrust of standing armies, rooted in the bitter controversies surrounding the army in seventeenth-century Britain and reinforced in America by the militia tradition and resentment of British use of the army to enforce unpopular imperial policies. Long before the colonies rose in rebellion, colonial legislatures had grown accustomed to restraining the military functions of the royal governors through their control of local taxation, and the bitter experience of British military occupation before and during the Revolutionary War transformed this tradition into a mainstay of American political culture.[3] Indeed, the military clauses of the Constitution largely confirmed established patterns of civil–military relations. Throughout the nineteenth century, the political dangers of standing armies, combined with adulation of the citizen-soldier tradition as a bulwark of American liberty, remained recurring features of popular ideology, especially as expressed by the Democratic Republican and Democratic parties. In the absence of a clear and compelling foreign threat, political antimilitarism guaranteed that the peacetime army would remain small and marginalized, totaling only 10,538 officers and men at mid-century and 27,532 on the eve of the Spanish-American War.[4]

A second factor influencing civil control has been the general stability of American social and political life: the relative absence of the bitter class, tribal, and religious conflicts that plague many developing nations; the centuries-long experience with the electoral process and early emergence of a stable system of party competition; and the density and perceived legitimacy of civilian institutions. While the armed forces have frequently functioned as a domestic constabulary force in the service of the federal government, they have neither seen the necessity nor been offered the opportunity for political intervention to restore order in time of domestic upheaval or arbitrate irreconcilable political controversies. Even the extraordinary conditions caused by the Civil War did not deprive the rival governments of broad popular support or create a power vacuum for the exploitation of an alienated military elite. Only briefly during Reconstruction did the army enter the mainstream of national politics, when Lieutenant General Ulysses S. Grant and other high commanders sided with congressional Republicans in their power struggle with President Andrew Johnson over control of policy toward the defeated southern states. They did so reluctantly, however, in the belief that Johnson's leniency toward the former Confederates threatened the fruits of the hard-won victory, and they returned to their traditional role as soon as Johnson's impeachment acquittal ended the constitutional impasse.[5]

Finally, the internal character of the American military establishment has contributed to the tradition of civil control. While hardly a mirror image of the population as a whole, American officers have generally derived from a broad social and geographic spectrum; thus military leadership has not been the preserve of a particular social class or region that might use military power to acquire or defend a privileged position. Moreover, the officer corps of both major services achieved a rather high level of professionalism during the first half of the nineteenth century, especially in terms of education, socialization, and civil–military interaction. In the army in particular, a major component of this professionalism, instilled at the U.S. Military Academy and reinforced by lengthening career patterns, was a service ethic: a collective sense of public duty and professional responsibility and a commitment to politically neutral service to duly constituted national authority. While officers frequently used political channels to push service and branch interests and seek personal advancement within the military hierarchy, their sense of professional propriety overwhelmingly restrained them from direct challenges to their civilian superiors or interventions into strictly civilian political controversies.[6] In any case, the small size and geographical dispersion of the permanent armed forces until well into the twentieth century insured that they would lack the power to dominate civilian institutions even if they had been so inclined.

The interplay of these factors has established the broad parameters of civil–military relations in the United States, precluding direct challenges to civilian authority. Within these boundaries, however, less threatening types of civil–military friction have been endemic. During the nineteenth century, these tensions were partly cultural, the mutual suspicions inevitably generated by the existence of a quasi-isolated and authoritarian military subculture in the midst of an economically expansive society professing individualistic and egalitarian values. Indeed, military officers' widespread sense of alienation from the civilian mainstream and their commitment to a unique and supposedly superior service ethic provided an important function for the emerging military profession, a means to preserve its identity and cohesion in the face of the disintegrating forces of America's democratic culture. More specifically, civil–military friction arose from the army's domestic constabulary role. Beginning shortly after the Revolution with the occupation of the trans-Appalachian West and continuing to the last decade of the nineteenth century, the peacetime army served mainly as a frontier police force, maintaining order on the Indian frontiers and international borders, establishing national authority in newly acquired regions, supplementing the militia in suppressing internal disorders, and enforcing controversial federal laws. At times, commanders also served temporarily as military and territorial governors, and for several years during Reconstruction they exercised great political power throughout the conquered South. Although regular officers generally acted with professional restraint and responsibility, the complex interaction between military authority and civilian aspirations produced recurrent tensions on the local level and periodically reinforced popular concerns about the dangers of standing armies.[7]

Another area of civil–military intersection may well have become the most problematic: the relationship between the army's chief officers and the nation's high civilian leadership. As Richard H. Kohn has suggested, by the nineteenth century this issue was more of an administrative matter than a constitutional or political issue, in that high commanders made no attempt to challenge the basic principle of civil supremacy.[8] Nevertheless the everyday conduct of military policy and administration produced a good deal of friction, and commanders sometimes did question the character and tightness of civilian control. The center of controversy was the office of commanding general of the army, or general-in-chief, a position occupied by the army's highest ranking officer from its formation in 1821 until its replacement with the army chief of staff in 1903. Though usually stationed in Washington, D.C., and in close contact with the president, secretary of war, and congressional leaders, this officer's powers and functions were never clearly defined, and the position remained throughout the century a source of recurring civil–military tension.[9]

Between the Revolution and the end of the War of 1812, the army's command system was fluid and decentralized. Except for the president, the only official with overall authority over the army was the civilian secretary of war. This office, modeled loosely on the British secretary at war, was a holdover from the Articles of Confederation government, adopted by the first United States Congress in 1789. Lacking constitutional standing, its incumbents exercised informally delegated powers, performing 'such duties as shall, from time to time, be enjoined on, or entrusted' to them by the president, a category that came to embrace the everyday administration of military affairs.[10] The army's senior officers were usually stationed in the West, where they directed the larger concentrations of troops and occasionally conducted quasi-political and diplomatic functions. Only during the undeclared naval war with France of 1798–1800, when George Washington briefly re-entered the army as lieutenant general, did a commissioned officer officially exercise command of the army as a whole, and Washington's service was largely nominal. During the War of 1812, the Madison administration further fragmented command by dividing the country into nine (later ten) military districts, each under a separate general reporting directly to the secretary of war, who continued to play the dominant role in planning and coordinating military operations.[11] In part this loose arrangement reflected the sprawling, amorphous character of American society and the absence of effective internal communication. It also mirrored the traditional suspicion of concentrated military power, a concern at least partially justified by the independent and erratic behavior of some high-ranking officers. The most notorious was James Wilkinson, the army's senior general throughout most of the early national period, who was a Spanish agent, co-plotter with Aaron Burr in Burr's western conspiracy, and a consummate political intriguer.[12]

The army's stumbling performance during the War of 1812 inspired a period of military reform in the postwar years, one aspect of which was a renovation of military administration. Largely through the efforts of John C. Calhoun, James Monroe's secretary of war, the government organized the formerly disjointed supply and support services into a cluster of centralized general staff bureaus – adjutant and inspector general, quartermaster, ordnance, engineering, subsistence, medical, and pay – with their headquarters in Washington, D.C., and headed by permanent chiefs. While legislation did not in all cases specify lines of authority, executive regulations and internal arrangements made these bureaus directly responsible to the secretary of war and through him to the accounting officers of the Treasury Department. Command of the line – the dispersed combat units of infantry and artillery – remained divided between two major generals commanding geographical divisions (northern and southern), who also reported to the secretary of war and who had only limited and indirect control over the staff personnel attached to their commands. By concentrating logistical operations at the capital and imposing tight controls based on the regular submission of standardized reports and returns, this arrangement contributed to an unprecedented degree of efficiency and accountability in routine army administration. It also caused deep resentment among division commanders and other line officers, who claimed that the staff-line dichotomy and the virtual autonomy of the bureaus undermined their authority, violated the hierarchy of command, and was unsuited to the demands of active service.[13]

The office of commanding general was a late and unintended byproduct of post-War of 1812 military reform. In 1820, an economy-minded Congress called on Calhoun for a plan to reduce the army's enlisted strength from its postwar level of 11,709 to 6,000. In a famous report of December 1820, Calhoun opposed any cutback of the present force, strongly arguing the necessity for a relatively large professional officer corps and a regular army geared to preparation for a future war. If a reduction was inevitable, he favored confining it to the rank-and-file and leaving the officer corps, including the two major generals and four brigadier generals of the line then in service, at its present strength. Organized on a cadre basis, the army could thus expand quickly and efficiently in an emergency by filling its 'skeletonized' units with recruits.[14] After a debate laced with traditional anti-standing army rhetoric, the House of Representatives rejected Calhoun's reasoning and voted for an across-the-board cutback of officers and men, keeping only a single brigadier general. The Senate proved more supportive of the army, however, and the outcome was an act of 2 March 1821, which incorporated a diluted version of Calhoun's cadre plan. It cut the army's enlisted strength by over one half but the officer corps by only one fifth, preserved the staff apparatus and regimental structure of a considerably larger force, and retained a single major general and two line brigadiers. Although nothing in the legislation specified the duties of the generals, Calhoun ordered the surviving major general, Jacob Jennings Brown, to Washington, D.C., to assume command of the army, a move intended to bring 'the military administration of the army, as well as its pecuniary, through the several subordinate branches, under the immediate inspection and control of the Government.'[15]

From the very start, the commanding general occupied an uncertain and controversial position in the military hierarchy. Neither Congress nor the administration had anticipated the office, and neither made an initial attempt to define its functions. A strong-willed administrator with presidential ambitions, Calhoun was unwilling to transfer effective control over the army to a commissioned officer, and the already entrenched general staff bureaus resisted any attempt to erode their autonomy. Indeed, the army's General Regulations of 1821, compiled by Brigadier General Winfield Scott and the bureau chiefs prior to the reduction, made no reference to a commanding general, while they confirmed the bureaus' direct relationship with the secretary of war.[16] Even before Brown arrived in Washington, a move was afoot, allegedly abetted by high-ranking staff officers, to abolish the major general's slot as a superfluous sinecure; in 1822 the House debated an additional reduction bill that included a provision to this effect, though this attempt failed.[17] Personally, Brown was not in a position to assert his powers. A self-taught citizen soldier rather than a professional, he had served in the New York volunteers before attaining a direct appointment to the regular army as a brigadier general in 1813. Although he became a national hero for his aggressive leadership in the hard-fought Niagara campaign of 1814 and continued in the postwar army as the senior division commander, he resided mainly at his home in Brownville, New York, where he mixed military administration with farming, land speculation, and politics. Moreover he suffered a severe stroke in October 1821, which left him partially paralyzed and unable to perform his duties for a year and permanently weakened in health.[18]

In effect, the commanding general's role was shaped informally, through interaction among the army's central offices. Under Calhoun and his successor in John Quincy Adams's administration, James Barbour, the secretary of war remained firmly in charge of the army as a whole. Nominally, Brown was in direct command of the line regiments, now distributed between an eastern and a western department. But his command powers were circumscribed from above by the secretary of war and from below by the two brigadier generals commanding departments, who exercised considerable autonomy in stationing their troops and responding to frontier threats. With the exception of the army's two inspectors general, who reported to him on their periodic tours of inspection, and to a lesser extent the adjutant general, the army's executive secretary and chief record-keeper, Brown lacked jurisdiction over the general staff.

By default, Brown's main function was advisory: he served as the principal source of information for the executive branch and Congress on the dispositions, discipline, training, and health of the line army, and through this channel he played a significant role in shaping military policy. Concerned that the dispersion of troops at small and isolated garrisons would undermine the army's readiness, he pushed relentlessly to concentrate forces at a group of relatively large posts, where they could preserve discipline while responding to frontier crises. He also promoted professional military education and was instrumental in the formation of schools of practice for the artillery and infantry, modeled on the schools of application in the French service and intended to provide officers with specialized training in their branches. He regularly advised the president and secretary of war on subjects ranging from the technicalities of military rank and promotion to methods to quell desertion and the defense of the Canadian border. Beginning in 1822, the commanding general submitted an annual report to the secretary of war that evolved into the principal statement of the army's condition and needs for improvement, and it influenced both the secretary's and the president's annual reports to Congress.[19]

By providing a regular channel for the transmission of military information and advice between the increasingly professionalized army officer corps and the nation's civilian decision-makers, the commanding general's advisory role was of central importance in shaping civil–military relations at the high governmental level. Nevertheless, Brown was not altogether satisfied with the function of military counselor and hoped for more extensive powers of command. After Calhoun left the War Department, he expressed his intention to assert control over the general staff bureaus, and he successfully lobbied to have the Artillery School of Practice, which originally reported directly to the secretary of war, transferred to his command.[20] However, Brown's deteriorating health and his ongoing absorption in civilian politics prevented him from significantly expanding the authority of his office.

Brown's death in February 1828 sparked a second movement in Congress to abolish the commanding general's position. In part, the cause was persistent anti-army sentiment, but it may also have been a reaction against the bitter rivalry between the brigadier generals commanding departments, Winfield Scott and Edmund P. Gaines, both of whom lusted for the higher rank and had long engaged in a quasi-public struggle for precedence. Opponents of the office argued that a commanding general was superfluous and an unnecessary expense. In peacetime, his administrative duties were routine and could easily be performed by the secretary of war and adjutant general; retaining the office in time of war might leave the army in the hands of an old and decrepit commander unfit for active service. Dividing the command between two generals of equal rank might also enhance civilian control. In the opinion of one congressman, 'I hope, if we ever shall find a Caesar in the army, we shall also find a Pompey.'[21]

Defenders of the position maintained that a professional commanding officer was essential to the unity and efficiency of the army. In a report of 19 March 1828, the Senate Military Committee spelled out for the first time in detail the functions of a commanding general, stressing his role as 'medium of communication between the government and the army' for all that relates to the army's 'instruction, subordination, equipments, supplies and health.' He also directed the recruiting service and system of military justice and gathered information on the nation's terrain as a basis for advising the administration in case of war. Without a commanding general, these functions would fall to the secretary of war, whose tenure was temporary and who usually lacked military expertise, or to staff officers, 'a kind of substitution which is in all cases offensive, but to military men particularly odious.'[22]

Though approved by the House, the bill to abolish the major general's rank died in the Senate. Late in 1828, however, the House briefly revived the issue, and Adams's second secretary of war, Peter B. Porter, responded with another defense of the position that reflected directly on the civil–military nexus. Basing his argument on the assumption that the main mission of the peacetime army was preparation for a major war, Porter maintained the importance of having a single professional commander stationed at the capital, 'where he can most readily receive the advice and orders of the President, and where he can hold the most direct and expeditious communication with every part of his command.' In the absence of a commanding general, the secretary of war could not perform this function, as 'the Department of War does not form an integral part of the military machine. The numerous civil avocations of the secretary of war would put it wholly out of his power to attend to the daily orders and complicated routine of duties which appertain to the command and discipline of an army.' The result would be an army divided into two independent and potentially conflicting commands, each headed by a brigadier general. Porter's report suggested that the commanding general's functions were not entirely advisory but entailed actual command of the army under the president through a channel separate from the civilian secretary of war.[23]

On 29 May 1828, Alexander Macomb, formerly the army's chief engineer, assumed command of the army as Brown's successor. In appointing a staff officer, President Adams bypassed the brigadier generals commanding departments, whose contentious lobbying for promotion had thoroughly disgusted him. Forty-six years old at the time of his promotion, Macomb had entered the army as a cornet of dragoons in 1799 and served as an officer in the Corps of Engineers during the early nineteenth century. As acting adjutant general of the army in the early months of the War of 1812, Macomb helped direct the wartime mobilization. He subsequently rose to brigadier general and commanded the forces at Plattsburgh, New York, which, together with the navy's Lake Champlain flotilla, checked a powerful British offensive from Canada in the late summer of 1814. He continued in the postwar army as a departmental commander, then accepted a demotion to colonel and chief engineer in the reduction of 1821. In contrast to his predecessor, Macomb was a life-long professional soldier who largely avoided civilian politics and harbored strong opinions on the question of military management. His 13-year tenure as commanding general went far toward shaping the office and defining the issues of civil–military relations for the remainder of the nineteenth century.[24]

Macomb's goal was to command the army as a whole under the president, with at most only loose supervision by the secretary of war. In particular, he sought to bring the general staff bureaus directly under his jurisdiction. A letter to the secretary of war in July 1831 expressed his views. Under the present system, the staff departments had 'no connection with the General in command of the Army, but refer direct to the secretary of war on all matters connected with their duties.' Since the secretary's usually limited tenure in office and absorption in other functions prevented him from exercising close control, the bureaus were virtually independent – so much so 'that one would suppose they did not belong to the same service.' The War Department should make rules and regulations for the army and appoint officers, 'but the command of Troops under the Executive, the maintaining discipline, the preservation of order and economy, the carrying into effect the commands of the Executive in reference to Military movements, properly belongs to the Commander of the Army.'[25]

Macomb's efforts to control the staff bureaus made limited headway. In 1830, he brought the adjutant general, Colonel Roger Jones, before a court-martial for communicating directly with the secretary of war in defiance of Macomb's orders. In his opinion, the adjutant general should function as the commanding general's chief of staff, and the court upheld this position by convicting Jones of insubordination. Macomb ordered the other bureau chiefs to report regularly to him on the activities of their departments and to inform him whenever they left or returned to the capital. He asserted tight control over the inspectors general and, through his assignment of inspection tours, used them to establish his right to oversee staff operations outside the capital, including the military academy, a move that sparked bitter complaints from the elitist Corps of Engineers.[26]

Perhaps the most ambitious step to centralize control occurred in 1832, when Lewis Cass, Andrew's Jackson's second secretary of war and a long-time friend and supporter of Macomb, ordered the formation of the 'Military Board.' Chaired by the commanding general and composed of the bureau heads stationed in Washington, this panel was to meet at the discretion of the secretary to consider questions 'relating to the discipline, police, economy, or expenditures of the Army, or to any other subject connected with Military Affairs.'[27] The motivations for establishing this board are unclear; it may have been an attempt by Cass to provide the War Department with an advisory group comparable to the Board of Navy Commissioners in the Navy Department. However, it certainly conformed to Macomb's ideas on staff centralization, and it suggests the embryo of a modern army planning staff. Macomb likewise presided over other military boards, including the Ordnance Board, a panel consisting of the chief of ordnance and other high-ranking officers, which met on an intermittent basis between 1831 and 1837 to draft a uniform system of ordnance and ordnance equipment for the army.[28]

Most of the topics considered by the Military Board were technical and routine, relating to clothing, supplies, pay, and personnel. One important assignment, however, was revision of the army's General Regulations. Macomb assumed principal responsibility for this project, largely bypassing Winfield Scott, compiler of the earlier system, and he took the opportunity to include an expansive definition of the commanding general's authority that would influence the debate over army command for the remainder of the century:

> The military establishment is placed under the orders of the major general commanding in chief, in all that regards its discipline and military control. Its fiscal arrangements properly belong to the Treasury Department, under the direction of the Secretary of War. While the general in chief will not interfere with the concerns of the Treasury, he will see that the estimates for the military service are based upon proper data, and made for the objects contemplated by law, and necessary to the due support and useful employment of the army. The general will watch over the economy of the service, in all that relates to expenditure of money, supply of arms, ordnance, and ordnance stores, equipments, camp equipage, medical and hospital stores, barracks, quarters, transportation, fortifications, military academy, pay and subsistence; in short every thing which enters into the expenses of the military establishment, whether personal or material.

The commanding general could call on the staff for advice and assistance in performing these duties, and the bureaus were to transmit their annual reports and estimates through the general, who would examine and rework them before passing them on to the secretary of war. In addition, the inspectors general, who reported to the commanding general, were given authority to inspect the staff departments and installations under staff control, including the military academy.[29]

The Macomb regulations, approved with only slight changes by the president in 1836, suggested strongly that the commanding general was to be the actual commander of the army, staff as well as line.[30] With the exception of support for the militia and the civil works projects of the engineers and topographical engineers, the topics falling under the general's supervision embraced virtually all the functions of the bureaus. Most importantly, the manual did not clearly establish the commanding general's subordination to the secretary of war – and in fact separated the two offices' responsibilities, assigning to the general the 'discipline and military control' of the army while leaving the secretary with only its 'fiscal arrangements.' Moreover, no distinction was made between the secretary's fiscal responsibilities and the 'economy of the service,' including expenditures and estimates, supervised by the commanding general. The regulations implied that, in relation to the army at least, the secretary and the general were coequal offices under the president, the general in military command, and the secretary in control of financial administration, serving in effect as chief military accountant.

Macomb's ambitious conception of the commanding general's role, which was rooted of course in the very haziness of the position's legal status, would long influence the debate over civil–military relations at the high governmental level. In practice, however, the general failed to establish his powers of independent command. Beginning in 1834, the army faced a series of crises: a brief war scare with France over President Jackson's demand that France pay debts owed Americans from the Napoleonic wars; tensions with Great Britain over filibustering on the Canadian border during the rebellion in Upper Canada in the late 1830s and later over the disputed Maine–New Brunswick boundary; the conduct of Indian removal, including the bitter seven-year-long guerrilla war in Florida against the Seminoles. Probably because of the pressure of events, the Military Board ceased to meet as a formal body late in 1835, though its consultative and advisory functions continued to be performed informally. Likewise, the War Department restructured the Ordnance Board in 1837, replacing Macomb and the senior staff officers with lower-ranking personnel.[31]

Much of Macomb's early success in asserting his authority stemmed from his close relationship with Lewis Cass. Joel R. Poinsett, secretary of war in Martin Van Buren's administration, was less supportive of the commanding general's claims, and during his tenure the staff bureaus regained much of their former autonomy. In 1837, Poinsett recommended a partial consolidation of the bureaus into a 'staff corps' under a high-ranking chief of staff, a proposal that seems to have built on the precedent of the Military Board and that resembled a prototype of a modern general staff. However, he strongly opposed the idea that the commanding general should assume the role of chief of staff, because the duties of the latter office were incompatible with the 'high functions which the General in chief is called upon to exercise in the Cabinet, and in the field. In every well regulated service these duties are separate, and they cannot be united in one person without impairing the efficiency of both.'[32] Although Poinsett's proposed restructuring of the staff failed to pass, Congress expanded the permanent commissioned personnel of the staff departments by 50 percent in 1838, a move intended to improve the army's field performance by reducing the need for details of line officers for temporary staff duty.[33] One effect, however, was to insulate the bureaus further from the combat arms and lessen even the limited control of the commanding general.

What emerged was a tradition of dual jurisdiction in army management – but one that did not involve the coequal status of commanding general and secretary of war envisioned by Macomb. Instead, the secretary remained the effective head of the army as a whole, exercising powers tacitly delegated by the president, with the general's responsibility largely limited to the line regiments and the autonomous staff bureaus overseeing support, logistics, and financial administration. The separation was never complete: the adjutant general and the inspectors general still reported to army headquarters on most matters, and line officers commanding departments, divisions, and posts constantly strove to control the staff officers attached to their commands. But the basic dichotomy between *command*, the function of the commanding general and subordinate line commanders under both president and secretary of war, and *administration*, the responsibility of the staff chiefs, persisted throughout the nineteenth century, causing endless intraservice and frequent civil–military friction.[34]

Despite his failure to control the staff, Macomb proved to be an influential commanding general. While by no means a brilliant or original thinker, he was the first truly professional officer to hold the high command, and he developed further the advisory and administrative functions of his office. With the exception of brief trips to the Indian war in Florida in 1836 and 1839 and a five-month tour in 1838 to coordinate anti-filibustering operations on the Canadian border, Macomb remained almost entirely in Washington, D.C., in close contact with the president, secretary of war, and congressional leaders. In his annual reports and in numerous letters and memoranda, he provided the civilian leadership with sound professional advice on military policy and procedures, from methods to combat desertion and improve discipline to the adoption of an officer retirement system, the disposition of forces on the Indian and international frontiers, and the conduct of military operations in Florida. During the war scares with France and Great Britain, he oversaw efforts to gather intelligence and strengthen the seacoast defenses, and he advised the administration on expanding the army. Macomb also strove to tighten his authority over the line commanders of departments and other geographical commands, who had a long tradition of independent action and a habit of communicating directly with civilian leaders, bypassing prescribed channels. While a certain degree of autonomy continued, Macomb's persistent efforts, together with improving communication and the general trend in the officer corps toward professional standards, did strengthen the official lines of military subordination and sharply reduce freelancing by commanders in the field.[35]

During his tenure as commanding general, Macomb tested the limits of the office's command powers but in the end settled for a circumscribed role as chief military counselor to the president and secretary of war and conduit of professional information and advice between the army and the nation's civilian leadership – a role well suited to his tactful and ingratiating personality. Macomb died in 1841, and his successor, Brigadier General Winfield Scott, proved to be a far more volatile influence in civil–military relations. Appointed a captain of artillery in 1808, Scott rose to brigadier general in the War of 1812 and emerged as a national hero for his performance during the Niagara battles of 1814. He remained in the postwar army as a department commander and served frequently as an administration trouble-shooter, handling such difficult civil–military problems as the South Carolina nullification crisis, Cherokee removal, and the filibustering troubles on the Canadian border. He also compiled the army's first comprehensive set of general regulations and a manual on infantry tactics adapted from the French system that established his reputation as a military thinker. Despite his extensive military experience and expertise, Scott was something of a throwback in the increasingly West Point-trained, professionalizing officer corps of the antebellum era. He possessed an immense ego and an arrogant, disputatious temperament that embroiled him in continual feuds with public figures both inside and outside the army. Moreover, he was an ardent Whig who pursued the presidency during much of his long career.[36]

Scott's basic conception of his office resembled that of his predecessor. In an 1830 report opposing a reduction of the army, he had strongly argued the need for a professional military commander to insure the symmetry and efficient organization of the army. 'The Secretary of War has not, either by the act creating his department, the rules and articles of war, or any other act of Congress, any *direct* command over the army.' The secretary could only issue orders by authority of the president and in any case usually lacked the military knowledge and continuity in office essential to effective command. The commanding general, in contrast, was 'professionally and minutely acquainted with the history, actual condition, and wants of the service committed to his immediate charge.' After taking office, Scott replaced the Macomb regulations with a revised version of his earlier manual, but he incorporated into it the core of Macomb's ambitious definition of the commanding general's powers.[37]

The first few years of Scott's tenure were relatively smooth: he had the support of the Whig administrations of William Henry Harrison and John Tyler, and he was partially distracted from military affairs by an unsuccessful attempt to win the party's presidential nomination in 1844. The situation changed with the election of James K. Polk, a strong-willed and intensely partisan Democrat who, despite his militantly expansionist foreign policy, had little respect for the regular army or the professional officers who led it. In May 1846, after the outbreak of the Mexican War, Polk reluctantly offered Scott command of the main field army forming on the Rio Grande to invade northern Mexico. Scott accepted the command as his due but was slow to leave Washington for the scene of operations, claiming that he was laboring long hours at his desk to oversee logistics and the mobilization of forces.[38] In fact, the situation revealed a key dilemma concerning the commanding general's role: If he took a field command in time of war, as most commentators assumed, he would effectively forfeit his responsibilities as professional adviser to the government and chief army coordinator, leaving a vacuum at the center of military administration.

During the early stages of the war, this discrepancy did not materialize. Angry at Scott's slowness to take the field – and his tactless, abrasive style of addressing the administration – Polk revoked the general's field assignment, consigning him to pursue his stationary duties at the capital through the summer and fall of 1846. Late in the year, however, the president decided that an invasion of Mexico at Vera Cruz would be necessary to end the war. Scott had earlier submitted a detailed and thoughtful plan for attacking Vera Cruz, and, despite deep reservations, Polk succumbed to the advice of his cabinet to appoint him as the expedition commander.[39] From November 1846 to the spring of 1848, Scott was absent from central headquarters, preparing for and then conducting his dramatic campaign against Vera Cruz and Mexico City. During this period, the administrative and advisory duties of the commanding general fell mainly to the adjutant general of the army, Colonel Roger Jones, who oversaw the mobilization of the volunteer and temporary regular forces and who personally drafted key wartime legislation relating to army organization.[40]

Moreover, President Polk proved to be an exceptionally active commander-in-chief, perhaps the most hands-on war president in American history. Convinced that high-ranking regular officers were opposed to his administration, indeed even obstructing the war effort, Polk intervened continually in the details of military management – planning strategy, selecting commanders, raising troops, directing military movements, overseeing logistics and internal War Department procedures, tracking military appropriations, and browbeating staff officers into enhancing their efforts.[41] He also initiated a bill to resurrect the rank of lieutenant general, last held by George Washington during the Quasi-war with France, with the intention of appointing Senator Thomas Hart Benton, a Democrat with very limited military experience, over the heads of the Whig major generals, Scott and Zachary Taylor. This effort, which might well have turned the army's high command into a political football, died quietly in the Senate.[42]

The war ended in a tangle of civil–military and political recrimination. Late in 1847, after the capture of Mexico City, Scott became enmeshed in a web of politically charged quarrels with high-ranking subordinates, arising largely from the publication of reports and letters intended to inflate the officers' contributions in the battles for the Mexican capital. Furious at what he considered to be Scott's persecution of Democratic officers, Polk removed the general from command of the army in Mexico in January 1848 and ordered a court of inquiry to investigate the controversy, though Scott was eventually cleared.[43] For several months in 1848 and early 1849, the administration divided overall army command between Scott and Zachary Taylor, Scott's rival as a war hero and the Whig presidential nominee and victor in the election of 1848. Scott directed the Eastern Division and Taylor the Western Division, each exercising within his jurisdiction the powers normally wielded by the commanding general.[44] On Taylor's inauguration, Scott resumed the unified command, and he renewed his bureaucratic struggle to assert control over the army as a whole, staff departments as well as line.[45] However,

Scott's decision to locate his headquarters in New York City in 1849–50 and in 1853–61, out of direct contact with the president and War Department, limited his effectiveness as military adviser to the government and chief army administrator. He was further distracted by his continuing political activities, which culminated in his disastrous defeat in the presidential campaign of 1852.

Scott's command ambitions reached a climax in 1855 in a bizarre and bitter controversy with Jefferson Davis, secretary of war under Franklin Pierce, Scott's victorious presidential opponent.[46] A strongly opinionated and rigid administrator, Davis clashed with the imperious commanding general on a number of minor issues, including Scott's application for a travel allowance to cover occasional trips on army business not specifically authorized by the War Department, and his claims to back pay on the basis of his promotion to brevet lieutenant general in 1855, which had been made retroactive to 1847. Most importantly for civil–military relations, Scott objected strongly to the secretary's practice of communicating directly with subordinate officers, bypassing Scott's New York City headquarters, and of issuing orders and instructions on his own authority, without specific reference to the president. In a series of legalistic and increasingly vituperative letters, the general carried forward the position implied in the Macomb regulations and his own earlier definition of the commanding general's powers: that the secretary of war lacked constitutional standing and an integral position in the military chain of command; that legislation and regulations limited his jurisdiction to logistical and administrative support; and that he had no authority to issue military orders or make independent decisions on military matters. Scott even questioned the president's constitutional ability to delegate his command powers to a civilian official.[47] In his equally strident replies, Davis cited many cases of previous secretaries of war communicating directly with officers in the field and issuing orders without reference to the president; moreover, Scott had voluntarily moved his headquarters out of close proximity to the War Department and thus could not expect to be consulted regularly on military orders. In Davis's opinion, the president regularly acted through the heads of the executive departments without the need for a formal delegation of authority, and 'the act of the Secretary of War is in legal contemplation the act of the President, and as such claims to be respected and obeyed' – a position sustained in a brief by Attorney General Caleb Cushing and approved by President Pierce.[48]

The Scott-Davis feud petered out in early 1856, leaving the relationship between commanding general and secretary of war without a permanent resolution. Late in his term, however, Davis struck a final blow at his adversary's command pretensions. In directing yet another revision of the army regulations, Davis had the section defining the powers and functions of the commanding general excised completely, leaving the office in a state of limbo. When Scott complained that the regulations amounted to an illegal usurpation of power, John B. Floyd, Davis's successor in the War Department, denied that the absence of a precise definition deprived the position of 'any power, authority, honor or command conferred upon that high office by law. Definitions are always difficult, sometimes impossible.'[49]

Chastened by his failure to establish his position's independent standing, Scott did work to define more precisely the commanding general's jurisdiction, albeit accepting now the primacy of the secretary of war. During discussions at the War Department in early April 1857, he submitted a memorandum to Floyd that attempted to distinguish the 'Usual line' separating the duties of the two offices. The secretary should exercise direct control over the U. S. Military Academy, the judge advocate of the army, and the '*disbursing branches*' of the general staff, a category that embraced nearly all the staff bureaus. While the inspectors general were usually subject to the commanding general's orders, jurisdiction over the adjutant general was divided, with that officer reporting directly to the secretary in matters relating to military commissions, army returns, and the militia. Scott agreed that the commanding general should obtain the secretary's approval before making any 'material change' in the stationing of troops, the arrangement of geographical commands, or the selection of recruiting superintendents. Moreover he acknowledged the impropriety of the general interfering when troops were employed 'to support civil authority, or any *politico-military* duty,' a common occurrence during the 1850s. In all other matters, 'it is supposed that the General-in-chief ought to be held responsible for the discipline & efficiency of the army & his ordinary authority not interfered with, except in cases of injustice, incompetency, misfeasance or negligence.'[50] Floyd appears to have agreed with this circumscribed interpretation of the general's powers, as no overt clash occurred between the two officials during the years preceding the Civil War.

By the late 1850s, Scott had largely forsaken his political ambitions, and, though aging, obese, and partially immobilized by gout, he continued to exert influence in military policy and administration. By telegraph and by periodic trips to Washington, D.C., he advised the government on military movements and dispositions. An opponent of Mormonism, a movement that he considered 'religiously hostile to the morals, the authority & laws of the U. States,' Scott took an enthusiastic part in organizing the expedition launched in 1857 to establish federal control over the refractory Mormon colony in Utah. In 1859 he traveled on special diplomatic assignment to Puget Sound to staunch a war scare with Great Britain, brought on by the unauthorized American occupation of disputed San Juan Island by orders of the local commander, Brigadier General William S. Harney. As he had done since taking the high command, Scott promoted the army's system of professional education, especially the re-establishment of schools of practice for the artillery.[51] During the secession crisis, he relocated his headquarters to Washington, D.C., and he provided sound professional advice to Abraham Lincoln's administration until pressured into retirement and replaced in November 1861 by the brash young commander of the Army of the Potomac, George B. McClellan.[52]

The civil–military tension over the role and powers of the commanding general was by no means settled by the outbreak of the Civil War. Indeed, it would continue with varying degrees of intensity throughout the remainder of the century, until partially resolved by the adoption of the modern general staff system in 1903. Generally the controversy remained within manageable limits – an administrative rather than a constitutional or political problem. Only under the extraordinary conditions of Reconstruction did a commanding general defy his constitutional commander-in-chief, and then it was to align the army with congressional leaders rather than to challenge the basic principle of civil control. Nevertheless, the controversy between general and secretary of war, and between line and staff, did involve the character and degree of civil control. In the eyes of most high-ranking line commanders, the increasingly professionalized army of the nineteenth century should be directly under a career military officer with the expertise and experience necessary to ensure its cohesion, efficiency, training, and readiness. While willing to accept the legitimacy of the secretary of war as an agent of the president, they maintained that his authority should be applied lightly and mainly confined to matters of logistical and financial administration, leaving the actual command of line and staff in the hands of a professional commander-in-chief. Civilian leaders generally resisted the commanding generals' pretensions to autonomous command, which they believed impinged on the constitutional powers of the president and the American tradition of civilian control, and they had influential allies in the staff chiefs, who sought to preserve their own independence and special relationship with the War Department. In the end, the commanding generals most successful in navigating the civil–military minefields were those who, like Alexander Macomb in the later years of his tenure, Henry Wager Halleck during the Civil War, and John M. Schofield during the 1890s, were willing to downplay active command and to focus on the more prosaic but equally vital role of chief military adviser to the government – a role that anticipated the functions of an army chief of staff.

Notes

[1] On the general topic of civil–military relations in the U.S., see: Huntington, *The Soldier and the State*; Smith, *American Democracy and Military Power*; Ekirch, *The Civilian and the Military*; Millett, *The American Political System and Civilian Control of the Military*; Kohn, ed., *The United States Military under the Constitution of the United States, 1789–1989*.

[2] Kohn, *Eagle and Sword*, 17–39.

[3] Schwoerer, 'No Standing Armies!'; Cress, *Citizens in Arms*; Leach, *Roots of Conflict*; Shy, *Toward Lexington*.

[4] Heitman, comp., *Historical Register and Dictionary of the United States Army, From Its Organization, September 29, 1789, to March 2, 1903*, 2:626.

[5] Simpson, *Let Us Have Peace*; Hyman, 'Johnson, Stanton, and Grant: A Reconsideration of the Army's Role in the Events Leading to Impeachment,' 85–100.

[6] Skelton, *An American Profession of Arms*, 282–304; Watson, 'Professionalism, Social Attitudes, and Civil–military Accountability in the United States Army Officer Corps, 1815–1846,' 888–1361.

[7] On the army's constabulary and governing role, see: Coakley, *The Role of Federal Military Forces in Domestic Disturbances*; Grivas, *Military Governments in California, 1846–1850*; Sefton, *The United States Army and Reconstruction, 1865–1877*.

[8] Kohn, 'Civil–military Relations: Civilian Control of the Military,' in *The Oxford Companion to American Military History*, edited by John W. Chambers II, 123–4.

[9] On the general history of the commanding general's office, see: Skelton, 'The Commanding General and the Problem of Command in the United States Army, 1821–1841,' 117–22; Stohlman, *The Powerless Position*; Bell, *Commanding Generals and Chiefs of Staff, 1775–1995*, 1–28.

[10] Act of August 7, 1789, in Hetzel, comp., *Military Laws of the United States*, 39–40; Ward, *The Department of War, 1781–1795*.

[11] Thian, comp., *Notes Illustrating the Military Geography of the United States, 1813–1880*, 31–4; Stagg, *Mr. Madison's War*, 278.

[12] Jacobs, *Tarnished Warrior*.
[13] Weigley, *History of the United States Army*, 134–7; White, *The Jeffersonians*, 236–250; Skelton, *American Profession of Arms*, 119–22, 232–3; Calhoun, *The Papers of John C. Calhoun*, vols. 2–3.
[14] John C. Calhoun to John W. Taylor, December 12, 1820, U.S. Congress, *American State Papers. Class V: Military Affairs*, 7 vols. Washington, D.C.: Gales and Seaton, 1832–1861, 2:188–91.
[15] Act of March 2, 1821, Hetzel, *Military Laws*, 213–15. For the congressional debate, see U.S. Congress, *Annals of the Congress of the United States, 1789–1824*, 42 vols. Washington, D.C.: Gales and Seaton, 1834–1856, 16th Cong., 2d sess. John C. Calhoun to James Monroe, November 27, 1822, *American State Papers: Military Affairs*, 2:450.
[16] U.S. War Department, *General Regulations for the Army; Or, Military Institutes*. Philadelphia: M. Carey and Sons, 1821.
[17] Samuel A. Storrow to Major Gen. Jacob Jennings Brown, October 5, 1821, Jacob Jennings Brown Papers, Massachusetts Historical Society; Annals of Congress, 17th Cong., 1st sess., 896, 1565–1610, 1615–18.
[18] Morris, *Sword of the Border*.
[19] Ibid., 234–48; Skelton, 'Commanding General,' 118–19; Brown's official letterbooks, Jacob Jennings Brown Papers, Library of Congress. Brown's annual reports are printed with the secretary of war's annual reports to the president, *American State Papers: Military Affairs*, 2,3. The diary of John Quincy Adams indicates that Brown met frequently with Adams throughout his presidency to discuss military matters as well as politics. John Quincy Adams, *Memoirs of John Quincy Adams, Comprising Portions of His Diary from 1795 to 1848*, edited by Charles Francis Adams, 12 vols. Philadelphia, 1874–1877, 6, 7.
[20] Adams, *Memoirs*, 6:537; Major Gen. Jacob Jennings Brown to James Barbour, November 8, 1825, Brown Papers, Library of Congress; Christopher Vandeventer's diary entries for November 4 and 8, 1825, Christopher Vandeventer Papers, William L. Clements Library, Ann Arbor, Michigan; General Orders No.1, January 2, 1826, National Archives, Records of the Office of the Adjutant General (Record Group 94), General Orders and Circulars of the War Department and General Headquarters of the Army, 1809–1860.
[21] For the debate on the bill to abolish the commanding general's position, see U.S. Congress, *Register of Debates in Congress, 1827–1837*, 29 vols. Washington, DC, 1825–1837, 20th Cong., 1st sess. Quotation on p. 2683.
[22] Report of Sen. William Henry Harrison to the Senate, March 19, 1828, *American State Papers: Military Affairs*, 3:820–22.
[23] Extract of letter of Secretary of War to the chairman of the House Committee on Military Affairs, January 14, 1829, ibid., 4:91–2.
[24] Everest, *The Military Career of Alexander Macomb*; Richards, *Memoir of Alexander Macomb*.
[25] Major Gen. Alexander Macomb to the Secretary of War, July 28, 1831, National Archives, Records of the Headquarters of the Army (Record Group 108), Letters Sent by the Headquarters of the Army, 1828–1903.
[26] Skelton. 'The United States Army, 1821–1837: An Institutional History,' 228–239; Skelton, 'Commanding General,' 119–20.
[27] National Archives, Records of the Headquarters of the Army (Record Group 108), Proceedings of the Military Board, 1832–1835. For Macomb's relationship to Cass, see Klunder, *Lewis Cass and the Politics of Moderation*, 55, 66–7.
[28] General Orders No. 74, December 24, 1831, Adjutant General's Office: General Orders and Circulars.
[29] U.S. War Department, *General Regulations for the Army*. Washington: Francis P. Blair, 1834, 115–16, 126.
[30] The only change involving the commanding general's powers was omission of review by the general of the staff bureaus' annual statements. U.S. War Department, *General Regulations for*

the Army of the United States; Also, the Rules and Articles of War, and Extracts from Laws Relating to Them. Washington, D.C., 1835, 119–20.

[31] General Orders No. 44, June 22, 1837, Adjutant General's Office: General Orders and Circulars.

[32] Joel R. Poinsett to Martin Van Buren, December 5, 1837, *American State Papers: Military Affairs*, 7:574; Poinsett to Thomas Hart Benton, December 18, 1837, National Archives, Office of the Secretary of War (Record Group 107), Reports to Congress from the Secretary of War, 1803–1870. On Poinsett as secretary of war, see also Putnam, *Joel Roberts Poinsett*, 149–95.

[33] Act of July 5, 1838, Hetzel, *Military Laws*, 261–7.

[34] Roberts, 'Loyalty and Expertise,' 128–207.

[35] Skelton, 'United States Army,' 287–97; Macomb's official correspondence in Headquarters of the Army: Letters Sent. Through 1837, Macomb's annual reports, included with the secretary of war's annual reports, are in the *American State Papers: Military Affairs*. After that date, they appear in the serial set of congressional documents.

[36] Elliott, *Winfield Scott*; Johnson, *Winfield Scott*; Peskin, *Winfield Scott*.

[37] Brig. Gen. Winfield Scott to Col. Roger Jones, October 15, 1830, *American State Papers: Military Affairs*, 4:649–50; U.S. War Department, *General Regulations for the Army of the United States, 1841*. Washington, DC: J. and G. S. Gideon, Printers, 1841, 84–5.

[38] Elliott, *Winfield Scott*, 420–32; Johnson, *Winfield Scott*, 149–56; Peskin, *Winfield Scott*, 137–8.

[39] Elliott, *Winfield Scott* , 435–41; Peskin, *Winfield Scott*, 138–42.

[40] On Jones's wartime policy role, see especially National Archives, Adjutant General's Office (Record Group 94), Reports to the Secretary of War, 1825–1870. See for example, Jones to William L. Marcy, July 30, 1846; Jones to Armistead Burt, December 28, 1846; Jones to Marcy, December 31, 1846, January 5, 1847, February 27, 1847, February 10, 1848. On the War Department during the Mexican War, see also Spencer, *The Victor and the Spoils*, 137–74.

[41] Polk, *The Diary of James K. Polk*, 2, 3. On Polk as war leader, see also Bergeron, *The Presidency of James K. Polk*, 65–111; Winders, *Mr. Polk's Army*, 186–201.

[42] Polk, *Diary*, 2: 226–8, 231, 261–2, 268–71, 275–6, 293, 352.

[43] Elliott, *Winfield Scott*, 565–90; Peskin, *Winfield Scott*, 197–203.

[44] General Orders No. 49, August 31, 1848, Adjutant General's Office: General Orders and Circulars.

[45] Major Gen. Winfield Scott to George W. Crawford, May 12, 1849, July 18, 1849, Capt. William G. Freeman to Adjutant General, June 18, 1849, Scott to Crawford, September 27, 1849, September 28, 1849, Brevet Capt. Irvin McDowell to Adjutant General, October 31, 1849, Freeman to Adjutant General, December 13, 1849, December 17, 1849, Headquarters of the Army: Letters Sent.

[46] Elliott, *Winfield Scott*, 649–59; Davis, *Jefferson Davis*, 228–30; Cooper, *Jefferson Davis, American*, 252–4; 34th Cong., 3d sess., Sen. Exec. Doc. No. 34.

[47] See especially, Lt. Gen. Winfield Scott to Jefferson Davis, July 17, 1855, July 30, 1855, July 31, 1855, September 29, 1855, 34th Cong., 3d sess., Sen. Exec. Doc. No. 34, 159–64, 180–81, 203–14.

[48] Jefferson Davis to Lt. Gen. Winfield Scott, July 25, 1855, Caleb Cushing to Davis, August 31, 1855, Franklin Pierce to Davis, Sept. 5, 1855, Davis to Scott, September 7, 1855, ibid., 166–80, 181–201. Quotation on 181.

[49] U.S. War Department, *Regulations for the Army of the United States, 1857* (New York: Harper, 1857); Lt. Gen. Winfield Scott, 'Remarks,' submitted to John B. Floyd, March 28, 1857, Headquarters of the Army: Letters Sent; Floyd to Scott, September 25, 1857, National Archives, Office of the Secretary of War (Record Group 107), Letters Sent by the Secretary of War Relating to Military Affairs, 1800–1889.

[50] Lt. Gen. Winfield Scott, memorandum submitted to secretary of war, April 3, 1857, Headquarters of the Army: Letters Sent. Scott seems to have drawn on the advice of his personal chief of staff, Assistant Adjutant General Lorenzo Thomas. Thomas, memorandum submitted to Scott, April 1, 1857, ibid.

[51] Scott played a more active role in military administration than several of his biographers have acknowledged. See his official correspondence for the 1850s in Headquarters of the Army: Letters Sent, and annual reports in the serial set of congressional documents. For quotation, see Lt. Gen. Winfield Scott, 'Garrison for Salt Lake City,' submitted to secretary of war, May 26, 1857, Headquarters of the Army: Letters Sent. On the San Juan Island mission, see Elliott, *Winfield Scott*, 664–71; Peskin, *Winfield Scott*, 228–30; 36th Cong., 1st sess., Sen. Exec. Doc. No. 2, 39–90. On the War Department during James Buchanan's administration, see also Pinnegar, *Brand of Infamy*, 53–102.

[52] Elliott, *Winfield Scott*, 675–715; Johnson, *Winfield Scott*, 222–33; Peskin, *Winfield Scott*, 233–56.

References

Bell, William G. *Commanding Generals and Chiefs of Staff, 1775–1995: Portraits & Biographical Sketches of the United States Army's Senior Officer*. Washington, D.C.: Center of Military History.

Bergeron, Paul H. *The Presidency of James K. Polk*. Lawrence: University Press of Kansas, 1987.

Calhoun, John C. *The Papers of John C. Calhoun*, edited by Robert L. Meriwether et al., 27 vols. Columbia: University of South Carolina Press, 1959–2003.

Coakley, Robert W. *The Role of Federal Military Forces in Domestic Disturbances, 1789–1878*. Washington, D.C.: Center of Military History, 1988.

Cooper, William J., Jr., *Jefferson Davis, American*. New York: Alfred A. Knopf, 2000.

Cress, Lawrence D. *Citizens in Arms: The Army and Militia in American Society to the War of 1812*. Chapel Hill: University of North Carolina Press, 1982.

Davis, William C. *Jefferson Davis: The Man and His Hour*. New York: Harper Collins, 1991.

Ekirch, Arthur A., Jr., *The Civilian and the Military*. New York: Oxford University Press, 1956.

Elliott, Charles W. *Winfield Scott: The Soldier and the Man*. New York: Macmillan, 1937.

Everest, Allan S. *The Military Career of Alexander Macomb and Macomb at Plattsburgh, 1814*. Plattsburgh, N.Y.: Clinton County Historical Association, 1989.

Grivas, Theodore. *Military Governments in California, 1846–1850; With a Chapter on Their Prior Use in Louisiana, Florida, and New Mexico*. Glendale, CA: Arthur H. Clark, 1963.

Heitman, Francis B. comp., *Historical Register and Dictionary of the United States Army, From Its Organization, September 29, 1789, to March 2, 1903*, 2 vols. Washington, D.C.: Government Printing Office, 1903.

Hetzel, Abner R. comp., *Military Laws of the United States*. Washington, DC: G. Templeman, 1846.

Huntington, Samuel P. *The Soldier and the State: The Theory and Politics of Civil–Military Relations*. New York: Harvard University Press, 1957.

Hyman, Harold M. 'Johnson, Stanton, and Grant: A Reconsideration of the Army's Role in the Events Leading to Impeachment.' *American Historical Review* 66 (October 1960): 85–100.

Jacobs, James R. *Tarnished Warrior: Major-General James Wilkinson*. New York: Macmillan, 1938.

Johnson, Timothy D. *Winfield Scott: The Quest for Military Glory*. Lawrence: University Press of Kansas, 1998.

Klunder, Williard Carl. *Lewis Cass and the Politics of Moderation*. Kent, Ohio: Kent State University Press, 1996.

Kohn, Richard H. *Eagle and Sword: The Federalists and the Creation of the Military Establishment in America, 1783–1802*. New York and London: The Free Press, 1975.

———. 'Civil–Military Relations: Civilian Control of the Military.' In *The Oxford Companion to American Military History* edited by John W. Chambers II. New York: Oxford University Press, 1999: 123–4

Kohn, Richard H., ed. *The United States Military Under the Constitution of the United States, 1789–1989*. New York and London: New York University Press, 1991.

Leach, Douglas Edward. *Roots of Conflict: British Armed Forces and Colonial Americans, 1677–1763.* Chapel Hill: University of North Carolina Press, 1986.

Millett, Allan R. *The American Political System and Civilian Control of the Military: A Historical Perspective.* Columbus: Mershon Center of The Ohio State University, 1979.

Morris, John D. *Sword of the Border: Major General Jacob Jennings Brown, 1775–1828.* Kent, Ohio: Kent State University Press, 2000.

Peskin, Allan. *Winfield Scott and the Profession of Arms.* Kent, Ohio: Kent State University Press, 2003.

Pinnegar, Charles. *Brand of Infamy: A Biography of John Buchanan Floyd.* Westport, CT: Greenwood Press, 2002.

Polk, James K. *The Diary of James K. Polk,* edited by Milo M. Quaife, 4 vols. Chicago: A.C. McClurg & Company, 1910.

Putnam, Herbert E. *Joel Roberts Poinsett: A Political Biography.* Washington, DC: Mimeoform Press, 1935.

Richards, George H. *Memoir of Alexander Macomb, the Major General Commanding the Army of the United States.* New York: M'Elrath, Bangs, 1833.

Roberts, William R. 'Loyalty and Expertise: The Transformation of the Nineteenth-Century American General Staff and the Creation of the Modern Military Establishment.' Ph.D. diss., Johns Hopkins University, 1980.

Schwoerer, Lois G. *'No Standing Armies!': The Antiarmy Ideology in Seventeenth-Century England.* Baltimore and London: Johns Hopkins University Press, 1974.

Sefton, James E. *The United States Army and Reconstruction, 1865–1877.* Baton Rouge: Louisiana State University Press, 1967.

Shy, John. *Toward Lexington: The Role of the British Army in the Coming of the American Revolution.* Princeton, N.J.: Princeton University Press, 1965.

Simpson, Brooks D. *Let Us Have Peace: Ulysses S. Grant and the Politics of War and Reconstruction, 1861–1868.* Chapel Hill: University of North Carolina Press, 1991.

Skelton, William B. 'The United States Army, 1821–1837: An Institutional History.' Ph.D. diss., Northwestern University, 1968.

——— . 'The Commanding General and the Problem of Command in the United States Army, 1821–1841,' *Military Affairs* 34 (December 1970): 117–22.

——— . *An American Profession of Arms: The Army Officer Corps, 1784–1861.* Lawrence: University Press of Kansas, 1992.

Smith, Louis. *American Democracy and Military Power: A Study of Civil Control of the Military Power in the United States.* Chicago: University of Chicago Press, 1951.

Spencer, Ivor D. *The Victor and the Spoils: A Life of William L. Marcy.* Providence: Brown University Press, 1959.

Stagg, J. C. A. *Mr. Madison's War: Politics, Diplomacy, and Warfare in the Early American Republic, 1783–1830.* Princeton, N.J.: Princeton University Press, 1983.

Stohlman, Robert F., Jr., *The Powerless Position: The Commanding General of the Army of the United States, 1864–1903.* Manhattan, KS: Kansas State University, 1975.

Thian, Raphael P. comp., *Notes Illustrating the Military Geography of the United States, 1813–1880.* Washington, D.C.: Government Printing Office, 1881.

Ward, Harry M. *The Department of War, 1781–1795.* Pittsburgh: University of Pittsburgh Press, 1962.

Watson, Samuel J. 'Professionalism, Social Attitudes, and Civil–Military Accountability in the United States Army Officer Corps, 1815–1846.' Ph.D. diss., Rice University, 1996.

Weigley, Russell F. *History of the United States Army.* New York and London: Macmillan Company, 1967.

White, Leonard D. *The Jeffersonians: A Study in Administrative History, 1801–1829.* New York: Macmillan Company, 1951.

Winders, Richard Bruce. *Mr. Polk's Army: The American Military Experience in the Mexican War.* College Station: Texas A&M University Press, 1997.

John M. Schofield and the 'Multipurpose' Army

Robert Wooster

In a 1980 essay, 'The Multi-Purpose Army on the Frontier: A Call for Further Research,' historian Michael L. Tate, building upon themes suggested earlier by Francis Paul Prucha, called attention to the United States Army's considerable non-martial accomplishments in the American West. No one having heeded his call for additional study, Tate eventually tackled the task himself, his *The Frontier Army in the Settlement of the West* (1999) drawing together published works into an intelligent, manageable synthesis. Tate shows that by distributing disaster relief, protecting national parks, conducting scientific research, improving rivers, roads, and harbors, preserving order during domestic disturbances, bringing federal dollars, and carrying with it the beliefs, values, and culture of the society it represented, the regular army influenced western development in ways far more diverse than simply fighting American Indians.[1]

But limiting such analysis to the West tells only part of the story, for the multipurpose army extended beyond the Mississippi River and the economic, cultural, and intellectual spheres emphasized by Tate. The regular army typically accounted for about 15 percent of all federal spending between 1865 and 1885, with its implementation of Reconstruction, intervention to maintain order in the strikes of 1877, and oversight of various civil engineering projects being the most visible examples of its diverse roles. And as John M. Gates noted two decades ago, army officers were by no means isolated from the larger American society, despite the strictures of such contemporary critics as Representative Fernando Wood (D-N.Y.), who insisted that army officers were 'idle vagabonds who are so well paid and do nothing.' In fact, the army and its officers were engaged in the very fabric of American public life. A re-assessment of Maj. Gen. John M. Schofield's involvement in a range of diplomatic, administrative, and political responsibilities and initiatives in the two decades following the Civil War illustrates the extent of that engagement.[2]

Born in 1831, Schofield graduated seventh in his West Point class of 1853. After two years with the First Artillery Regiment, he returned to West Point as a temporary instructor in the Department of Natural and Experimental Philosophy. There Schofield courted and married Harriet ('Rittie') Bartlett, daughter of his department head, Professor William H. Bartlett, an internationally acclaimed scientist whose subsequent work as an actuary for a New York insurance company offered his son-in-law special inroads into the halls of the eastern establishment.[3]

The outbreak of the Civil War found Schofield in St. Louis, Missouri, concluding a one-year leave of absence from the army while teaching physics at Washington University. Once again donning his uniform, he played a key role in ensuring that the state remained under Union control. For his heroic (but unsuccessful) bayonet charge during the fighting at Wilson's Creek, he was later awarded a Medal of Honor. Subsequent appointments eventually left him in command of all Union forces in Missouri. President Abraham Lincoln came to rely on his steadiness; during the Vicksburg campaign, Schofield's willingness to endanger his own command by sending 20,000 reinforcements won Ulysses S. Grant's esteem as well.[4]

But Schofield was anxious to leave what one state figure described as the Missouri 'tangle.' Nearly two years' involvement in this contentious environment, whose authority often extended into neighboring Kansas, had generated many enemies. Conservatives charged that Schofield's anti-guerrilla measures had violated too many civil liberties; radicals countered that he had not gone far enough in crushing resistance to federal authority. In January 1864 he was transferred, eventually coming to command the Army of the Ohio. Cautiously capable during William T. Sherman's Atlanta campaign, the former artillery officer then successfully fended off John Bell Hood's Confederates at the Battle of Franklin (30 November 1864), inflicting heavy enemy casualties in the process. By war's end, Schofield had moved to North Carolina, where troops in his command captured Wilmington and linked up with Sherman's army at Goldsboro.[5]

Prematurely balding and a bit overweight, the bewhiskered, cigar smoking Schofield looked more like a corporate lawyer than a veteran of four hard years of Civil War. Perhaps this irony was suitable for one who would be dispatched on so many unusual government assignments over the next two decades. Indeed, a general who had earned the trust of Lincoln, Grant, and Sherman seemed an ideal fit for a post that even the most bureaucratic of governments – much less that of the United States in 1865 – would have had trouble filling. In 1863–64, Napoleon III of France had used Mexico's failure to repay its debts as an excuse to install the Hapsburg Archduke Ferdinand Maximilian as emperor of a puppet government there. The Civil War had delayed an immediate United States response, but the Confederacy's collapse gave Matías Romero, head of the Mexican government-in-exile's legation in Washington, the opportunity to re-energize his lobbying efforts. True Mexican loyalists, suggested Romero, would welcome an army of *Norteamericanos* that would help them oust the European interlopers.[6]

A respected general was needed to lend the scheme credibility. Grant and Sherman both rejected the offer, but the former suggested Schofield, who was then handling Reconstruction duties in North Carolina, as a substitute. 'Grant told me that after Generals Sherman and [Philip H.] Sheridan,' Romero explained in summer 1865, 'he considered General Schofield... as the most meritorious general produced by the Civil War. From the political point of view and as a man of talent,' continued the minister, 'Grant classified him superior to Sherman.' Discrete personal meetings affirmed the high recommendation. 'The more I deal with Schofield, the better I realize that Grant's praise of him was not exaggerated,' proclaimed Romero. The restored Mexican government would pay Schofield to lead an army of Union and Confederate veterans formed into three infantry divisions, one cavalry division, and nine artillery batteries into Mexico. To lend Schofield the necessary cover for an operation that he believed would serve national interests, Grant planned to dispatch him to the Rio Grande 'on an inspection tour' with a one-year leave of absence.[7]

But Secretary of State William Seward steadfastly opposed the proposed expedition. Dubious about the reception that these northern intruders would receive in Mexico, confident that diplomacy could oust French troops, and suspicious of outside meddling in State Department business, Seward arranged a meeting with Schofield. Rather than leading an army of questionably funded mercenaries into a foreign country, reasoned the secretary, why not go to Paris and take up the matter personally? There, as Schofield later described it, Seward encouraged him to 'get your legs under Napoleon's mahogany, and tell him he must get out of Mexico.' A prudent man who undoubtedly recognized the risks inherent in leading American troops into Mexico, Schofield agreed to undertake Seward's informal mission as his 'army' was being organized.[8]

With a deft touch, Seward managed to delay Schofield's departure until November. After a brief stay in London, the general arrived in Paris in early December, ensconcing himself in the splendor of the city's Grand Hotel. 'All Paris is in a ferment about my visit here,' wrote Schofield to his wife. 'Newspaper editors are besieging the legation to learn what it means... These French are a most excitable people but they will boil down pretty soon. Meanwhile I shall amuse myself.' As U. S. ministry officials fended off queries about the nature of the mission, Schofield made a noncommittal public toast at an annual Thanksgiving dinner sponsored by Americans in Paris, initiated communications with the French war ministry, and met with Prince Napoleon, the emperor's cousin. But Schofield soon concluded that budget shortages and diplomatic pressure would cripple France's ability to sustain an army in Mexico. No official meeting with

Napoleon, save for a chance encounter at a Tuileries ball, was deemed necessary. After six restless months visiting with French officials and touring Paris, the continent, and Scotland while waiting for new instructions, he returned to Washington in late May. Stripped of French support, Maximilian was captured and executed in 1867, his empire having collapsed.[9]

Although State Department officials downplayed his role in influencing French policy, Schofield's tact, judgment, and discretion had once again impressed Grant, thus reinforcing the personal alliance formed during the Civil War. Schofield's appearance in Paris in 1865–66 probably had only a minimal impact on French policy; still, his presence symbolized the possibility of a difficult contest against an army of veteran troops fought far from French shores. And it averted the need for the Mexican government-in-exile to bring a foreign army south of the Rio Grande. For his part, Minister Romero was pleased enough with Schofield's performance to recommend continued payments for the services he had rendered.[10]

Three months after returning from Europe, Schofield was assigned command of reconstruction in Virginia, where he would remain until May 1868. The post held many challenges, for Civil War memories would die hard in the Old Dominion. The flower of the state's white male population had been decimated and thousands of former slaves were now free. A social conservative, Schofield wanted to preserve order and encourage economic growth by ensuring that white moderates of the better sort dominated state offices. Jobs and economic recovery, rather than social justice, were in his view the South's most pressing needs. But Schofield was also a pragmatist. Any reasonable person could see that blacks required protection from white supremacists. And although he privately opposed the measure, he advised Virginians to accept the Fourteenth Amendment so as to spare themselves from the intervention of an increasingly impatient Congress.[11]

Despite Schofield's lobbying, the Virginia legislature rejected the Fourteenth Amendment. Enraged by such Southern obstructionism and President Andrew Johnson's refusal to offer blacks even minimal federal protection, Congress asserted its authority, carving much of the former Confederacy into five military districts, whose commanders were directed to insure state compliance and authorized to remove officials who they deemed impediments to Reconstruction. Even with these new powers, Schofield still tried to chart a conservative course in Virginia. General Orders No. 1 proclaimed that existing government officers would remain in place except 'in individual cases.' The exercise of the army's power should be 'as slight as possible,' as long as justice was administered impartially 'to all classes.' Civilians were 'requested' to 'confer' with military authorities when filling vacant offices. In Schofield's view, while 'the color of a man's skin ought to have no more to do with it than the color of his hair,' rule by the uneducated and unqualified would prove fatal to the Republicans, who would be blamed for the government's misdeeds. Thus he allowed talented 'men who would aid in restoration' to remain in office, even if they had once taken up arms against the United States.[12]

By October 1867, voter registration had proceeded well enough to elect delegates to a new convention charged with writing a constitution that might restore the Old

Dominion to the Union. To Schofield's chagrin, a Republican/Radical majority dominated the convention and wrote a charter that disfranchised former Confederates and required strict loyalty oaths from prospective officeholders. Fearing that the latter provisions would galvanize conservatives into political action, Schofield hastened the process of finding 'respectable and competent' Republicans for civil offices. He also replaced the governor, Francis H. Pierpont, whose influence was waning, with Henry Horatio Wells, a former Union officer who had resettled in Virginia after the war. Combining army and state patronage might 'give additional strength and influence to respectable republicans,' Schofield reasoned. As a last resort, the general made a dramatic personal appearance before the convention, warning that the stringent requirements for voting and office-holding would lead to bad government and political disaster. Noisy debate followed his departure. 'King Schofield,' charged critics, was 'going back' on blacks. In April 1868, the convention approved the constitution with the restrictive voting and test oath clauses intact.[13]

This tack having failed, Schofield took his case to commanding general Grant. Extremists from both sides would dominate any government resulting from the proposed constitution, he reasoned. To avert this crisis, Schofield suggested that the army ignore the convention's work 'until the friends of reconstruction get control of the State' as it continued to replace former Rebels with qualified Unionists. Money – or rather the lack of it – provided the necessary excuse for delay. The convention had already spent the $100,000 set aside to cover the costs of the convention and the resulting election. Recognizing that a flawed government would result from such a document, Schofield predicted that Congress would refuse to appropriate the additional funds needed to hold the constitutional referendum.[14]

Events seemed to verify the wisdom of Schofield's proposals. Congress indeed delayed the money for another 13 months, and when it released the funding, it mandated that the test-oath and disfranchising clauses of the proposed constitution be subjected to separate votes. Voters overwhelmingly approved the constitution but rejected both clauses that Schofield had found so odious. Judge Alexander Rives, a Virginia moderate, credited the general with having done 'a great service.' And by averting a bitter conservative backlash, Schofield's policies had, however unwittingly, helped to lay the groundwork for continuing biracial involvement in Virginia politics for three decades.[15]

Like so many of his comrades, Schofield had mixed feelings about the army's role in Reconstruction. Long suspicious of extremists of any political bent, he would later proclaim his work 'in staying the tide of fanaticism in Virginia' to be 'one of the most satisfactory portions of my official career.' But the federal government's deployment of military forces in the former Confederate states left him deeply troubled, particularly when that government and those troops challenged the traditional ruling classes at the expense of what he deemed to be proper public order. In any event, Schofield had demonstrated a deft ability to protect his own position. Of the five generals originally appointed to command military districts in the South – Philip Sheridan (Texas and Louisiana); Dan Sickles (Carolinas); John Pope (Georgia, Florida, and Alabama); and E. O. C. Ord (Arkansas and Missouri) – Schofield enjoyed the longest tenure. Although

President Andrew Johnson frequently disagreed with Schofield's implementation of Reconstruction, the chief executive found no pretext to remove him.[16]

But Schofield had already turned his attentions elsewhere. On 28 May 1868, the Washington *Evening Star* had described Schofield, a recent arrival in the capital, as 'a gentleman of high integrity' who 'has never taken any active part in politics.' Already, in fact, Schofield had immersed himself in high-level politics, becoming involved in the struggle between Congress and President Johnson. As the impeachment case against Johnson dragged on into April, Republicans doubtful of the propriety of such a move sought from the president confidence-building gestures regarding his future intentions. Armed with assurances that Johnson would cooperate, Senators James Grimes (R-Iowa) and William P. Fessenden (R-Maine) had suggested to William M. Evarts, the president's lead defense counsel, that John M. Schofield – known to have close relations with Grant and considered to have done well in postwar Virginia – might be an acceptable compromise choice to replace the controversial Edwin M. Stanton as secretary of war.[17]

On 21 April, Evarts requested a private meeting with Schofield at Willard's Hotel, long a Washington gathering point for congressmen, visitors, lobbyists, and intrigue. Moderate and conservative Republicans, predicted Evarts, would interpret his nomination as a sign that the president would no longer interfere in reconstruction. If this were not done and Johnson removed from office, the Republicans – including Grant, soon to be the party's nominee for president – would go down to defeat once the flimsy nature of the impeachment case became known. With Grant's approval, Schofield agreed to the scheme. Johnson, who regarded Schofield as 'cold and selfish' but 'entirely competent,' forwarded his nomination as Secretary of War along to the Senate as per the unwritten agreement. Described as an 'extraordinary development' by the *New York Times*, the proposal helped to slow the momentum against Johnson. In mid-May, proposals to convict the president failed by one vote, seven Republicans (including Grimes and Fessenden) joining Johnson's allies. Schofield's nomination as Secretary of War was approved later that month.[18]

Johnson was wary of his new cabinet officer, whose moderate course in Virginia had clashed with his more conservative agenda. But even the fiercely obstinate president understood that any direct challenge to Schofield would precipitate another congressional crisis. A test case came almost immediately. Johnson wanted Brig. Gen. Lovell Harrison Rousseau, who had publicly denounced the Radicals, to take over Schofield's old command in Virginia. But Schofield favored his current subordinate, the more moderate Col. George Stoneman. Senator James R. Doolittle (R-Wisc.), who had voted against impeachment, advised Johnson to back down. 'If done now against the wish of the new secretary [Schofield],' warned Doolittle, 'it would lead to great and fierce excitement in Congress.' Stoneman received the appointment.[19]

Secretary Schofield worked closely with Evarts, the recently appointed attorney general, in developing guidelines that would allow the army to support local authorities in the former Confederate states during 'extraordinary emergencies.' Officers should prevent problems by stationing troops at potential trouble spots. They were also instructed to 'exercise, upon their own responsibility, a wise decision, to the end that in any event the peace may be preserved.' Presidential approval for army intervention was 'only a formality.' Though he continued to oppose radical measures, Schofield's directives encouraging officers to act without the president's specific orders helped to balance the administration's more conservative approach. Johnson, Schofield believed, inevitably 'acquiesced' – if only after a good deal of angry bluster – to his position on the army's involvement in Reconstruction.[20]

During his ten-month tenure as war secretary, Schofield also supported Philip Sheridan's aggressive campaigns against Indians of the Southern Plains. 'The races *cannot* live together,' insisted the secretary, 'and it is the Indians who must yield.' But other initiatives went nowhere. Like virtually all of his comrades in arms, Schofield believed that shifting the Bureau of Indian Affairs, which supervised the reservations, from the Interior Department to the War Department would reduce corruption and improve the implementation of Indian policy. Congress, however, rejected this transfer. Even more disappointing was his failure to resolve the contentious relationship between the secretary of war, commanding general, and the heads of the army's ten administrative bureaus. Constitutionally, the president was commander in chief of the nation's armed forces. As the president's deputy, the secretary of war could communicate directly with the staff bureaus and issue orders to the army without going through the commanding general's office, thus undercutting the influence of the nation's highest ranking military officer. Permanently stationed in the capital, the bureau chiefs adroitly exploited the resulting power vacuum to forge strong alliances with Congress and operate their departments like semi-independent fiefdoms.[21]

Grant understood the problem, and upon assuming the presidency had delayed naming his own new war secretary to give Schofield time to make the necessary changes. Schofield promptly instructed staff officers to report to Sherman, who succeeded Grant as commanding general, and insisted that 'all orders... be transmitted through the General of the Army.' But John A. Rawlins, who was slated to replace Schofield in the War Department, disliked the prospect of serving in a position diminished by Schofield's recent order. Rawlins was terminally ill with tuberculosis and Grant was not about to deny the wishes of an aide who had stood resolutely behind him throughout the Civil War. In the face of noisy objections from the bureau chiefs, their congressional patrons, and his dying friend, Grant backed down. Upon taking over, Rawlins promptly rescinded Schofield's recent orders.[22]

Grant's election had at least allowed Schofield's promotion to major general, a welcomed change which soon brought another series of public responsibilities and controversies. Schofield assumed command of the sprawling Department of the Missouri (including the states of Missouri, Kansas, and Illinois, the Indian Territory, and the territories of Colorado and New Mexico) in March 1869 and stepped up to the Division of the Pacific (encompassing the western third of the country) 14 months later. In those capacities, he loosely advised subordinates in the field who conducted several campaigns against Indians. Behind the scenes, he also headed a board of officers assigned to draw up new infantry, cavalry, and artillery tactics. After nearly two years of effort, the Schofield Board sent its report to the War Department, only to have its work filed in one of that office's 'pigeon holes.' More public was an unseemly controversy between Schofield and the allies of the recently-deceased George H. Thomas, his former commander in the Nashville campaign, over their roles in the defeat of Hood. Often fought through anonymous letters in newspapers, the long-running contest was only one of many vitriolic postwar public feuds between former brothers in blue.[23]

From his headquarters in San Francisco, Schofield's interests were also drawn to the Pacific Ocean and the possibility of another extraordinary government commission. In March 1872 he and Lt. Col. Barton S. Alexander, an engineer, proposed that they be dispatched to Hawaii to 'look into the defensive capabilities of the different ports and their commercial facilities.' President Grant approved the scheme in theory, but the opposition of domestic American sugar producers made any immediate moves to cement ties with Hawaii impolitic. There matters stood until December, when Rear Admiral Alexander M. Pennock, en route to escort King Kamehameha V on a state visit to the United States, had stopped off at California. Discussions with Pennock rekindled Schofield's interest in going to the islands. With the excuse that such a trip might help his old comrade to overcome a long bout with pneumonia, Sherman issued the necessary orders.[24]

News of Kamehameha's death magnified the mission's importance. Upon its arrival at Honolulu, the group met with Lunalilo, the new king, and surveyed the islands of Oahu and Hawaii. Schofield identified the harbor at Pearl River, Oahu, as the best site for a naval base in all the islands. 'The value of such a harbor to the commerce of the world and especially to that of the United States is too manifest to require discussion,' he explained to Sherman. 'It is the key to the Central Pacific Ocean.' Although a coral reef blocked large ships from entering the river's fine protected anchorage, a potential great power such as the United States had the resources to deepen the channel. Shore batteries could assure that the base was 'completely defended' from land or sea assault. Since Hawaiians opposed immediate annexation, Schofield favored a frequently ventured alternative: cession of the harbor and adjacent lands in return for a reciprocal trade agreement with the United States.[25]

Following several false starts and the death of King Lunalilo, the Hawaiians agreed to offer exclusive reciprocity in exchange for a promise not to make territorial concessions to another nation. Schofield joined the lobbying effort, explaining to his former army comrade, Senator Ambrose E. Burnside (R-R.I.), 'control of those Islands in time of war would be a necessity to us.' To Representative Gilbert C. Walker (D-Va.), who he had come to know while on Reconstruction duty in Virginia, the general declared that 'control of those Islands in time of war would be indispensably necessary to command of the Pacific Ocean and the security of our commerce on this coast.' Schofield took a similar vein with Representative John K. Luttrell (D.-Cal.). The Hawaiian Islands 'constitute the only natural outpost to the defenses of our Pacific Coast.' Any delay might allow Great Britain or another foreign power to get a foothold instead. The treaty finally took effect in September 1876; 11 years later, Hawaii granted the United States the right to establish a naval base at Pearl Harbor. Advocates on both sides of the Hawaiian annexation issue would continue to cite excerpts from Schofield's work for years to come.[26]

As the Hawaiian reciprocity treaty wound its way through Congress, Schofield returned to the Division of the Pacific, where Indian affairs in California, Oregon, and

Arizona consumed most of his attention. But in 1876 Sherman again solicited Schofield's assistance in resolving several nagging concerns. Revelations that he had sold lucrative post sutlerships for personal profit had disgraced Secretary of War William Belknap; with the influence of that office weakened, there might still be the opportunity to insure that the commanding general could really command. Further, the United States Military Academy needed a thorough review. The scholarly Schofield, a West Point alumnus with first-hand knowledge of the inner-workings of Washington, seemed ideally suited for both tasks. With much trepidation, he returned East that summer.[27]

That fall's presidential contest soon diverted Schofield's attention from his other special duties. Rutherford B. Hayes, the Republican governor from Ohio, was pitted against the Democratic candidate, Samuel J. Tilden, governor of New York. Disputed results in four states had left Tilden one electoral vote short of the necessary majority. Fearing anarchy, Sherman made contingency plans to bring 4,000 troops to Washington and asked Maj. Gen. Winfield Scott Hancock and Schofield to develop the army's position should the Republican Senate insist upon Hayes and the Democratic House demand Tilden. Although officers should in most cases remain 'extremely cautious and circumspect' on political matters, in this instance Sherman concluded, 'we must use our force and influence to sustain the authorities legally in existence and recognized.'[28]

A strict constructionist and a Democract, Hancock labeled the matter 'simple.' The House should elect the president and the senate the vice-president. Schofield, by contrast, developed a subtler stance. He identified the greatest danger as stemming from a possible attempt by the president of the Senate, Thomas W. Ferry (R-Mich.), to claim sole jurisdiction over the counting of the disputed votes, a position favored by most Republicans. This, Schofield predicted, would lead to anarchy. Instead, Schofield concluded that the House and the Senate should 'agree to disagree' and call for new elections. Should this be impossible (and it certainly had little basis in the constitution itself), Schofield submitted a 'Proposed Joint Rule for counting the votes.' Pleased with Schofield's careful arguments, Sherman shared his correspondence with the imperious Senator Roscoe Conkling (R-N.Y.). Conkling echoed Sherman's praise for Schofield, noting that 'high as I thought of their writer before, they have raised him in my estimation.'[29]

Fortunately, Schofield's contingency plan proved to be unnecessary. In January 1877 a joint congressional committee (which included Conkling) set up an independent electoral commission to settle the dispute. Sherman once again called upon Schofield for an in-depth analysis. The latter pronounced it 'fair, honorable, and constitutional,' reinforcing Sherman's – and the army's – support for the process. With both parties wracked by internal divisions and Hayes (or his agents) having already promised certain concessions, southern Democrats agreed to accept the commission's judgment declaring the Republicans the victor.[30]

In mid-July, Schofield found himself detached on yet another special assignment. Stung by repeated pay cuts, workers for several railroads struck in mid-July. Attempts by police, private security forces, and state militias to break the strikes often turned bloody, with ugly riots erupting in Baltimore, Pittsburgh, and Chicago. President Hayes authorized the use of federal troops to restore order but insisted that they not break any strikes. Since commanding general Sherman was away from the capital on a western tour, on 22 July Schofield was ordered from West Point to Washington. There he temporarily assumed command of troops in the capital region and attended several cabinet meetings. He left eight days later, his troops having confined themselves to restoring order.[31]

As the election crisis tapered off and the strike cooled, Schofield redoubled his efforts to reform army regulations. The army's role in American life had become increasingly controversial, with impasses over its size, continued presence in the South, and administrative reorganization having forced the second session of the Forty-fourth Congress to adjourn without passing an appropriations bill, leaving soldiers without pay for five months. Sherman's insistence that new regulations give the commanding general 'absolute power' over the staff had also created a firestorm of opposition among the bureau chiefs. After another year of fruitless negotiation Congress formed another joint committee, to be chaired by Senator Burnside. Schofield provided considerable input to Burnside's committee, and the final proposal – a 724-page tome issued in December 1878 – placed the commanding general firmly in control of the staff and provided for rotation between line and staff officers. Although it also included sizeable budget cuts, many regulars concluded that it was about as good as they could expect.[32]

But the bill's immense size invited poison-pill amendments. Moreover, the staff opposed it 'tooth & nail,' according to Sherman. Amazed by the outpouring of protest from disgruntled army staff members, Senator Burnside proclaimed that one department in particular had been transformed 'into a bureau of newspaper correspondence.' In February 1879 the House rejected the entire measure; a stripped-down version that focused on reorganization failed to pass the Senate later that month. Schofield's efforts of nearly two years had thus come to naught. 'The difficulty seems to be that while we are resting in our 'impregnable fortress of reason,'' he told Sherman, 'those staff fellows quietly undermine us and blow us up!' Meaningful structural changes in the old army bureaus would not come until the early twentieth century, after Secretary of War Elihu Root abolished the office of commanding general in favor of a general staff.[33]

Affairs at West Point initially seemed more promising. Crucial to any real change at the Military Academy, argued Schofield, were a modernized curriculum and better instructors. Additional instruction in marksmanship, cavalry tactics, and English was also necessary. Spanish could be dropped and better instructors placed on the staff. Semi-annual exams should be required only of students of doubtful proficiency and be moved from early January to mid-December, thus giving most cadets a much-needed holiday. The superintendent also took on the practice of hazing, delivering 'a pretty sharp lecture' to the cadets in August 1879. Victims of such violations must report it immediately; at the same time, their 'manhood' demanded that they defend themselves from their assailants.[34]

The institution's only black cadet, Johnson C. Whittaker, had long been the focus of Superintendent Schofield's attention. Born a slave and ostracized by the other cadets, Whittaker's conduct was good but his academic preparation questionable. In January

1879, Schofield intervened to save him from flunking out. 'I may be influenced somewhat by the fact that he is the only one of his race now at the Academy,' explained Schofield, 'and has won the sympathy of all by his manly deportment, and earnest efforts to succeed. The Professors do not think he can ever master the course, but I am disposed to give him another chance.' But the black cadet's troubles were not over. On the morning of 6 April 1880, he was found in his room, bound to his bed and bloodied from cuts to his ears. With the other cadets avowing no knowledge of the deed, many concluded that Whittaker had staged the affair in a desperate effort to save himself from being dismissed for academic deficiencies. Indignant to such challenges to his own honor, Whittaker demanded a court of inquiry.[35]

The onslaught of handwriting experts, reporters, private investigators, jurists, lawyers, and curious townspeople transformed the proceedings into a media circus. On 28 May, the court of inquiry ruled against Whittaker. But the lurid tales of hazing and frequent cadet debauches at nearby watering holes revealed during the inquiry had reflected badly on the Academy, and Schofield's clumsy attempts to defend his charges did nothing to help. Two weeks into the trial, he had publicly absolved all cadets except Whittaker of any guilt. Interviews granted to reporters also seemed premature. Schofield saw the criticism as unfair, complaining that he had kept Whittaker, 'a poor colored boy,' at West Point 'in opposition to the unanimous recommendations of the Academic Board.' Whittaker had allowed himself to be exploited by those who wanted to make the Academy into 'the propagandist of political, religious, or social theories.'[36]

By August, widespread public skepticism of the investigation had convinced President Hayes to remove Schofield from command at West Point. Determined not to go quietly, Schofield vigorously defended his actions during a meeting with President Hayes and Secretary of War Alexander Ramsey on the morning of the 17th. Racial prejudice was hardly limited to West Point, thundered the old artilleryman; why should the Academy be expected to act in a manner inconsistent with American society? Further, Whittaker's inability to protect himself against this attack, as well as an earlier incident of hazing, demonstrated that he would never be fit to be an army officer. In the end, Hayes delayed action in regards to the superintendency and adopted Schofield's suggestion that Whittaker be given a leave of absence from his studies at West Point.[37]

Having averted his immediate removal, Schofield's fate at West Point now rested on the upcoming presidential election. His comrade in arms, Winfield Scott Hancock, had won the Democratic Party's nomination for the presidency; his victory might enable old soldiers like Schofield to begin with a clean slate. Hancock 'has ability, firmness, honesty, and courage,' explained Schofield, who also penned a strong defense of his colleague's actions during the controversies of 1876–77. But such was not to be the case, as James A. Garfield defeated Hancock by a narrow margin. As if to ensure his own removal, Schofield promptly insisted that blacks were not ready to attend the Academy and requested that he be given either a geographical command commensurate with his major general's rank or a leave of absence to visit Europe. Instead, the administration carved out for Schofield a new 'Division of the Gulf' – a nondescript command including Arkansas, the Indian Territory, Louisiana, and Texas – and named Brig. Gen. Oliver

O. Howard, long known as a champion of black rights, the new superintendent at West Point. Schofield concluded that his decision to accept this most recent special assignment had been 'the mistake of my life.'[38]

Whittaker was soon dismissed from West Point for academic deficiencies and the makeshift Division of the Gulf discontinued. Now perceived as a political liability, Schofield was trundled off on a military inspection of Europe, returning to various division commands until he became commanding general, by virtue of his seniority, in 1888. In that position he helped temporarily to improve relations between the army and civilian administrators, establishing especially effective relations with Secretary of War Redfield Proctor. Upon reaching his sixty-second birthday in 1895, Schofield accepted mandatory retirement, briefly returning to the public spotlight when called upon for military advice by President William McKinley during the opening days of the Spanish-American War. He died in 1906.

Respected for his intelligence and broad experiences in the sciences, the law, public administration, and military reform, John M. Schofield had taken part in several highly-charged controversies of the post-Civil War era. His record was mixed. Schofield had played his supporting role as the government's quasi-official military figurehead during Maximilian's ill-fated regime in Mexico as effectively as conditions allowed. Bigoted but not a Klansman, Schofield's middle-of-the-road approach to Reconstruction in Virginia helped to smooth the Old Dominion's transition back into the Union. Likewise, his presence as secretary of war did much to calm the political crisis surrounding the embattled Andrew Johnson administration. Schofield had quickly recognized the strategic importance of Pearl Harbor, although his nation delayed implementing his plans to secure rights to a naval base there for over a decade. His contingency plans during the political firestorms resulting from the disputed Hayes-Tilden presidential election of 1876, though of dubious constitutionality, reaffirmed his credibility in many political circles. Oddly, Schofield's greatest failures – his inability to meaningfully reform either army regulations or the U. S. Military Academy – had come in areas in which he might have been expected to have done better.

For his own part, Schofield had come to resent his role as the nation's miscellaneous agent in the two decades following the Civil War. A proud man, he knew that in several instances, especially in the matters of army reform and the place of blacks in the Military Academy, he had been on the losing side of the contest. In his darker moments, he came to see himself – and, more generally, the army as a whole – as having been unappreciated by American society. In 1880, for example, he penned an angry diatribe, published anonymously in *Harper's New Monthly Magazine*, lambasting the public's ingratitude toward its Civil War veterans. And on two occasions – once after his failed bid for promotion to major general in 1866; the second time after the debacle with the Hayes administration – he lashed out angrily against his friend, William Sherman.[39]

His own melancholy notwithstanding, John M. Schofield's activities reveal much about the way the United States government operated in the two decades following the Civil War. With only a small federal bureaucracy, army officers had to be generalists, capable of handling a variety of assignments and responsibilities. Wary of big government and a large standing army, torn over the role of blacks and former Confederates in national life, and eager to exert influence abroad without fully committing the nation's resources, most Americans would probably have been very satisfied by the use of one of their Civil War veterans in these non-combat roles. Theirs was a government of convenience and limits rather than bureaucracy and administrative structure, and Schofield and the army proved a convenient means for handling national concerns, whatever the effectiveness of their actions.[40]

Schofield's experiences also suggest that the personal and official papers of army officers offer fertile fields for future scholarship in a variety of non-military subjects. Beyond the dutiful coverage of Reconstruction, the wars against the Indians, and the 1877 strikes, general surveys of the early years of Gilded Age America too often overlook the activities of the army and its officers. Perhaps this stems from an overemphasis on 'business pacifism,' the potent combination of influences that led some of the nation's late-nineteenth century capitalists and philosophers to conclude that progressive industrial societies could eliminate war. Or perhaps historians have been too ready to assume that all officers followed William T. Sherman's well-known admonitions that the army divorce itself from politics.[41] Whatever the case, John M. Schofield's actions as unofficial ambassador for the removal of French troops from Mexico, director of Reconstruction in Virginia, temporary secretary of war, inspector for potential military bases in Hawaii, negotiator for army reforms, and superintendent at West Point suggest that the army, in stark contrast with Sherman's counsel, was actively involved in a wide range of public policy initiatives. Indeed, the reintegration of the multipurpose army in broader studies of the immediate post-Civil War period will yield a fuller, richer, and more deeply nuanced understanding of American history.

Acknowledgements

The author thanks Dr. David Blanke, Texas A&M University-Corpus Christi, and Dr. Alan Lessoff, Illinois State University, for their comments and suggestions on various sections of this paper, and Dr. Patrick J. Carroll, Texas A&M University-Corpus Christi, for sharing materials from the Benito Juárez Papers in Mexico City.

Notes

[1] Michael Tate, *The Frontier Army in the Settlement of the West*; Tate, 'The Multi-purpose Army on the Frontier: A Call for Further Research'; Prucha, *Broadax and Bayonet*.

[2] Laurie and Cole, *The Role of Federal Military Forces in Domestic Disorder*; United States Department of Commerce, Bureau of the Census, *Historical Statistics of the United States: Colonial Times to 1970*, Bicentennial Edition, 2 parts (Washington: Government Printing Office, 1975), 2, 1114–15; Gates, 'The Alleged Isolation of U.S. Army Officers in the Late 19th Century,' 32–45; Coffman, 'The Long Shadow of *The Soldier and the State*,' 69–82; *Congressional Globe*, 44th Congress, 1 session, 3780; Utley, *Frontier Regulars: The United States Army and the Indian, 1866–1891*, 60. Schofield has received relatively little scholarly attention. McDonough, *Schofield*, concentrates on the Civil War years, with a lone chapter on Reconstruction. Military

historians have generally concentrated on Schofield's interest in army reform; see especially Weigley, 'The Military Thought of John M. Schofield,' 77–84; Mixon, 'Pioneer Professional'; Swails, 'John McAllister Schofield.

[3] Schofield, *Forty-Six Years in the Army*, 1–31; 'Memoir Drafts' file, box 93, John M. Schofield Papers, Library of Congress, Washington, D. C.

[4] McDonough, *Schofield*, 11–68; Schofield, *Forty-Six Years*, 70–71, 110; *War of the Rebellion: A Compilation of the Official Records of the Union and Confederate Armies*, Washington: Government Printing Office, 1880–1901, 22, pt. 2, 306–8, 355, 604–7; Neely, '"Unbeknownst" to Lincoln,' 212–16.

[5] Edward Bates to James Eads, Mar. 23, 1863, box 1–2, James B. Eads Collection, Missouri Historical Society (St. Louis); Schofield, *Forty-Six Years*, 68–112; McDonough, *Schofield*, 69–156.

[6] Schoonover, *Mexican Lobby*, 31; Hanna and Hanna, *Napoleon III and Mexico*, 210–11; Miller, 'Matías Romero: Mexican Minister to the United States During the Juárez-Maximilian Era,' 228–45.

[7] Schofield, *Forty-Six Years*, 378–82; Schoonover, *Mexican Lobby*, 50–51, 64, 66, 71–3, 83–5, 89–90; Ignacio Mariscal to Schofield, 6, 12, 15 June 1865, box 77, Schofield Papers, LC; Matías Romero to Schofield, 2, 12, 21 July 1865, ibid.; Matías Romero to Pedro Santacilia, 13 June 1865, exped. 1281, fs. 1–2, Archivo Benito Juárez, Biblioteca Nacional (México City); Matías Romero to Benito Juárez, 9 August 1865, exped. 1327, fs. 1–2, ibid.

[8] Hanna and Hanna, *Napoleon III and Mexico*, 241–5; Schofield, *Forty-Six Years*, 382–5; 'French Occupation of Mexico,' box 77, Schofield Papers, LC; Edwin Stanton to William Seward, 28 July 1865, roll 90, William R. Seward Papers; John Schofield to William Seward, 4 August 1865, ibid.; Schoonover, *Mexican Lobby*, 50–51, 89, 102.

[9] Schofield, *Forty-Six Years*, 385–92; John Schofield to Rittie Schofield, 28, 30 November, 5, 12, 22 December 1865, 2, 24 January 1866, box 77, Schofield Papers, LC; J. Edward Wilkins to John Schofield, 9 December 1865, ibid.; *New York Times*, 19, 28 December 1865; John Schofield to Ulysses Grant, 8 December 1865, 7, 19 January 1866, *The Papers of Ulysses S. Grant*, edited by John Y. Simon, 16 (Carbondale: Southern Illinois University Press, 1988), 129–31; William Seward to John Schofield, 23 December 1865, roll 92, Seward Papers; John Bigelow to William Seward, 8 December 1865, roll 92, ibid.

[10] Schoonover, *Mexican Lobby*, 131; Hanna and Hanna, *Napoleon III and Mexico*, 247.

[11] Schofield, *Forty-Six Years*, 394–5; 'Reconstruction,' in Reconstruction in Virginia File, box 86, Schofield Papers, LC.

[12] Lowe, *Republicans and Reconstruction in Virginia*, 76; Schofield, *Forty-Six Years*, 397–401; General Orders No. 1, Secretary of War, Annual Report, 1867, House Executive Document No. 1, 40th Cong., 2 sess., serial 1324, 243; Report of Schofield, 5 October 1867, ibid., 240–41; 'Schofield on Reconstruction,' box 86, Schofield Papers, LC; John Schofield to Adjutant General, 22 March 1867, ibid.; John Schofield to Edwin Stanton, 6, 10 April 1867, box 47, ibid.; John Schofield to Adjutant General, 15 April 1867, Letters Sent, First Military District, RG 393, National Archives, Washington, D. C.; John Schofield to Ulysses Grant, 2 June 1867, *Grant Papers* 17, 183.

[13] Lowe, *Republicans and Reconstruction*, 122–3, 142–4; Maddox, *The Virginia Conservatives*, 57–9; Lowe, 'Virginia's Reconstruction Convention: General Schofield Rates the Delegates,' 341–60; John Schofield to Ulysses Grant, 2 April 1868, *Grant Papers*, 18, 218–20; John Schofield to Ulysses Grant, 24 April 1868, box 48, Schofield Papers, LC; clipping of *Richmond Dispatch*, 18 April 1868, box 88, ibid.; *Richmond Whig*, 22 April 1868; *Daily Enquirer and Examiner* (Richmond), 18 April 1868.

[14] John Schofield to Ulysses Grant, 18, 19 April 1868, *Grant Papers* 18, 222–3; John Schofield to Ulysses Grant, 21 March 1868, filed in letterbook under 'X,' box 47, Schofield Papers, LC; John Schofield to Adjutant General, 27 March 1868, Letters Sent, First Military District; Lowe, *Republicans and Reconstruction*, 158–60.

[15] Alexander Rives to John Schofield, 12 September 1868, box 8, Schofield Papers, LC; John Schofield to Alexander Rives, 15 September 1869, box 49, ibid.; Dailey, *Before Jim Crow*.
[16] Schofield to Rives, 15 September, 1869, box 49, Schofield Papers. For the best general surveys of the army in Reconstruction, see Sefton, *The United States Army and Reconstruction*; Dawson, *Army Generals and Reconstruction*; and Dawson, 'Reconstruction as Nation-Building: The U.S. Army in the South,' in *Armed Diplomacy*.
[17] *Evening Star* (Washington), 28 May 1868; Trefousse, *Andrew Johnson*, 323–4; Castel, *Presidency of Andrew Johnson*, 187–8; Barrows, *William M. Evarts*, 150–51.
[18] William Evarts to John Schofield, 21 April 1868, box 4, Schofield Papers, LC; Moore Diary, 23, 24 April 1868, roll 51, Andrew Johnson Papers, Library of Congress, Washington, DC; McDonough and Alderson, eds. 'Republican Politics and the Impeachment of Andrew Johnson,' 178–83; *New York Times*, 25, 26 April, 26–30 May 1868; *Evening Star* (Washington), 25, 28 April 1868; Schofield, *Forty-Six Years*, 418; Edwin Stanton to Andrew Johnson, 26 May 1868, roll 12, Edwin Stanton Papers, LC. Grant later changed his mind, but Schofield had already allowed his name to go forth.
[19] James Doolittle to Andrew Johnson, undated [ca. 31 May 1868], *The Papers of Andrew Johnson*, edited by Paul H. Bergeron, 14, Knoxville: University of Tennessee Press, 1997, 141.
[20] George Schofield to John Schofield, 28 June 1868, box 8, Schofield Papers, LC; Edward Townsend to Robert Buchanan, 10 August, SW, AR, 1868, House Ex. Doc. No. 1, 40th Cong., 3 sess., serial 1367, xxi; William Evarts to Magruder, 20 August, ibid., xxiii–xiv; John Kelton to George Thomas, 25 August, ibid., xxii; John Kelton to George Meade, 25 August, ibid., xxv; Schofield, *Forty-Six Years*, 419–20; Coakley, *The Role of Federal Military Forces in Domestic Disorders*, 300–301.
[21] Report of Schofield, 20 November, SW, AR, 1868, i–xvii; Utley, *Frontier Regulars*, 11–12, 31, 139–41, 189–91; Wooster, *Military and United States Indian Policy*, 77–84; Weigley, *History of the United States Army*, 190–92, 246–50; Ulysses Grant to Edwin Stanton, 28 January 1866, roll 10, Stanton Papers.
[22] Ulysses Grant to William Sherman, 18 September 1867, roll 12, Sherman Papers; Smith, *Grant*, 468–9, 477; Marszalek, *Sherman*, 384–5; 'The War Department,' box 82, Schofield Papers, LC; *Memoirs of General W. T. Sherman* (Library of America ed., 1990), 931–2; Wilson, *The Life of John A. Rawlins*, 354–6; John Schofield to Ulysses Grant, 11 March 1869, box 86, Schofield Papers, LC; William Sherman to President, 26 March 1869, roll 45, Sherman Papers; John Rawlins to General of the Army, 26 March 1869, roll 4, Letters Sent by the Secretary of War to the President and Executive Departments, microcopy M 421, National Archives.
[23] Jamieson, *Crossing the Deadly Ground*, 6–9. For Schofield's description of the feud, see *Forty-Six Years*, 290–98, and many letters in his personal papers, especially in John Schofield to Campbell, January 24, Feb. 9, 25, 1870, box 49, Schofield Papers, LC.
[24] Tate, *Hawaii*, 83; John Schofield to John Porter, 10 November 1872, box 89, Schofield Papers, LC; Barton Alexander to Andrew Humphreys, 11 March 1872, box 78, ibid.; John Schofield to Andrew Humphreys, 12 March, ibid.; William Belknap to Hamilton Fish, 18 March, ibid.; Hamilton Fish to William Belknap, 25 March, ibid.; Andrew Humphreys to John Schofield, 21 May, ibid.; William Belknap to John Schofield, 24 June, ibid.; John Schofield to William Sherman, 24 December 1872, ibid.; William Sherman to John Schofield, 27 December, ibid.
[25] John Schofield to William Sherman, 15 February 1873, box 78, Schofield Papers, LC; John Schofield and Barton Alexander to William Belknap, 30 September 1873, ibid.; Tate, *Hawaii*, 82–7. Their official report has been published in the *American Historical Review* 30 (1925), 561–5.
[26] Tate, *Hawaii*, 92–108, 113–17; John Schofield to Ambrose Burnside, 25 February 1875, box 49, Schofield Papers, LC; Charles Allen to John Schofield, 18 December 1875, 16 February 1876, box 2, 8 January 1876, box 10, ibid.; John Schofield to Gilbert Walker, 2 December 1875, box 49, ibid.; John Schofield to John Luttrell, 30 December 1875, ibid.; Bell, *Last Among Equals*, 22–3; John Schofield to John Morgan, 13 Jan. 1898, Senate Doc. 62, 55th Cong., 2 sess., serial 3592; Eaton, *Hawaiian Annexation Scheme, A Sugar Trust Plot*, 17–18.

[27] William Sherman to John Schofield, 28, 30 March, 8 April, 4, 25 May, 1 June 1876, box 42, Schofield Papers, LC; John Schofield to William Sherman, 29 March, 7, 8 April, 4, 10 May, 26 July, 4 August 1876, ibid.; Private Military Journal, June–August 1876, box 1, ibid.; John Schofield to William Sherman, 23, 25 May 1876, roll 49, Sherman Papers; John Schofield to William Sherman, 26 July 1876, roll 23, ibid.; William Sherman to John Schofield, 13 July 1876, box 28, Hiram Barney Collection, Huntington Library, San Marino, Ca.

[28] Marszalek, *Sherman*, 428; William Sherman to John Schofield, 13 November, 19, 20 December 1876, box 28, Barney Collection; William Sherman to John Schofield, 28 December 1876, box 93, Schofield Papers, LC.

[29] John Schofield to William Sherman, 26, 28 December 1876, 4, 10 January 1877, boxes 10 and 93, Schofield Papers, LC; William Hancock to William Sherman, 28 December 1878, roll 23, Sherman Papers; John Schofield to William Sherman, 2 January 1877, ibid.; William Sherman to John Schofield, 4, 10 January 1877, box 93, Schofield Papers, LC; Roscoe Conkling to William Sherman, 9 January, ibid.

[30] William Sherman to John Schofield, 19, 26 January 1877, box 93, Schofield Papers, LC; John Schofield to William Sherman, 20 January 1877, ibid.

[31] Private Military Journal, July 24–30, 1877, box 1, Schofield Papers, LC; Proclamation of the President, July 18, 1877, 4042 AGO 1877, roll 346, Letters Received by the Office of the Adjutant General (Main Series), 1871–1880, Microcopy 666, National Archives; John Schofield to Secretary of War, July 22, 1877, roll 347, ibid.; Edward Townsend to William Hancock, 27 July 1877, ibid.; John Schofield to William Forney, 27 July 1877, ibid.; Laurie and Cole, *Role of Federal Military Forces*, 29–55.

[32] 'Reply to objections offered by Chiefs of Bureaux, etc.,' August 1876, box 71, Schofield Papers, LC; William Sherman to John Schofield, 24 August, 19 December 1876, 15, 20 June, 6 August, 18, 29 December 1878, box 28, Barney Collection; John Schofield to William Sherman, 28 January 1877, 13 March, 5 July 1878, John M. Schofield Papers, United States Military Academy (West Point, NY); Private Military Journal, 22, 29 January, 1 March 1877, box 1, Schofield Papers, LC; Utley, *Frontier Regulars*, 62–63; John Schofield to Henry Banning, 10 February 1878, roll 45, Sherman Papers; Philip Sheridan to William Sherman, 4 January 1878, roll 25, ibid.; William Sherman to Philip Sheridan, 7 April 1878, roll 17, Philip Sheridan Papers, LC; John Schofield to Ambrose Burnside, 11 July 1878, box 89, Schofield Papers, LC; John Schofield to Robert Scott, 26 September 1878, box 50, ibid.; Emory Upton to William Sherman, 19 December 1878, roll 45, Sherman Papers; John Schofield to William Sherman, 20, 24 December 1878, ibid.; Langley, 'The Democratic Tradition and Military Reform' 192–200.

[33] William Sherman to John Schofield, 18, 23, 29 December 1878, 19 January 1879, box 28, Barney Collection; *Cong. Record* 45th Cong., 3 sess., pt. 2, p. 1758; Boylan, 'The Forty-fifth Congress and Army Reform,' 173–86; John Schofield to William Sherman, 29 May 1879, roll 26, Sherman Papers; Marszalek, *Sherman*, 435–6.

[34] John Schofield to William Sherman, 27 February, 4 April 1878, Schofield Papers, USMA; John Schofield to William McCrary, 30 August 1877, 16 April 1878, 22, 25 July 1879, box 50, Schofield Papers, LC; Report of Schofield, 8 November, SW, AR, 1877, House Ex. Doc. No. 1, pt. 2, 45th Cong., 2 sess., serial 1794, 150; 'Suggestions for the Consideration of the Academic Board,' 22 December 1879, box 13, Schofield Papers, LC; 'An Address Delivered by Maj. Gen. J. M. Schofield,' box 91, ibid.; John Schofield to Rutherford Hayes, 15 August 1879, Schofield Papers, USMA; John Schofield to William Lazelle, 19 August 1879, ibid.

[35] John Schofield to Adjutant General, 15 January 1879, box 50, 6, 7 April 1880, box 13, Schofield Papers, LC; Marszalek, *Assault at West Point*, 13–14, 39–41, 63–5; Charles Barth Diary, 6 April 1880, USMA; Private Military Journal, 6, 7 April, 5, 29 May 1880, box 1, Schofield Papers, LC.

[36] Marszalek, *Assault*, 63–131; *The Nation*, 15, 29 April, 6 May, 1880; Proceedings of the Court of Inquiry in the case of Johnson C. Whittaker, QQ 1858, RG 153, National Archives; Private Military Journal, box 1, Schofield Papers, LC; John Schofield to William Sherman, 11 April

1880, box 50, ibid.; William Sherman to John Schofield, 11, 18 April, 18, 24 May 1880, box 28, Barney Collection; John Schofield to Bullitt, 9 May 1880, box 50, Schofield Papers, LC; John Schofield to William Sherman, 19 April, 29, 31 July, 14 August 1880, ibid.; 'Relative Social Status of Colored Cadets,' May 1880, box 89, ibid.; Private Military Journal, 3 June 1880, box 1, ibid.; William Sherman to John Schofield, 9, 15 August 1880, box 50, ibid. For the Fitz-John Porter board, see the voluminous correspondence in the Schofield Papers, LC. The original charges against Porter may be found in O. R. 12, pt. 2, 506–12. The Schofield board's report is in ibid., 514–34.

[37] Private Military Journal, 17 August 1880, box 1, Schofield Papers, LC; Marszalek, *Assault*, 145–7; Schofield, *Forty-Six Years*, 445–6.

[38] William Hancock to John Schofield, 22 January 1880, box 18, Barney Collection; John Bigelow to John Schofield, 6 July, 10 August 1880, box 10, Schofield Papers, LC; John Schofield to John Bigelow, 11 July, 11 October 1880, box 50, ibid.; John Schofield to Flood, 29 September, 17 October 1880, box 13, ibid.; Private Military Journal, 3 November 1880, box 1, ibid.; Flood to John Schofield, 8 October 1880, box 11, ibid.; John Schofield to William Hancock, 4 November, 12 December 1880, box 50, ibid.; John Schofield to William Sherman, 1 September, 5, 7, 13, 29 November 1880, ibid.; John Schofield to Adjutant General, 12 November 1880, ibid.; William Sherman to John Schofield, 12, 27 November, 13 December 1880, box 42, ibid.; Schofield, *Forty-Six Years*, 439.

[39] Memoranda Lot A, 27–35 file, box 89, Schofield Papers, LC; 'Ingratitude of the Republic,' *Harper's New Monthly Magazine* 61 (June 1880), 118–22; McMahon to John Schofield, 18 December 1879, box 12, Schofield Papers, LC; John Schofield to William Sherman, 16 February 1868, box 45, ibid.; Private Military Journal, 17 August 1881, box 1, ibid.

[40] For a cogent analysis of public perceptions of the role of government during the Gilded Age, see Calhoun, 'The Political Culture: Public Life and the Conduct of Politics,' 185–213. For the growth in the federal government, see Bensel, *Yankee Leviathan*; Skowronek, *Building a New American State*.

[41] William Sherman to Preston, 17 April 1873, roll 45, Sherman Papers; Marszalek, *Sherman*, 444. For anti-military sentiment, see Huntington, *The Soldier and the State*, 222–6. For examples of good recent accounts of the period that include the army only tangentially, see Painter, *Standing at Armageddon*; Thompson, *The 'Spider Web,'* 256–62; Campbell, *The Human Tradition*; Richardson, *The Death of Reconstruction*; and the excellent essays in Calhoun, ed. *The Gilded Age*.

References

Barrows, Chester L. *William M. Evarts: Lawyer, Diplomat, Statesman.* Chapel Hill: University of North Carolina Press, 1941.

Bell, Roger. *Last Among Equals: Hawaiian Statehood and American Politics.* Honolulu: University of Hawaii Press, 1984.

Bensel, Richard Franklin. *Yankee Leviathan: The Origins of Central State Authority in America, 1859–1877.* Cambridge: Cambridge University Press, 1990.

Boylan, Bernard L. 'The Forty-fifth Congress and Army Reform,' *Mid-America* 41 (July 1959): 173–86.

Campbell, Ballard C., ed. *The Human Tradition in the Gilded Age and Progressive Era.* Wilmington: Scholarly Resources, 2000.

Calhoun, Charles W. 'The Political Culture: Public Life and the Conduct of Politics.' In *The Gilded Age: Essays on the Origins of Modern America*, edited by Charles W. Calhoun. Wilmington: Scholarly Resources, 1996.

Castel, Albert E. *Presidency of Andrew Johnson.* Lawrence: Regents Press of Kansas, 1979.

Coakley, Robert W. *The Role of Federal Military Forces in Domestic Disorders, 1789–1878.* Washington: Center of Military History, United States Army, 1988.

Coffman, Edward M. 'The Long Shadow of *The Soldier and the State.*' *Journal of Military History* 55 (1991): 69–82.

Dailey, Jane E. *Before Jim Crow: The Politics of Race in Postemancipation Virginia.* Chapel Hill: University of North Carolina Press, 2000.

Dawson, Joseph G., III. *Army Generals and Reconstruction: Louisiana, 1862–1877.* Baton Rouge: Louisiana State University Press, 1982.

———. 'Reconstruction as Nation-Building: The U.S. Army in the South.' In *Armed Diplomacy: Two Centuries of American Campaigning,* U.S. Army Training and Doctrine Command and Combat Studies Institute. Fort Leavenworth: Combat Studies Institute Press, 2004.

Eaton, Dorman B. *Hawaiian Annexation Scheme, A Sugar Trust Plot, Exposed by General Schofield.* New York: 1897

Gates, John M. 'The Alleged Isolation of U.S. Army Officers in the Late 19th Century.' *Parameters: The Journal of the U.S. Army War College* 10 (1980): 32–45.

Hanna, Alfred Jackson and Kathryn Abbey Hanna. *Napoleon III and Mexico: American Triumph over Monarchy.* Chapel Hill: University of North Carolina Press, 1971.

Huntington, Samuel P. *The Soldier and the State: The Theory and Politics of Civil–Military Relations.* New York: Vintage Books, 1964.

Jamieson, Perry D. *Crossing the Deadly Ground: United States Army Tactics, 1865–1899.* Tuscaloosa: University of Alabama Press, 1994.

Langley, Lester D. 'The Democratic Tradition and Military Reform, 1878–1885.' *Southwestern Social Science Quarterly* 48 (1967): 192–200.

Laurie, Clayton D., and Ronald H. Cole. *The Role of Federal Military Forces in Domestic Disorders, 1877–1945.* Washington: Center of Military History, United States Army, 1997.

Lowe, Richard G., ed. 'Virginia's Reconstruction Convention: General Schofield Rates the Delegates.' *Virginia Magazine of History and Biography* 80 (1972): 341–60.

———. *Republicans and Reconstruction in Virginia, 1856–1870.* Charlottesville: University of Virginia Press, 1991.

Maddox, Jack P. *The Virginia Conservatives: A Study in Reconstruction Politics.* Chapel Hill: University of North Carolina Press, 1970.

Marszalek, John F. *Assault at West Point: The Court-Martial of Johnson Whittaker,* rpt 1994. New York: Macmillan Co, 1972.

———. *Sherman: A Soldier's Passion for Order.* New York: Free Press, 1993.

McDonough, James Lee, and William T. Alderson. 'Republican Politics and the Impeachment of Andrew Johnson.' *Tennessee Historical Quarterly* 26 (1967): 178–83.

———. *Schofield: Union General in the Civil War and Reconstruction.* Tallahassee: Florida State University Press, 1972.

Miller, Robert Ryal. 'Matías Romero: Mexican Minister to the United States During the Juárez-Maximilian Era.' *Hispanic American Historical Review* 45 (1965): 228–45.

Mixon, Robert W. 'Pioneer Professional: General John M. Schofield and the Development of a Professional Officer Corps, 1888–1895.' M.A. thesis, Rice University, 1982.

Neely, Mark E., Jr. '"Unbeknownst" to Lincoln: A Note on Radical Pacification in Missouri During the Civil War.' *Civil War History* 44 (1998): 212–16.

Painter, Nell Irwin. *Standing at Armageddon: The United States, 1877–1919.* New York: W. W. Norton, 1987.

Prucha, Francis Paul. *Broadax and Bayonet: The Role of the United States Army in the Development of the Northwest, 1815–1860.* Madison: University of Wisconsin Press, 1953.

Richardson, Heather Cox. *The Death of Reconstruction: Race, Labor, and Politics in the Post-Civil War North, 1865–1901.* Cambridge: Harvard University Press, 2001.

Schofield, John. *Forty-Six Years in the Army,* rpt 1998. Norman: University of Oklahoma Press, 1897.

Schoonover, Thomas. *Mexican Lobby: Matías Romero in Washington, 1861–1867.* Lexington: University Press of Kentucky, 1986.

Sefton, James E. *The United States Army and Reconstruction, 1865–1877*. Baton Rouge: Louisiana State University Press, 1967.

Skowronek, Stephen. *Building a New American State: The Expansion of National Administrative Capacities, 1877–1920*. Cambridge: Cambridge University Press, 1982.

Smith, Jean Edward. *Grant*. New York: Simon and Schuster, 2001.

Swails, Thomas W. 'John McAllister Schofield: Military Diplomat.' M.A. thesis, University of Hawaii, 1966.

Tate, Merze. *Hawaii: Reciprocity or Annexation*. East Lansing: Michigan State University Press, 1968.

Tate, Michael L. *The Frontier Army in the Settlement of the West*. Norman: University of Oklahoma Press, 1999.

———. 'The Multi-purpose Army on the Frontier: A Call for Further Research.' In *The American West: Essays in Honor of W. Eugene Hollon*, edited by Ronald Lora. Toledo: University of Toledo Press, 1980.

Thompson, Margaret Susan. *The 'Spider Web:' Congress and Lobbying in the Age of Grant*. Ithaca: Cornell University Press, 1985.

Trefousse, Hans L. *Andrew Johnson: A Biography*. New York: W. W. Norton, 1989.

Utley, Robert M. *Frontier Regulars: The United States Army and the Indian, 1866–1891*. New York: Macmillan, 1973.

Wilson, James H. *The Life of John A. Rawlins*. New York: Neale Co., 1916.

Weigley, Russell. *History of the United States Army*, enlarged ed. Bloomington: Indiana University Press, 1984.

———. 'The Military Thought of John M. Schofield.' *Military Affairs* 23 (1959): 77–84.

Wooster, Robert. *Military and United States Indian Policy, 1865–1903*. New Haven: Yale University Press, 1988.

A Part or Apart: The Alleged Isolation of Antebellum U.S. Army Officers

Robert P. Wettemann, Jr.

Isolation or Internal Improvements

> In a few days I will leave this place to *mingle with the world*. I must throw aside the difference [and] *mingle in society* and endeavor to push my fortune. For years to come so good an opportunity may never come again. I have some acquaintances in Washington, Philadelphia and New York. If I cultivate them now beside the present advantage I may desire future benefit. The society here is contemptible.
>
> Second Lieutenant Samuel Heintzelman
Second U. S. Infantry Regiment
Fort Gratiot, Michigan, 1832[1]

With these words, Heintzelman bid farewell to a backwater frontier post, hoping that a return to American society would prompt opportunity to knock at his door. The anticipated prospects never materialized, and after two years' topographical duty, Heintzelman returned to his regiment to continue an ultimately lengthy military career.[2] Like Heintzelman, many U. S. Army officers left garrison life to pursue military 'duty' in the civilian realm between 1815 and 1845, with a significant number taking advantage of the terms of the General Survey Act of 1824. The act authorized the president to employ officers of the U. S. Army on surveys for 'such roads and canals as he may deem of *national importance, in a commercial or military point of view*,' to facilitate the construction of a network of internal improvements to more effectively bind the republic together.[3] Demand for this type of assistance, coupled with a broad interpretation of 'national importance' at the hands of the chief executive brought an increasing number of West Point-educated army officers into contact with the civilian world prior to the act's repeal in 1838. This intersection between civil and military circles, realized as the nation was experiencing what historians have labeled the 'Market Revolution,' had profound effects upon the form and function of military service in the decades preceding the Mexican War, thereby calling into question notions of an antebellum United States Army that was isolated, either in whole or part, from American society.[4]

Historian William Skelton asserts that 'by the eve of the Civil War, the officer corps had developed into a distinct subculture that was partially isolated, both physically and intellectually, from the main currents of the civilian world.'[5] Likewise, Samuel Watson notes that '[officers] did share a certain degree of isolation or even alienation from [civilian society's] values, and a sense of community derived from their vital but seemingly thankless mission.' As a consequence, Watson suggests that 'many officers in the years 1815 and 1846 were attempting to insulate themselves from the market revolution that caused so much anxiety and stress in the civilian world.'[6]

In light of the General Survey Act, the duties undertaken by army officers between 1824 and 1838 raise significant questions regarding the validity of the 'isolation thesis' embraced by many scholars of the antebellum army. This thesis is best delineated by Samuel P. Huntington and Russell F. Weigley. Huntington argues that prior to the American Civil War, an American 'liberal tradition' shaped a military establishment distinctly at odds with the social and intellectual mainstream of American society. Huntington casts the Jacksonian rejection of a professional establishment as anti-intellectual opposition to the officer corps as an aristocratic institution.[7] Weigley took these notions of isolation one step further. Describing the antebellum army, he writes, 'a gulf far wider than anything the eighteenth century had known came to separate the Army from the rest of America in attitudes, values and beliefs,' as the U.S. Army 'was sufficiently isolated to resemble sometimes a monastic order, isolated often physically as it patrolled the distant Indian frontiers, and isolated still more in mind and spirit as it cultivated specialized skills with in a sprawling nation of jacks of all trades.'[8] Edward M. Coffman's more recent study of the nineteenth century U.S. Army in peacetime furthers the isolation thesis. Chapters titled 'Buried in Oblivion: Officers, 1815–1860,' 'Companions of Our Exile: Women and Children 1815–1860,' and 'Wanderers in the Land: Enlisted Men, 1815–1860,' certainly imply a physical, if not intellectual, separation from American society.[9] Moving ahead chronologically, John M. Gates convincingly refutes clichéd notions of an officer corps isolated from American society though his focus is on the officers of the late nineteenth century. Examining published antebellum officer's letters and memoirs, it is possible to find numerous examples of cordial relations with members of American society on a variety of levels, suggesting that Gates's ideas may be extended backward into the antebellum period.[10]

During the early decades of the nineteenth century, army officers played an influential role in advancing the transportation revolution. The consequences of this interaction were increased contact with American society and a blurring of military roles at a time when Jacksonian Democrats tended to define martial duty in terms of their citizen-soldier figurehead. Professing that the favors of government should fall upon the people 'like rain,' Jackson and his followers decried the seemingly unfair extension of the privileges of government, and the favored position of U.S. Army officers.[11] Democratic criticism of federal-sponsored internal improvements and a supposedly aristocratic officer corps led to the repeal of the General Survey Act at a time when the onset of the Second Seminole War called officers to command troops in the Florida swamps. Before the 1840s were over, the Army would be flung back to isolated corners of the continent to spend the next ten years policing territory gained by Democrats touting Manifest Destiny. In the interim, however, there existed a time when the army, and its officers in particular, maintained close relations with American society. It is, consequently, this brief period of contact, and the political discord that ensued, that must be considered as an additional source of an isolated antebellum officer corps.[12]

'To the Public Prosperity'

The Military Peace Establishment Act of 1815 represented a significant milestone in the history of the United States, as it did, for the first time, mark the acceptance of the need for a peacetime regular army. Recognition of the need for this force was not accompanied by a precise definition of what duties this army would undertake and how the military would work to defend the nation. Opponents of a standing army, believing in the innate military ability of the 'the yeomanry of the country,' professed that the militia could provide 'the great security' for the nation. Even those who favored a small regular army envisioned that most of it would be stationed at isolated garrisons on the nation's frontier, as 'no gentleman would *employ our soldiers in opening roads, or making canals,*' as those did not represent typical martial duties.[13]

As the army struggled to find peacetime acceptance, it did so under the aegis of a secretary of war whose vision of military duty and service would earn him a place of distinction among those who held the post during the first half of the nineteenth century. Shortly after President James Madison vetoed the 'Bonus Bill' to finance a network of internal improvements, the bill's architect, South Carolinian John C. Calhoun, became President James Monroe's secretary of war. Throughout his eight years in the War Department, Secretary Calhoun reconciled the Republican resistance to a standing army with the military needs of the nation, and supported improvements in the U.S. Military Academy curriculum and the beginning of professionalization within the army officer corps. More importantly, he sought to justify the existence of this professional officer corps by putting their newly acquired scientific and technical education to use in preparing surveys, plans, and estimates for a national system of roads and canals. His plan would strengthen the nation militarily and promote national growth on a Jeffersonian model, but do so with the consequence of bringing army officers into unprecedented contact with American society.

Less than two weeks after assuming his portfolio, Calhoun stated that he would be 'amply rewarded' if his efforts in the department 'should tend in any degree to advance the growing prosperity of the Republick [sic].'[14] Three days later, Calhoun expressed similar sentiments to General Jacob Brown. 'In accepting the office,' he wrote, '...I was actuated by a strong desire to contribute as much as possible to the publick [sic] prosperity, by giving our military establishment the strongest utility and perfection.'[15] As an earlier advocate of the Bonus Bill, Calhoun saw no reason why the army could not exercise a role in the development of a national network of internal improvements, provided their actions both contributed to the common defense and promoted the general welfare.[16] This became doubly important after the military reduction in 1821, as a small number of regulars would make the nation's ability to concentrate force paramount. Consequently, Calhoun sought to hitch the supernumerary officers who remained in uniform after 1821 to the wagon of national development, actions which would dramatically change the relationship between American society and its 'isolated army.'[17]

Calhoun's belief in the utility of a network of internal improvements came well before the 1821 reduction in force, for he had lauded this notion in his 1819 'Report on Roads and Canals.' Stating that the interests of the military and the national economy were virtually indistinguishable, he professed that 'A judicious system of roads and canals, constructed for the convenience of commerce and the transportation of the mail only... is itself among the most efficient means for "the more complete defense of the United States".' These lines of communication would not only link the nation together and increase the national wealth, but would add to 'our resources in war.' Citing the provisions that placed responsibility for the common defense and promotion of the general welfare upon the shoulders of the federal government, Calhoun ignored constitutional limitations expressed by more conservative members of his party, and wholeheartedly recommended a national system of internal improvements.[18]

Calhoun proposed using army engineers trained at a recently revitalized United States Military Academy to survey routes that would contribute to a more effective defense of the 'the eastern, or Atlantic Frontier; the northern, or Canadian Frontier; and the southern, or the frontier of the Gulf of Mexico.'[19] Furnishing 'able military and topographical engineers,' the military could be 'brought in aid of the moneyed resources of the country.'[20] Where 'incorporated companies are already formed, or the road or canal company commenced [work] under the supervision of a State,' Calhoun recommended a union between civil and military leaders, with work being 'done by contract, under the superintendence and inspection of officers of the engineer corps.' Citing successes enjoyed by the military in directing private contracts for fortifications at Mobile and New Orleans, Calhoun claimed that by extending this system to 'military roads and canals, combined with a careful inspection and superintendence by skilful [sic] engineers,' the government could 'complete them with economy, durability and dispatch.'[21]

On 30 April 1824, President Monroe signed the General Survey Act, authorizing the employment of 'two or more skillful engineers, and such officers of the Corps of Engineers, or who may be detailed to duty with that Corps, as he may think proper,' to conduct surveys and prepare plans and estimates for routes of 'national importance, in a commercial or military point of view.'[22] For Secretary Calhoun, the passage of the General Survey Act represented the culmination of his departmental goals, as he established a role for the army by introducing them to domestic national economic development. At the same time, it opened a door between the army and civilian America as uniformed officers began conducting surveys for an integrated system of roads and canals and supervising other civil works of 'national importance.'[23]

In carrying out the Survey Act, President Monroe ordered military officers into the civilian realm based upon a strict interpretation of what was national, usually with an eye toward the effective defense of the country.[24] Presented in conjunction with Calhoun's report of the War Department for 1824, Monroe's Eighth Annual Message called upon Congress to increase the strength of 'both the corps of engineers – the military and the topographical,' to improve 'the execution of the powers of Congress, and in the aid of the States,' giving the nation the greatest advantage of 'their talents and services' in peace and war. As a result of the peacetime employment of these officers on national projects outside the scope of purely defensive works, '*the military will be incorporated with the civil*, at the same time removing 'injurious distinctions and prejudices of every kind,' for by assuming a nation-building role, the army, and particularly its officer corps, would possess an important peacetime function.[25]

Petitioning the United States government for aid, many state-sponsored and private companies solicited and received technical expertise from the U.S. Army. During his final year in office President Monroe carefully considered the definition of what was national in approving projects under the General Survey Act and detailing officers accordingly. His successor, John Quincy Adams, entertained a more expansive vision of 'national importance' with regards to construction projects.

Capitalizing upon the fact that West Point represented America's only source of scientifically trained engineers, Adams's policies soon made Benjamin Latrobe's 1816 observation that 'nothing is so easily converted to civil use, as the science common to both the profession of a civil and military engineer' a controversial reality.[26] Upon his election, President Adams claimed that the 'roads and aqueducts of Rome have been the admiration of all after ages.'[27] With no increase in the ranks of the Corps of Engineers forthcoming, he ordered line officers away from their regiments for service on internal improvements projects to better secure the future of the American republic. Where more shrewd politicians might have retreated from potential controversy, Adams's 'latitudinarian doctrines' with regards to internal improvements, coupled with an increased martial role in their prosecution, would contribute to the undoing of a president whose very election in 1824 was characterized by partisan rancor and electoral dispute.[28]

Many in Congress criticized the expanded role for the army from the outset. Virginia Congressman William Rives moved to strike an early Survey Act appropriations measure, claiming the union of civil and military interests to be 'radically vicious.'

Rives reasoned that when Americans 'see the officers of the United States [Army] among us,' they would 'naturally associate them with the idea of the vast fiscal power and resources of this Government.' Rives contended that the basis for the injection of the military into the civilian realm was inextricably linked to the 'paternal solicitude' of the executive, who, in suffering from political miscalculations associated with the 'Corrupt Bargain' of 1824, was attempting to use the military to ensure his reelection in 1828.[29] In like fashion, William Smith of South Carolina condemned a Senate report detailing 'sixty-nine distinct surveys of roads, of canals, of rivers, of creeks, and of harbors' conducted by the military.[30] By using military engineers in civilian circles, Smith alleged that the Adams administration, conscious of the challenge it would face in the next presidential election, was seeking to 'buy the people with their own money.' Expressing similar contempt for the regular army, he cast these officers, the 'sons of members of Congress, and the sons of their friends and favorites' as men not performing their military duties, and simply, 'amusing themselves through the country.'[31]

Although President Adams initially approved work on five new 'national' projects, his army soon looked to other requests that brought an ever increasing number of uniformed officers into civilian circles.[32] Seeking an 'experienced engineer' to aid in the development of a project in his district, Congressman Thomas Metcalfe of Kentucky secured the services of Lieutenant Colonel Stephen Long to survey a road linking Zanesville, Ohio, and Lexington, Kentucky, in March 1827.[33] Baltimore & Ohio Railroad President Philip Thomas met with President Adams on 1 May 1827 and quickly received promises of Long's expertise to chart a route for the proposed rail line, with additional assistance to be provided by Captain William G. McNeill, and Lieutenants William Cook, Walter Gwynn, Joshua Barney, Isaac Trimble, R. Edward Hazzard, John Dillahunty, and Henry Thompson, line officers deemed 'conversant with the details of civil engineering.'[34] Later that summer, Lieutenant Colonel John Anderson received orders to survey a canal route between Taunton and Weymouth, Massachusetts.[35] Upon the request of the Pennsylvania Canal Commissioners, Lieutenant John Findlay received a furlough to assist them in charting a route during the winter of 1827–28.[36] While Long, McNeill, and Anderson were Topographical Engineers, the lieutenants detailed to service were not, and were part of a growing number of line officers detailed to serve within the confines of American society during the Adams presidency (see Table 1).

Table 1 Line Officers Detached to Engineering Duty, 1824–29.

Year	1824	1825	1826	1827	1828	1829
Officer Corps (size)	540	540	540	540	540	540
Topographical duty	17	25	30	29	35	36
% of Officer Corps	3.1	4.6	5.5	5.3	6.5	6.6
Engineering duty	1	2	2	1	1	8
% of Officer Corps	0.2	0.4	0.4	0.2	0.2	1.5
Total Officers on detached duty	18	27	32	30	36	44
Total % of Officer Corps on detached duty	3.3	5.0	5.9	5.5	6.6	8.1

Those who opposed this expanded presence of the U.S. Army in American society soon found a champion in the man jilted by Adams in the 1824 election. Shortly after the 1824 presidential debacle, proponents of democracy looked to Andrew Jackson, hoping that hero of New Orleans could deliver the nation from the forces of privilege, promote equality in government and impose a limit on federal involvement with internal improvements.[37] His election in 1828 would not only mark the dawn of a new era of American democracy, but would lead to a dramatic shift in policy regarding American civil-military relations, a shift that would limit the military's role *in* American society and return serving officers to their normally recognized place commanding troops in the field.

Few could deny that Andrew Jackson lacked formal experience in military affairs. However, by virtue of his victory over the British at New Orleans, many regarded him as the ultimate example of the citizen-soldier. Although Jackson believed that West Point-trained officers promoted the 'moral and intellectual character' of the regular army, 'their knowledge of the military art will be advantageously employed in the militia service.'[38] That would be the limit of their contact with American society, as Jackson, still much the general, believed that an officer's place was in front of soldiers, not engaged in works of internal improvements. In a comparable vein, not only did Jackson believe that 'all internal improvements funded by the national government' should be 'opened to the enjoyment of all our fellow citizens,' but he rejected any union of the financial or corporate concerns of the federal government (i.e., the military) with those of the 'States or individuals' as 'inconsistent with its institutions' and highly 'impolitic.'[39]

The union of federal and private interests represented one of Andrew Jackson's greatest fears, a fear expressed in the Maysville and other internal improvements vetoes.[40] If the federal government financed intrastate improvements, or detailed officers to conduct surveys for state or private projects, these actions not only ran contrary to the notion that the 'majority is to govern,' but represented the extension of federal privilege to either a specific locality or incorporated company. From Jackson's perspective, the continued employment of serving army officers in the private sector would lead to 'prejudice to the public interest or an alienation of the affectations to the general discredit,' a practice dangerous to the liberties of the people.[41] By limiting federal privilege to states and private companies and only approving appropriations (or assistance) for projects he considered national, he hoped to 'prevent m'ch logg-rolling [sic] legislation,' and 'put down the corrupting system of [government] union with corporations and appropriations for local objects.'[42]

So initially, Jackson sought to confine projects surveyed or directed by the army to those of national significance, thereby curtailing the 'pernicious consequence of a scramble for the favors of government' that had taken place during the Adams administration.[43] However, as officers took advantage of the exclusive opportunities made possible by a West Point education and continued conducting surveys for roads, canals, and railroads throughout the early years of Jackson's presidency, they soon became targets for Democratic criticism. Not only did the Jacksonians believe that the academy was generating an exclusive, aristocratic officer corps, but this prop for Henry Clay's

American System simply detailed officers throughout the country to assist those best able to secure political patronage for private gain. When these 'privileged' academy graduates were not ordered to the line, but instead found employment developing new communications routes for state governments and private companies, surely, many Democrats reasoned, this did not represent the most effective use of a military dedicated to the common defense.

The opposition to continued civil–military collaboration notwithstanding, officers continued performing yeoman service in advancing the nation's infrastructure throughout Jackson's first term. In June 1830, Major General Alexander Macomb informed Lewis Coryell of the Pennsylvania Canal Company that the leave of absence granted to Brevet Second Lieutenant Antes Snyder of the Second Infantry would be extended, and he would effectively be on furlough until 1 September, allowing him to continue his 'indispensable' work on the Delaware division of the canal.[44] On 30 November 1831 New Jersey Governor Peter Vroon successfully solicited the continued assistance of Fourth Artillery Lieutenant William Cook, who up to that point had been serving as the superintending engineer on the Camden and Amboy Railroad. August 1831 found Topographical Engineer Captain James Graham and two assistants charting a railroad route between Winchester and Harpers Ferry, Virginia.[45] In addition, other officers served in assignments with a number of eastern railroads, including the Baltimore and Susquehanna, the Patterson and Hudson River, and the Catskill and Conajoharie.[46]

While Jackson launched his attack on internal improvements in general with the Maysville veto, his crusade against officers working in the civilian realm took on other forms. The employment of an ever-increasing number of West Point graduates on these projects came to change Jackson's opinion of what he once called 'the best school in the world.'[47] Professing that 'the bulwark of our national defense is the national militia,' Jackson, like so many of his political allies, soon came to question the form and utility of a military academy that had strayed from its Jeffersonian roots.[48] Not only did the automatic promotion of graduating cadets to brevet second lieutenant foster an apparent military aristocracy, but critics claimed a West Point education now led to a personal benefit from the public purse, as officers' technical skills allowed them to extend privileges to those who employed military engineers on private and local improvement projects being launched throughout America.

In an effort to reduce this contact, Jackson's Secretary of War, Lewis Cass, issued Order No. 63, on 15 November 1831, ordering all officers 'absent from their military duties, with the sanction of the War Department, and engaged in any employment not under its direction' to return to their regiments.[49] The directive represented a reaction to an earlier report prepared by Cass's predecessor, John Eaton, showing the magnitude of civil–military contact. Of the 511 infantry and artillery officers, 320 (63 percent) were on duty with their regiments, while 140 of them (27 percent) were on staff or other detached service (including recruiting, topographical duty, instruction at West Point, and quartermaster and commissary duties with their regiments) and 51 (10 percent) were on furlough. Of those on staff duty, 30 were with the engineer branches: eight with the Corps of Engineers and 22 on topographical duty.[50]

Cass's order represented an attempt to apply the equalitarian principles of the Jacksonian Democrats to the operations of the army engineers in two ways. Ordering all officers on extra duties back to their regiments represented a great step towards limiting the need for the large number of supernumerary officers then in service. By forcing officers to return to their regiments, the company duties formerly assumed by superfluous officers would now be carried out by those officers assigned to the regiment. This practice would not only eliminate the need for the extra officers produced by West Point, but it would promote economy, frugality, and small government, as the enrollment at this 'privileged' institution could be reduced.

At the same time, Cass's Order No. 63 also represented an attempt to apply the principles outlined in the Maysville Veto to War Department engineers. No longer would officers be freely detailed to projects of national importance under the loosely defined terms of the General Survey Act. By limiting this extension of military assistance, the number of army officers working in American society would be strictly curtailed. In the future, the secretary of war could limit their operations to three classes of national projects, as outlined by Colonel John J. Abert, commander of the Topographical Bureau. The bureau's first priority should be surveys 'directed by resolutions of Congress,' as they were supposed to be an expression of the needs of the people. Second, attention would be directed to any incomplete surveys. When completed, work would shift to a third class of surveys, namely those 'requisite to ascertain the military peculiarities of our frontier and for position of fortifications.'[51]

Despite the restriction imposed on officers detached from their regiments, some continued working on civilian projects. Just days after Cass's order, Abert reported that Captain William McNeill, Second Artillery Lieutenant George Whistler, and First Artillery Lieutenant John Dillahunty continued to superintend work on the Baltimore and Ohio Railroad, having been previously 'relieved' from Cass's directive.[52] On 27 April 1832, Fourth Artillery Lieutenant Augustus Canfield was ordered to assist Sixth Infantry Lieutenants Drayton and Whistler on the additional 'public duties' already assigned to McNeill.[53] Later that summer, McNeill was directed to other projects outside the purview of those 'national' works, surveying planned rail routes connecting New London, Connecticut, and Providence, Rhode Island, between New London and Worcester, Massachusetts, as well as examining obstructions in the Providence River, Rhode Island. To assist him, First Artillery Lieutenant William Swift and Third Artillery Lieutenant Edward White were placed under McNeill's command.[54]

Despite Cass's order, a significant number of officers continued to blur the lines between military and civilian roles, as many remained actively involved in civil affairs. These activities were not confined solely to engineering officers, as some of the officers so engaged were on leave from their respective regiments and consequently absent from their troops in the field.

The continued absence of these officers led to more directives from the War Department, with General Order No. 48, issued on 18 May 1833, perhaps being the most explicit notice of the alleged ills facing the antebellum officer corps. In an effort to prevent recently commissioned academy graduates from pursuing lucrative employment opportunities on civilian projects through furlough or detachment to the staff,

Table 2 Line Officers Detached to Engineering Duty, 1830–38.

Year	1830	1831	1832	1833	1834	1835	1836	1837	1838
Officer Corps (size)	540	540	589	599	599	599	647	647	647
Topographical duty	27	25	30	23	27	26	18	1	0
% of Officer Corps	5	4.6	5.1	3.8	4.5	4.3	2.8	0.1	0
Engineering duty	10	10	11	15	16	21	23	13	1
% of Officer Corps	1.9	1.9	2.0	2.5	2.7	3.5	3.6	2.0	0.1
Officers detached on Special Engineering Assignment*	4	4	3	4	3	6	5	2	0
% of Officer Corps	0.7	0.7	0.5	0.6	0.5	1.0	0.8	0.3	0
Total Officers on detached duty	41	39	44	42	46	53	46	16	1
Total % of Officer Corps on detached duty	7.6	7.2	7.5	7.0	7.7	8.8	7.1	2.5	0.1

*Includes service with one or more of the following engineering projects: Virginia Railroad, Baltimore and Susquehanna Railroad, New Orleans Canal, New Jersey Internal Improvements, Ohio and Mississippi River Survey, Patterson and Hudson Railroad, Boston and Providence Railroad, Florida Military Road, Stonington and Providence Railroad, Cumberland Road, Potomac Aqueduct, U. S. Coast Survey, Florida and Alabama Railroad, Taunton and New Bedford Railroad, Norwich and Wooster Railroad, Niagara Ship Canal, Charleston and Cincinnati Railroad, Connecticut River Survey, Fayette Railroad, Atlanta, Florida and Georgia Railroad, and Saybrook Harbor Navigation.

Cass tried to confine the services of junior officers to the regiments to which they were posted. His order specified that no officer would be 'allowed to fill any Staff appointment, the duties of which will detach him from his regiment, until he has served, at least three years with his regiment,' expressly noting that the order would apply to future postings in the Engineer and Topographical departments. Subsequent paragraphs of the order limited the duration of detached service to a maximum of two years, noting that all officers operating contrary to these orders were to be 'relieved and ordered to rejoin their respective regiments and stations' by 1 May 1834 or 'as soon as public service will, in the opinion of the general-in-chief, permit.'[55]

These orders came as a number of Democratic congressmen renewed their objections to the military academy. Among the more well-known critics, 'Colonel' David Crockett of Tennessee introduced a Congressional resolution in 1830 that the academy should be abolished altogether, as it granted 'exclusive privileges to its cadets,' and was 'a downright invasion of the rights of the citizens and a violation of the civil compact called "the constitution".'[56] Early in the first session of the Twenty-third Congress, Kentucky Democrat Albert G. Hawes called upon the House Committee on Military Affairs to consider abolishing West Point.[57] Condemning the academy in 1836, New Hampshire Democrat Franklin Pierce opposed the schooling of 'any number of young men who, on the completion of their education' did not form a portion of the military force, but returned 'to the walks of private life,' going on to recommend a drastic restructuring of the academy.[58]

During the course of these attacks, a number of officers responded, either publicly or in private. Writing under the pseudonym 'Truth,' one officer questioned the policies established by Order No. 48 in the *Army and Navy Chronicle*. Observing that he was 'not aware of the regulation having been revoked,' he knew of 'a number of officers now on detached service' who had not fulfilled the requisite three years service with their regiment. 'Truth' challenged the extension of special privileges to other officers who violated the regulation by serving in a detached capacity for more than two years. The anonymous writer pointed a finger at the general-in-chief, Alexander Macomb, arguing that his position 'endow[ed] him with a source of patronage and unlimited discretion,' allowing him to act 'to his, and his friends' pleasures and interests.' Macomb's orders, the unidentified scribe professed, failed to promote the 'efficiency of the army; but what will best consist with personal feeling, personal bias – what will best bolster up self!' adding that 'these, it would seem, are the motives to the present unjust policy observed towards the army.'[59]

Some officers, conscious of these attacks and wondering why the Jacksonians could not see the military utility of officers advancing the nation's internal development, questioned their future in the military, particularly when their engineering skills would be profitable elsewhere. During the summer of 1836, Lieutenant George Cullum, angered by efforts to close the academy, expressed his frustrations to his family. Serving as Colonel Joseph G. Totten's assistant in the construction of Fort Adams, Rhode Island (near Newport), Cullum discovered that after 30 years service, his superior received only $1,700 per year. Faced with such limited prospects and tiring of the repeated attacks against the Military Academy, he dejectedly wrote, 'I am broken in spirits by the niggardly treatment we have received during the few past years.' In light of the poor working conditions, and the machinations of the 'filthy politicians,' he entertained other options for employment. Having worked within the civilian realm

Table 3 Officer Resignations, 1830–44[63]

Year	Number	% Total	Total Officer Corps	% Corps
1830	15	3.7	546	2.7
1831	18	4.4	546	3.3
1832	23	5.7	594	3.9
1833	37	9.1	603	6.1
1834	14	3.4	603	2.3
1835	47	11.6	603	7.8
1836	117	29.1	648	18.1
1837	44	10.8	648	6.8
1838	26	6.4	648	4.0
1839	22	5.4	735	2.9
1840	13	3.2	735	1.8
1841	10	2.4	735	1.4
1842	10	2.4	733	1.4
1843	4	1.0	733	0.5
1844	6	1.4	733	0.8
TOTAL	406	100.0	N/A	N/A

constructing of coastal works, he recognized that 'there is at present a great demand for civil engineers throughout the country, and from the offers that have been made I know that I could advance my pecuniary affairs much.' He warned his brother-in-law not to 'think it strange.... if after getting a little more practical information' he saw him 'doff the chapeau and epaulets for money.'[60] Cullum's search for alternate employment was not unique. 'The Officer's Friend,' writing to the *Army and Navy Chronicle* in September, observed that young officers educated at West Point 'can get handsome salaries by attaching themselves to companies engaged in carrying on works of internal improvement, such as rail roads, canals, mining, &c.,' a notion that echoed in the *Chronicle*'s pages well into the next year.[61]

In May 1836, the paper's editor wrote 'that the army is becoming (we might perhaps with more justice say, *has become*) unpopular with the officers, is manifested by the number of resignations which almost daily take place.' He went on to comment upon the cause of these resignations, observing that 'nearly all the employments in civil life offer better remuneration than the pay and chances of promotion in the army.'[62] Comments such as these were not hollow threats, as a number of officers had already left the ranks of the army for lucrative civilian employment both before and after the publication of Orders No. 43 and 69. Considering how rapidly they secured work, their new jobs could only have been possible as a result of the civilian contacts made while performing 'military' duties under the terms of the General Survey Act.

Before he formally joined the Second Infantry, Lieutenant Antes Snyder, having spent his post-West Point graduation leave of absence working on the Delaware division of the Pennsylvania Canal, left the army on 20 September 1830 for a permanent position as Assistant Engineer to continue working for the state of Pennsylvania. Lieutenant William Cook of the Fourth Artillery resigned in January 1832 after having spent the preceding two years in uniform working on a variety of internal improvements projects in New Jersey (and prior to that on detached duty under Captain William McNeill). Having established significant connections in those pursuits, he quickly secured employment with the nearby Camden and Amboy Railroad. Lieutenant George Whistler discarded his uniform in December 1833, having spent the previous 11 years engaged on topographical duty and working on no fewer than three different railroads. Immediately upon his resignation, he became the associate engineer of the Stonington, Connecticut, and Providence Rhode Island Railroad, capitalizing upon connections established while working as a military engineer for the other railroad companies.[64]

These departures were part of a larger resignation crisis of the mid-1830s, for a number of officers left the army, having been made aware of the opportunities present in civilian society as a product of their employment under the General Survey Act. Capitalizing upon the opportunities presented by internal improvements and seeking to avoid service in the Second Seminole War, their collective loss, coupled with the continued absence of other officers employed both within the army and in the civilian realm, placed the regular establishment in dire circumstances. As Cullum contemplated the attacks levied against the army, conditions forced Adjutant General Roger Jones to inform political leadership of the staff shortages suffered by field commanders.

In Florida, Major General Winfield Scott 'was without a single officer for duty on his personal staff, no-one to act as adjutant general, inspector general, or even aide-de-camp,' with General Edmund P. Gaines facing comparable manpower difficulties on the Mexican border.[65]

On 24 June 1836 the War Department struck back, issuing General Order No. 43, designed to force those officers on detached duty to return to their regiments at a time when their engineering expertise was desperately needed by the military and actively sought by state governments and private companies. The adjutant general informed the army that at the direction of President Jackson 'the several Captains now absent from their companies and not on duty with the Army, nor employed in military service proper' should rejoin their regiments without delay, specifically naming 37 junior officers, 25 of whom were on engineering or topographical duty.[66]

Even with this explicit directive, many officers continued to work in civilian society, with their actions being defended by the chief of the Topographical Bureau. In a report of active topographic officers and their assistants forwarded to Secretary Cass, Colonel Abert explained that if these state and private projects languished, it would amount to nothing less than 'a prohibition of the improvement of the country and divests the Government of its paternal and patronizing character.'[67] Acting at Abert's direction, the following officers remained employed on civil works: Lieutenant Seneca Simmons of the Seventh Infantry and Third Infantry Lieutenant James Cooper assisted Lieutenant Colonel Stephen Long in developing the surveys, plans and estimates for a railroad route from Belfast, Maine, to Quebec, Canada, acting at the request of the governor and legislature of Maine; Seventh Infantry Lieutenant Roger Dix aided Major Hartman Bache in preparing drawings based upon their survey of Georgetown, South Carolina; Fourth Artillery Lieutenant John Macomb worked with Captain James D. Graham in superintending the railroad construction from the Alabama state line to the Appalachicola River, in addition to preparing the surveys, plans and estimates for a railroad that the governor of Florida requested be made between Pensacola, Florida, and Columbia, Georgia; Fourth Artillery Lieutenant Joseph E. Johnston joined Captain William Turnbull in overseeing construction of the Potomac aqueduct; and Lieutenant Thomas Drayton of the Sixth Infantry and Seventh Infantry Lieutenant James Reed were employed under the direction of Captain William G. Williams in a state survey of a rail route from Charleston, South Carolina, to Cincinnati, Ohio.[68]

These line officers violated War Department orders under the sanction of immediate superiors who were active agents in ensuring the success of the very state entities and private corporations for which their surveys were made. In late August, a *Washington Globe* advertisement offered $200 a year for laborers willing to assist in the construction of the Alabama, Florida and Georgia Railroad that ran from Pensacola, Florida, to Columbia, Georgia.[69] Not only did Captain James Graham survey that route, but the advertisement listed him as company engineer under company President William H. Chase, who also held a commission as captain in the Corps of Engineers.[70]

This continuing union of public and private interests in spite of War Department orders to the contrary soon motivated President Jackson to take action. Making a more concerted effort to suspend permanently the detachment of line officers for engineer duty on state and private projects, Adjutant General Jones issued General Order No. 69, on 13 October, containing forceful words straight from the president's pen. Due to the failure of Order No. 43 and the 'destitute condition of the service owing to the absences of so many platoon officers,' Jackson proclaimed that 'this condition of the Army must no longer be permitted to exist.' The old general pronounced that an officer's duty was commanding men in the field, not taking jobs in civilian circles that separated them from their troops. To these ends, Jackson ordered 'the several captains and subalterns who are not on duty with their companies' to 'immediately… join their regiments.' Specifically naming those officers who should return to service, he decreed that in the future, no more than two officers from an artillery company and one from an infantry company would be simultaneously detailed for detached duty, without presidential approval. Moreover, Jackson insisted, 'Topographical Engineers will be employed with the army in the field, and hereafter be assigned to duty under the orders of the proper commander.'[71]

To remove any possibility of misinterpretation of this order, Jackson specifically named the field officers to whom the Topographical Engineers were to report. Of the eight topographical engineers sent to the frontier, all were called away from established civilian projects of considerable import, projects that Colonel Abert believed 'could not be entrusted to men other than officers of great experience and diligence.'[72] Informing Jackson's new Secretary of War, Benjamin Butler, of the situation, Abert convinced Butler to rescind at least part of Order No. 69, as the colonel later informed all officers under his direction except two that they would be allowed to remain on civilian construction projects until 1 February 1837. At that time, they were expected to have concluded their surveys, and were requested to report to the officers previously specified.[73]

Despite Jackson's best efforts, West Point graduates continued to be employed on state and private projects. When directed to return to their regiments, many officers left the army, translating their federally-funded West Point education into lucrative employment in a growing domestic economy. The extension of technical assistance by army officers, as well as the speedy departure of officers educated at the public expense to the civilian realm, remained a thorn in the side of the Jacksonians. Though not opposed to Jefferson's idea of educating young men in the military arts, the self-serving actions of these technically trained officers represented the antithesis of Jacksonian views on privilege, equality, and the propriety of the union of public aid and private enterprise.

Reacting to these developments, Jacksonians in Congress launched a new round of criticism upon what they asserted was the aristocratic nature of West Point, a political offensive set against the backdrop of conflict in Florida and Texas. In May 1837, these events would be further complicated by the downturn of the American economy and the onset of the Panic of 1837. While the prospect of campaigning in the swamps of Florida provided a powerful deterrent to continued military service, the moribund domestic economy ended what had been an internal improvements boom.

Thus, it was Jackson's hand-picked successor, Martin Van Buren, who would ultimately be forced to deal with these issues in an effort to end military participation in the development of a national network of internal improvements. In doing so, a number of factors worked collectively not only to make the repeal of the General Survey Act a possibility, but to ensure that army officers would remain in command positions in the future. These events had the net result of forcing army officers to return to more active military service with their regiments, as changing circumstances, not to mention a changing national landscape, placed new demands upon the War Department.

Jacksonian Victory

As he prepared his first annual message, Van Buren received word of the 'enmity' that existed 'on the part of a large portion of the officers of the Army towards the late and present administration, and the unfavorable influence which they exercise against them.' In a private and confidential letter addressed to the president and subsequently forwarded to Secretary of War Joel R. Poinsett, Ver Planck Van Antwerp, writing from Calhoun, Tennessee, informed Van Buren that the 'manner in which [army] operations had been conducted, and appropriations made' on the National Road in Indiana during the last three years cost [their] Democratic party at least 'two thousand votes in the election in November last and an equal number in the late Congressional election.' Van Antwerp accused Captain Cornelius Ogden, acting as superintendent of the Cumberland Road, of interfering in local politics by appointing 'a large number of persons… avowedly and in many cases actively and influentially, opponents of the Administration,' to serve in different capacities in Illinois and Indiana. To solve these problems Van Antwerp not only advocated breaking up Ogden's headquarters and ordering him to some fortification or isolated coastal project, but the ardent Western Democrat offered more general suggestions with regard to military policy.[74]

Claiming to have been a former cadet,[75] Van Antwerp asserted that no man had been a 'warmer friend than myself' of the Military Academy, though the 'anti-democratic principles, and the contempt in which some of them [academy-educated officers] held the intelligence and political right of the "Citizens"' had forced him to change his opinion. As a consequence of the 'power and patronage thrown into the hands of officers of the Army,' Van Antwerp recommended that to better serve the 'wishes of the great mass of the people, and the true interests of the Democratic Party… steps can not too speedily be taken, for ridding the settled parts of the country of the presence of the Military.' Force them 'to the frontier, or *upon the sea coast or the Lakes.*'[76]

It is not known the degree to which Van Antwerp's letter influenced Van Buren, but other Democrats in Congress certainly echoed the notions he brought to the president. During the course of the debate to increase the military establishment to allow them to fight more effectively the growing Seminole War in Florida, Democratic Senator James Buchanan of Pennsylvania agreed that 'some increase of the topographical and military engineers was necessary.' However, he inquired as to whether or not the expansion would include 'any provision' to 'prevent the employment of engineers by private companies.' While he understood that civil engineers had been 'scarce' in 1824, such was not the case in 1838. Railroad and canal companies employed army officers 'to a great extent, and that [army officers] had accumulated large fortunes under the service of their country while the business of the government was neglected.' Although he may have exaggerated the matter of 'fortunes,' Buchanan successfully amended the bill so that 'no officers of the said corps [of Engineers] shall be employed in any service, for any state or company, for which he shall receive any compensation except his pay from the United States.' No senator questioned his amendment, tacitly recognizing the need to solve problems posed by military participation on state and private internal improvement projects, and no debate was offered when the Senate approved the bill and sent it to the House.[77]

In debating the measure, the House added a section to the bill that barred the door between the U.S. Army and civilian America first opened by the General Survey Act. The House amendment explicitly prohibited 'the separation of officers from their regiments and corps for employment on civil works of internal improvement,' or further work in the service of private companies, giving officers so employed one year to sever their relations with any company that employed them. Within a few days, differences between the two versions were ironed out and the bill was passed on for presidential approval.[78]

When Van Buren signed the 'Act to Increase the Present Military Establishment of the United States, and for Other Purposes,' and a second supplemental act approved three days later, he ended the U.S. Army's active role in promoting domestic prosperity.[79] Prohibiting officers from being separated from their regiments for employment on civilian internal improvement projects and blocking those same officers from offering their services to incorporated companies while in uniform, halted a practice that allowed academy graduates to extend federal privilege, and dissolved most connections between the national government and private companies that Jackson had decried since the Maysville Veto. This move effectively made illegal the most prominent means by which officers could, while remaining in uniform, execute broadly interpreted 'martial' duties in American society, ensuring that continued contact between the active-duty army officers and private enterprise would be limited at best. Naturally, numerous former officers retained their lucrative jobs as engineers with railroads and construction companies.

The acts of July 1838 did not, however, mark the immediate end of military participation on internal improvements, as a few officers still found a way to benefit from detached duties on internal improvements, albeit on a limited basis. On 25 August 1838, Brevet Lieutenant Colonels James Kearney and Stephen Long, and Captains William Swift and George Hughes, were allowed to continue working, but were requested to 'terminate' their 'present connection' with the state or company for whom they worked within one year after the act of 5 July 1838 was signed by the president.[80] Although a handful of officers were granted these limited exceptions, the new statutes halted all work for states and private companies, as well as redefined the form, focus, and function that military engineering would take in the future. No longer would officers extend privileges to states and private companies through their engineering aid, receive financial benefit or job opportunities from this association, or, to recall Heintzelman's phrase, 'mingle with society' while receiving pay for being a U.S. Army officer.

The survey, design, and construction of the projects undertaken by military engineers after 1838 reflected the position articulated by President Jackson in his veto of the Maysville Road Bill. As he had written to Martin Van Buren in 1830, national routes should be limited to 'those great leading and navigable streams from the ocean, and passing through two or more states, and [clearing] an obstruction that prevents commerce from passing thro' other states, which when removed will give an uninterrupted passage to those other states.'[81] In December 1838, the duties of the Corps of Topographical Engineers were formalized in General Order No. 11, as Commanding General Alexander Macomb assigned the Topographical Engineers to prepare 'surveys for the defense of the frontier, inland and Atlantic, and of positions for fortifications, in reconnaissance of the country through which an army has to pass… the examination of all routes of communication by land or water, both for supplies and for military movement: [and] in the construction of military roads and bridges, and of fieldworks, for the defenses of encampments, fords, ferries, and bridges.' In carrying out these duties, 'Officers of the Corps of Topographical Engineers,' and by implication, any additional line officers assigned to assist them, 'should *always* accompany Armies in the field.'[82]

Redefined Martial Duties

By the end of the next decade, the acquisition of Oregon and the lands gained at successful conclusion of the Mexican War would double the size of the United States. In short order, the U.S. Army would be ordered to the far reaches of the continent to police the recently acquired territories and make them safe for settlement. In performing these new tasks, much of the army would be physically isolated from the remainder of the nation, and officers commanding frontier posts would have little contact with American society. Those in positions of leadership continued to be products of West Point, but unlike previous graduates, those receiving their commissions after 1838 were now required to serve in the military for four years after graduation instead of a single year, as had been the case previously. Most remained in service throughout the 1850s, and it was only the Civil War that would generate a mass exodus from the commissioned ranks anywhere close to that which occurred during the mid-1830s.

The new ideas of martial service that emerged following the repeal of the General Survey Act were accompanied by a redefinition of what it meant to be a military officer. As a product of increased civilian contact, those officers uncomfortable with notions of service to country over self replaced their army blue with civilian mufti in pursuit of personal gain. Many of those officers who remained in uniform did so in a physically isolated army, but chose to perform their duties nurturing seeds of nascent professionalism, recognizing that an army officer's primary duty was to the country. Through this conscious choice of service to country, these officers demonstrated that personal interests were secondary to the national defense.

The return of line officers to their regiments also contributed to an increased acceptance for the military at the hands of those who had formally opposed it. With the Mexican War proving the value of a West Point education, the academy would never again be a target of the Jacksonian Democrats who sought its elimination. Under their new definitions of duty, the Corps of Topographical Engineers continued land surveys after the war ended in 1848. In 1853, the Corps performed the single largest surveying project to date when Congress approved the Pacific railroad survey.[83] Although the Pacific railroad was widely regarded as a national project, the roadblock to internal improvements projects imposed by the 1838 statutes failed to prevent officers returning from Mexico from seeking employment with other companies building railroads in both older states and the new territories. However, this employment came with an important caveat, as it was dependent upon an officer securing an officially-sanctioned leave of absence or a furlough freeing him from other military duties. Under no circumstances could officers seek work of this nature if they were engaged in military service in the field. This prohibition against service in American society bred isolation, isolation that came with the recognition of the need for a U.S. Army that once again performed purely martial duties as a part of American society, while remaining apart from it.

Notes

[1] Heintzelman Diary, 4 August 1831 through 30 March 1832, Samuel P. Heintzelman Papers, United States Military Academy Library, West Point, NY, emphasis added.

[2] During a 43-year career, Heintzelman fought in Florida, Mexico, California, and in the Civil War, and served in garrison in Wisconsin, Kansas, Missouri and New York. He remained ambitious even while on the frontier, blurring his martial roles as president of the Sonora Exploring and Mining Company in the 1850s. See Thompson, *Fifty Miles and a Fight*, and North, *Samuel Peter Heintzelman and the Sonora Exploring and Mining Company*. For his military record, see Cullum, *Biographical Register*, 2: 372–74.

[3] 'An Act to Procure the Necessary Surveys, Plans and Estimates upon the Subject of Roads and Canals,' *United States Statutes at Large* vol. 4, 22–23 (1824), emphasis added.

[4] See Sellers, *The Market Revolution*. In his study of the transformation of American economic relationships that followed the War of 1812, the author argues that beginning in 1817, John Calhoun's War Department, and specifically the younger generation of officers educated at a West Point recently remodeled along the lines of the French Ecole Polytechnique, was central to developing a network of roads, canals and railways that summarily facilitated a national transportation revolution. Although Sellers is correct in noting the dramatic expansion of civil engineering operations directed by army officers during the Adams administration, he fails to make a distinction between local and national internal improvements, and how Andrew Jackson objected to the use of military officers on local projects, yet permitted their employment on national projects relating to interstate commerce. My analysis of Jacksonian-era internal improvements and the role of the U.S. military in their prosecution is based upon the research for Wettemann, 'To The Public Prosperity.'

[5] See Skelton, *An American Profession of Arms*, 181. In 'Professionalization of the U.S. Army Officer Corps During the Age of Jackson,' Skelton contends that by the 1830s and 1840s, 'officers were becoming more circumspect in their political activities' as their 'political actions' focused mainly on issues within the service,' 462–463. Skelton further lays out this notion in 'Officers and Politicians: The Origins of Army Politics in he United States before the Civil War.'

[6] See Watson, 'Flexible Gender Roles During the Market Revolution.' However, Watson claims that 'Army officers were not isolated from society, though its values sometimes irritated and even alienated them,' an apparent contradiction from his earlier position, 99, note 9. In addition to addressing notions of isolation, Skelton's *An American Profession of Arms*, and

Watson's earlier 'Professionalism, Social Attitudes and Civil-Military Accountability in the United States Army Officer Corps,' were central in articulating the emergence of a professional military ethic prior to the American Civil War. They challenge Coffman's 'The Long Shadow of *The Soldier and the State*,' which reviews the historiographical evolution of the argument, positing that American military professionalism was the product of a post-Civil War military establishment. Unlike Coffman, Skelton persuasively contends that a distinctive 'military mind' emerged before 1861, with officers, possessing 'a complex of ideas concerning their collective role, civil-military relations, foreign and Indian affairs, and other matters,' including, as initially outlined a certain circumspection when it came to issues of politics, Skelton, *An American Profession of Arms*, xiii, notions further developed by Watson, 'Professionalism, Social Attitudes and Civil-Military Accountability.' My analysis builds upon the work of Skelton and Watson, establishing that the General Survey Act and the ensuing political debate over the role of the U.S. Army in internal improvements served as a catalyst in defining at least one aspect of the 'military mind' outlined by Skelton, doing so well before the advent of the Civil War, see Wettemann, 'To The Public Prosperity': The U.S. Army and the Market Revolution, 1815–1844.'

[7] Huntington, *The Soldier and the State*, 193–221.

[8] Weigley, *History of the United States Army*, 157–58. The entire relevant passages from Weigley are as follows: 'For the future, however, the most important result of the divergence between civilian egalitarianism and military professionalism was an increased isolation of the Army from the rest of American life... a gulf far wider than anything the eighteenth century had known came to separate the Army from the rest of America in attitudes, values, and beliefs... Henceforth... the Regular army was sufficiently isolated to resemble sometimes a monastic order, isolated often physically as it patrolled the distant Indian frontiers, and isolated still more in mind and spirit as it cultivated specialized skills within a sprawling nation of jacks-of-all trades.'

[9] Coffman, *The Old Army*. Although Millett and Maslowski, *For the Common Defense*, recognize the importance of the 1824 General Survey Act and the economic impact of military posts to nearby settled areas, their comparison of junior officers 'shut away in frontier posts' to naval officers on 'distant ships' suggests both physical and intellectual isolation from American society.

[10] Gates, 'The Alleged Isolation of U.S. Army Officers in the Late 19th Century.'

[11] Framing Jacksonian Democracy in the context of a struggle between privilege and equality is not new. Other historians have relied upon similar themes to explain the political, economic and social developments of the period, but in doing so have generally neglected any part played by the U.S. Army and its officer corps. Schlesinger, *The Age of Jackson*, casts Jacksonian democracy as a product of a class struggle in which the many supported Jackson as their champion, who sought to harness the power of the national government to curb the power of a small but powerful business elite. Myers *The Jacksonian Persuasion*, concludes that the Jacksonians sought a return to 'old republican virtues' of the Jeffersonian era, viewing the president's struggle in terms that would not be lost to opponents of the flexible doctrines of the Adams administration or to critics of the Military Academy and the expansion of an aristocratic officer corps. Similar theses may be found in Ashworth, 'Agrarians' and 'Aristocrats' and Kohl, *The Politics of Individualism*. Harry L. Watson, *Liberty and Power*, establishes a clear connection between the class struggle presented by Schlesinger with the ideological motivations introduced by Meyers, Ashworth and Kohl, but, like the others, ignores the contribution made by the U.S. Army to facilitating the transportation revolution.

[12] The role and consequences of the military in advancing a national system of internal improvements has been largely ignored in biographies of the prominent political personalities of the Jacksonian era. Studies of James Monroe emphasize the constitutional questions he grappled with in dealing with internal improvements, not the prospective actions of the U.S. Army, as typified in Ammon, *James Monroe*, 387, 394. Likewise, analyses of the Adams administration

consider both the call for national improvements outlined in his First Annual Message as well as attempts to halt his ambitious programs, but spend little time on the specific subject of internal improvements, as seen in Nagel, *John Quincy Adams*, 301–303. Remini, *John Quincy Adams*, notes the grants of money or land extended by the Adams administration to internal improvements projects, but ignores the expertise offered by U.S. Army officers. In *Andrew Jackson and the Course of American Freedom, 1822–1832*, Remini argues that Jackson's veto of the Maysville Road Bill may have appeared to mark the end of all federal internal improvements, the president nonetheless made a careful distinction in that he favored national improvements, not those that benefited a single state or private corporation, again ignoring a potential role to be played by the military, 255–56. The sole exception to this trend of omission may be found in some studies of John C. Calhoun, as it is virtually impossible to separate the subject of internal improvements from his tenure as secretary of war. Bartlett, *John C. Calhoun*, posits that after the veto of the Bonus Bill, Calhoun knew that the military could use its resources to advance a system of internal improvements. As secretary, it became his long term goal to develop a professional army with a core of competent, scientifically-trained officers who would be capable of building roads and improving waterways for purposes of both defense and national growth. Although Bartlett recognized Calhoun's realization that West Point would be central to this program, that was the extent of his analysis. Establishing this vital link between army officers and a national network of internal improvements moves the argument beyond that offered by Wiltse, *John C. Calhoun*, who saw the military and commercial practicality to Calhoun's efforts in forwarding the call for a network of roads and canals, but only considered constitutional questions regarding its implementation, ignoring altogether a potential role of army officers and the U.S. Military Academy in binding the republic together, 132–35, 172, 202, 298.

[13] *Annals of Congress*, 13th Cong., 3rd Sess., 1200, 1202.
[14] John C. Calhoun to Charles Jared Ingersoll, 14 December 1817, in Meriwether, Hemphill, Wilson, eds., *The Papers of John C. Calhoun*, 24 vols. 2: 16–7 (hereafter referred to as Meriwether et al., eds. *Calhoun Papers*).
[15] Calhoun to General Jacob Brown, 17 December 1817, ibid., 1: 22–23.
[16] Calhoun, 'Speech on Internal Improvements,' 4 February 1817, ibid., 1: 403.
[17] See Spiller, 'Calhoun's Expansible Army: The History of a Military Idea,' 189–203. Although the reduction of 1821 did not truly create an expansible army as Calhoun envisioned, the retention of supernumerary officers in each of the army's regiments made employment of officers on civil projects a possibility. With only a captain and the first and second lieutenants necessary for the command of a company of forty-two men (often company strength was much lower), the potential certainly existed for supernumerary officers (usually junior officers recently graduated from West Point and holding a brevet rank) beyond the aforementioned three called for by regulation to be employed elsewhere.
[18] Calhoun to Henry Clay, 7 January 1819, in Meriwether, et al., eds., *Calhoun Papers*, 3: 461–62
[19] Ibid., 3: 463
[20] Ibid., 3: 469–70.
[21] Ibid., 3: 470–71.
[22] 'An Act to Procure the Necessary Surveys…,' *United States Statutes at Large*, vol. 4, 22–23 (1824).
[23] Limited surveys were carried out prior to the passage of the General Survey Act. In 1823, Calhoun informed George P. MacCullogh, commissioner for the Morris Canal in New Jersey, that 'The aid which you request from this department will be cheerfully afforded so soon as the Board of Engineers, consisting of General [Simon] Bernard and Lieutenant Colonel [Joseph G.] Totten shall return from Erie in Pennsylvania'; Calhoun to MacCullogh, 14 August 1823, Meriwether, et al., ed. *Calhoun Papers*, 8: 230. The report prepared by Bernard and Totten was forwarded to Major General Alexander Macomb on 5 November 1823, and may be found in Letters Received, Office of the Chief of Engineers, 1819–1825, E-14, box 20,

Records of the Office of Chief of Engineers, Record Group 77, National Archives and Records Administration, Washington, D.C. (hereafter RG 77, NARA).

[24] In Secretary Calhoun's final departmental report, he carefully defined four national projects: the survey of the Chesapeake and Ohio Canal; improvements connecting the Ohio River with Lake Erie; a canal uniting the bays of the North Atlantic states; and a national road from Washington to New Orleans. See 'Condition of the Military Establishment and the Fortifications,' *American State Papers: Military Affairs* 7, vols. (Washington: Gales and Seaton, 1832–61), 2: 699 (hereafter referred to as *ASP:MA*).

[25] James Monroe, Eighth Annual Message, 7 December 1824, Richardson, ed. *Messages and Papers of the President*, 2: 255–56, emphasis added.

[26] Benjamin H. Latrobe, quoted in Calhoun, *The American Civil Engineer*, 38.

[27] John Quincy Adams, Inaugural Address, 4 March 1825, Richardson, ed. *Messages and Papers of the President*, 2: 298–99.

[28] Fitzpatrick, *The Autobiography of Martin Van Buren*, 449.

[29] *Annals of Congress*, 19th Cong., 2nd Sess., 3: 1275.

[30] Smith was reading from *House Doc. No. 172*, 20th Cong., 1st Sess., 'A letter from the Secretary of War in relation to the Works of Internal Improvement which have been undertaken or projected by the General Government from the year 1824 to 1826 inclusive,' brought before the House of Representatives on 4 March 1828.

[31] *Register of Debates of Congress*, 20th Cong., 1st Sess., 4: 634–43.

[32] These surveys were as follows: Reconnaissances for a canal across the Florida peninsula, between Lake Pontchartrain and the Mississippi River, and between the Tennessee and headwaters of the Alabama rivers, an examination of the Muscle Shoals on the Tennessee River, and a survey of the western route of the National Road through West Tennessee, Mississippi and Louisiana. See Macomb to Bernard, 12 March 1827, Letters Sent, Internal Improvements, M 65, roll 1, RG 77, NARA.

[33] Barbour to Thomas Metcalfe, 2 March 1827; Macomb to Stephen Long, 23 March 1827, ibid.

[34] Entry of 26 April 1827, Minute Book of the Baltimore and Ohio Railroad Company, 24 April 1827 to 26 August 1830, Baltimore and Ohio Railroad Museum, Baltimore, MD; Adams, ed. *Memoirs*, 7: 266. Barbour to Peter Little, 2 May 1827, Letters Sent, Internal Improvements, M65, roll 2, RG 77, NARA; Macomb to Captain William G. McNeill, 9 May 1827, Macomb to Lieutenant Colonel Stephen H. Long, 10 May 1827, ibid. Few officers were as conversant with military engineering and its applications to American society as were Long and McNeill. In Charles F. O'Connell, Jr, 'The Corps of Engineers and the Rise of Modern Management, 1827–1856,' in Smith, *Military Enterprise and Technological Change*, 87–116, the author argues that the pair, as well as Captain William Swift and Lieutenant George Whistler, and eventually Brevet Second Lieutenant Herman Haupt, who resigned his commission in 1835, were responsible for supplying modern business managers with bureaucratic management techniques first developed for the army.

[35] General Alexander Macomb to Lieutenant Colonel John Anderson, 16 June 1827, Letters Sent, Internal Improvements, M65, roll 2, RG 77, NARA.

[36] Macomb to Lieutenant John K. Findlay, 27 June 1827, ibid.

[37] Andrew Jackson, First Inaugural Address, 4 March 1829, Richardson, ed. *Messages and Papers of the President*, 2: 438, emphasis in the original.

[38] Jackson, First Annual Message, 8 December 1829, ibid., 2: 456.

[39] Jackson, Second Annual Message, 6 December 1830, Richardson, ed., ibid., 2: 508–10.

[40] For a discussion of Jackson's vetoes, see Jackson, 'The Internal Improvements Vetoes of Andrew Jackson.'

[41] Jackson, Second Annual Message, 6 December 1830, Richardson, ed. *Messages and Papers of the President*, 2: 510.

[42] Jackson to Brigadier General John Coffee, 28 December 1830, Bassett, ed. *Correspondence of Andrew Jackson*, 4: 215–17.

[43] Jackson, Sixth Annual Message, 1 December 1834, Richardson, ed. *Messages and Papers of the Presidents*, 3: 122.
[44] Macomb to Lewis Coryell, 15 June 1830, Cooling, *The New American State Papers*, 15: 200.
[45] Colonel John J. Abert to J. Bruce, 16 August 1831; Abert to J. D. Graham, 16 August 1831, ibid.
[46] 'Annual Report of the Secretary of War,' 21 November 1831, *ASP:MA*, 4: 766 (hereafter referred to as SWAR).
[47] Jackson to Andrew Jackson Donelson, 5 March 1823, Bassett, ed. *Correspondence of Andrew Jackson*, 3: 190–91.
[48] Andrew Jackson, Inaugural Address, 4 March 1829, Richardson, ed. *Message and Papers of the Presidents*, 2: 438.
[49] Order No. 63, 15 November 1831, Orderly Book, Entry 128, vol. 2, RG 77, NARA.
[50] 'Statement of the Number and Rank of Officers of the Army on Duty in the Line, Staff, or Detached Service, and Those Absent on Furlough,' 8 February 1831, *ASP:MA*, 4: 683–86.
[51] Abert to Lewis Cass, 3 February 1832, Letters Sent, Topographical Bureau, M 66, roll 1, RG 77, NARA.
[52] Abert to Cass, 16 November 1831, Letters Sent, Topographical Bureau, ibid.
[53] Abert to McNeill, 27 April 1832, ibid.
[54] Abert to McNeill, 4 July 1832, ibid.
[55] Order no. 48, 18 May 1833, General Orders and Circulars, M 1094, roll 3, RG 94, NARA.
[56] *Annals of Congress*, 21st Cong., 1st Sess., 6: 583–84.
[57] *Register of Debates*, 23rd Cong., 1st Sess., 10: 2549–51.
[58] Ibid., 24th Cong., 1st Sess., 12: 4571, 4574–76.
[59] *Army and Navy Chronicle*, 3 December 1835, 389 (hereafter referred to as *ANC*).
[60] George W. Cullum to Alfred Heidekoper, 20 August 1836, George Washington Cullum Papers, Manuscript Division, Library of Congress.
[61] *ANC*, 1 September 1836, 138. The 5 January 1837 issue of the *ANC*, reprinted an article from the *New York American* citing the 'insufficiency of the pay' and 'higher rates of compensation in civil life,' that were driving officers from the service,' 7.
[62] Ibid., 19 May 1836, 313.
[63] Data for this table was compiled from one or more of the following: 'Statement of the number of company officers in the army in service against the Creek and Seminole Indians in Florida in 1836; The number and rank of those who resigned; The number of companies of the several arms in service there during that year,' 2 March 1837, *ASP:MA*, 7: 110–15; Cullum, *Biographical Register*; Gardner, *Dictionary of All Officers*; Hamersly, *Complete Regular Army Register*; Heitman, *Historical Register and Dictionary of the U.S. Army*, 2 vols.
[64] For a summary of the military career of these officers, consult Cullum, *Biographical Register*, 2: 440, 280, 214–22.
[65] Abert to Cass, 27 April 1836, Letters Sent, Topographical Bureau, M66 roll 2, RG 77 NARA; Roger Jones to Cass, 24 June 1836, Letters Received, Secretary of War, M221, roll 116, RG 107, NARA.
[66] General Order No. 43, 28 June 1836, General Orders and Circulars, M1094, roll 4, RG 94, NARA.
[67] Abert to Cass, 6 July 1836, Letters Sent, Topographical Bureau, M66, roll 2, RG 77, NARA ; Abert to Butler, 24 January 1837, ibid.
[68] Ibid. Briefs outlining the actions of officers employed by the Louisville, Cincinnati and Charleston Railroad Company also appeared in *ANC*, 7 April 1836, 216, and 28 April 1836, 263.
[69] *Washington Globe*, 29 August 1836.
[70] Ibid.; Gordon, *Compilation of Registers of the Army of the United States*, 548.
[71] General Order No. 69, 15 October 1836, General Orders and Circulars, M1094, roll 4, RG 94, NARA.
[72] Abert to Acting Secretary of War Carey A. Harris, 24 October 1836, Letters Sent, Topographical Bureau, M66, roll 2, RG 77, NARA. Abert to Benjamin F. Butler, 5 November 1836, ibid.

This group of assignments showed that army engineers were providing assistance to projects all over the nation, but primarily in the North and East.

[73] Abert to Kearney, Long, Bache, McNeill, Turnbull and Williams, 28 December 1836, ibid.
[74] Ver Planck Van Antwerp to Van Buren, 20 November 1837, roll 25, Lucy Fisher West, ed. *Papers of Martin Van Buren* 55 rolls (Alexandria, Va.: Chadwick-Healey, 1987).
[75] Regarding his education, a J. P. Van Antwerp, is listed among cadets accepted to West Point in 1823 provided in 'History of the military academy,' 1 March 1837, *ASP:MA* 7: 33. Van Antwerp was accepted into West Point with Abraham Van Buren, which would link him to the president. Originally from Albany, New York, he was 'well reported' in the 'U.S. Military Academy Cadet Application Papers, 1805–1866,' M2037, roll 1, Records of the Adjutant General's Office, RG 94, NARA.
[76] Van Antwerp to Van Buren, 20 November 1837, emphasis in the original. Van Buren forwarded this message to his secretary of war, Joel Poinsett, as the original letter can be found in his papers in the State Historical Society of Pennsylvania, Philadelphia.
[77] *Register of the Debates of Congress*, 25th Cong., 2nd Sess., 6: 133, 136.
[78] Ibid., 25th Cong., 2nd Sess., 6: 482–84, 485–88, 489.
[79] 'An Act to Increase the Present Military Establishment of the United States, and for Other Purposes,' 5 July 1838, and 'An Act Supplemental to the Act to Increase the Military Establishment of the United States, and for Other Purposes,' 7 July 1838, in Callan, *Military Laws of the United States*, 329–39, 340–41. Specifically, the act authorized increasing the Corps of Engineers by adding one lieutenant colonel, two majors, six captains, six first lieutenants and six second lieutenants, to be paid the same as officers of the dragoon regiments. The act also organized the Corps of Topographical Engineers on an equal footing, establishing a corps composed of one colonel, one lieutenant colonel, four majors, ten captains, ten first lieutenants and ten second lieutenants, to be compensated identically to the Corps of Engineers.
[80] Abert to Kearney, Long, Swift and Hughes, 25 August 1838, Letters Sent, Topographical Bureau, M66, roll 2, RG 77, NARA.
[81] Jackson to Martin Van Buren, 18 October 1830, Bassett, ed. *Correspondence of Andrew Jackson*, 4: 185.
[82] General Order No. 11, 2 March 1840, General Orders and Circulars, M1094, roll 4, RG 94, NARA, emphasis added.
[83] See 'The Pacific Railroad Surveys,' chapter in Goetzmann, *Army Exploration in the American West*, 262–304. The thirteen-volume report prepared by the members of the Corps of Topographical Engineers may be found in *Senate Exec. Doc. No. 78*, 33rd Cong., 2nd Sess..

References

Ammon, Harry. *James Monroe: The Quest for National Identity*. New York: McGraw-Hill, 1971.
Ashworth, John. *'Agrarians' and 'Aristocrats': Party Political ideology in the United States, 1837–1846*. Cambridge, UK: Cambridge University Press, 1987.
Bartlett, Irving H. *John C. Calhoun: A Biography*. New York: W.W. Norton, 1993.
Bassett, John Spencer, ed. *Correspondence of Andrew Jackson*, 7 vols. Washington, DC: Carnegie Institution of Washington, 1926–35.
Calhoun, Daniel H. *The American Civil Engineer: Origins and Conflict*. Cambridge, MA: Harvard University Press, 1960.
Coffman, Edward. *The Old Army: A Portrait of the American Army in Peacetime, 1784–1898*. New York: Oxford University Press, 1986.
——— 'The Long Shadow of *The Soldier and the State*.' *Journal of Military History* 55 (January 1991): 69–82.
Cooling, Benjamin Franklin, ed. *The New American State Papers: Military Affairs*, 19 vols. Wilmington, Del.: Scholarly Resources, 1979.

Cullum, George W. *Biographical Register of the Officers and Graduates of the U.S. Military Academy at West Point*, 2 vols. Boston: Houghton Mifflin & Co, 1891.

Fitzpatrick, C., ed. *The Autobiography of Martin Van Buren, Vol. 2, Annual Report of the American Historical Association*. Washington: Government Printing Office, 1920.

Gardner, Charles K., comp. *Dictionary of All Officers, who have been Commissioned, or have been Appointed and Served, in the Army of the United States... Including the Distinguished Officers of the Volunteers and Militia of the States*. New York: G.P. Putnam & Co., 1853.

Gates, John. 'The Alleged Isolation of U.S. Army Officers in the Late 19th Century.' *Parameters: Journal of the U.S. Army War College* 10 (September 1980): 32–45.

Goetzmann, William. *Army Exploration in the American West, 1803–1863*. New Haven: Yale University Press [1959]. Reprint, Austin: Texas State Historical Association, 1991.

Hamersly, Thomas H.S., comp. *Complete Regular Army Register of the United States Army for One Hundred Years (1779–1879)*, 2 vols. Washington, D.C., Government Printing Office, 1903.

Heitman, Francis. *Historical Register and Dictionary of the U.S. Army*, 2 vols. Washington, D.C.: Government Printing Office [1903] Reprint, Gaithersburg, MD: Olde Soldiers Books, 1988.

Huntington, Samuel P. *The Soldier and the State: The Theory and Politics of Civil-Military Relations*. Cambridge: The Belknap Press of Harvard University Press, 1957.

Jackson, Carlton. 'The Internal Improvements Vetoes of Andrew Jackson.' *Tennessee Historical Quarterly* 25 (Fall 1996): 261–80.

Kohl, Lawrence F. *The Politics of Individualism: Parties and the American Character in the Jacksonian Era*. New York: Oxford University Press, 1989.

Meriwether, Robert L., W. Edwin Hemphill, and Clyde N. Wilson, eds. *The Papers of John C. Calhoun*, 24 vols. Columbia, SC: University of South Carolina Press, 1959–1998.

Millett, Allan R., and Peter Maslowski, *For the Common Defense: A Military History of the United States*. New York: The Free Press, 1984.

Myers, Marvin. *The Jacksonian Persuasion: Politics and Belief*. Stanford: Stanford University Press, 1957.

Nagel, Paul C. *John Quincy Adams: A Public Life, A Private Life*. New York: Alfred A. Knopf, 1997.

North, Diane M.T. *Samuel Peter Heintzelman and the Sonora Exploring and Mining Company*. Tucson: University of Arizona Press, 1980.

O'Connell, Charles F., Jr. 'The Corps of Engineers and the Rise of Modern Management, 1827–1856.' In *Military Enterprise and Technological Change: Perspectives on the American Experience*, edited by Merritt Roe Smith. Cambridge, MA: The MIT Press, 1985.

Remini, Robert V. *Andrew Jackson and the Course of American Freedom, 1822–1832*. New York: Harper & Row, 1981.

———. *John Quincy Adams*. New York: Henry Holt, 2002.

Richardson, James D., ed. *Messages and Papers of the Presidents*. New York: Bureau of National Literature, 1897.

Skelton, William. 'Professionalization of the U.S. Army Officer Corps During the Age of Jackson.' *Armed Forces and Society* 1 (Summer 1975): 443–71.

———. 'Officers and Politicians: The Origins of Army Politics in he United States before the Civil War.' *Armed Forces and Society* 6 (Fall 1979): 22–48.

———. *An American Profession of Arms: The Army Officer Corps, 1784–1861*. Lawrence: University Press of Kansas, 1992.

Schlesinger, Arthur, Jr. *The Age of Jackson*. Boston: Little Brown & Co., 1945.

Sellers, Charles. *The Market Revolution: Jacksonian America, 1815–1844*. New York: Oxford University Press, 1991.

Smith, Merritt Roe, ed. *Military Enterprise and Technological Change: Perspectives on the American Experience*. Cambridge, MA: The MIT Press, 1985.

Spiller, Roger J. 'Calhoun's Expansible Army: The History of a Military Idea.' *South Atlantic Quarterly* 79 (Spring 1980): 189–203.

Thompson, Jerry D., ed. *Fifty Miles and a Fight: Major Samuel Peter Heintzelman's Journal of Texas and the Cortina War*. Austin: Texas State Historical Association, 1998.

Watson, Harry L. *Liberty and Power: The Politics of Jacksonian America.* New York: Hill & Wang, 1990.
Watson, Samuel J. 'Flexible Gender Roles During the Market Revolution: Family, Friendship, Marriage and Masculinity Among U.S. Army Officers, 1815–1846.' *Journal of Social History* 29 (Fall 1995): 81–106.
———. 'Professionalism, Social Attitudes and Civil-Military Accountability in the United States Army Officer Corps, 1815–1846.' Ph.D. Diss., Rice University, 1996.
Weigley, Russell F. *History of the United States Army.* New York: Macmillan Publishing Co., 1967.
Wettemann, Robert. '"To The Public Prosperity": The U.S. Army and the Market Revolution, 1815–1844.' Ph.D. Diss., Texas A&M University, 2001.
Wiltse, Charles M. *John C. Calhoun: Nationalist, 1782–1828.* Indianapolis: Bobbs-Merrill Co., Inc., 1944.

PART 2: SPECIAL SUBJECTS

How the Army Became Accepted: West Point Socialization, Military Accountability, and the Nation-State During the Jacksonian Era

Samuel J. Watson

Notions of professionalism were unevenly developed, and widely contested, in antebellum America. Professionalism is a shifting status, asserted and defined both through professional efforts and the external social and political relationships specific to particular historical contexts. Professionalism is also a process, and the cultures of the society and the profession – or of the organizations claiming professional authority – play as important a role as the profession's presumed function in this process. The social sources and characteristics of the aspirants may be just as significant as their expertise and the demand for their services, an expertise and a demand that are themselves socially constituted. That opposition to standing armies and an officer corps of privileged placemen slowed the development of a professional army is a cliché in nineteenth-century U.S. history.[1] Yet the officers of the early national and Jacksonian army were actually better situated to claim and gain professional status than civilians, both those seeking military posts and those seeking recognition in other professions. This was the case not so much because of their claim to a distinctive function defending society – which was debated by the politicians who controlled the army's destiny – as because of their ability to secure recognition as gentlemen and their material sponsorship by the state. Recognition, sponsorship, and the privilege that came with them were rooted more in the officer's accountability to civil society – his ability to present himself as a representative of values associated with the national center, such as rationality, cohesion, order, and national expansion – than in his military expertise per se.[2]

The demand for accountability came from three sources, each both fiscal, political – meaning responsiveness to the policies chosen by Congress and the executive – and practical. The first source was a parsimonious Congress, always eager to gain votes through appeals to a public antagonistic to taxation and jealous of political privilege, yet demanding a variety of expensive tasks and a rigorous accounting for public funds in addition to the preservation of the army's warfighting capability. Second were the logistical needs of the organization itself, of its officers and enlisted soldiers, who had suffered severely from the inefficiency and corruption of civilian contractors before and during the War of 1812, needs that led the army to assume greater purchasing responsibilities afterwards. Third were the demands of U.S. foreign policy and international order, which required a reliable force responsive to national civilian authorities. All three sources were joined in the development of a military force capable of projecting effective power over international distances – a capability the United States lacked in 1815. Thirty years later the Regular Army provided this capability, which made the conquest of northern Mexico possible; during the Civil War Regular Army administrative and logistical skills did the same for national reunification. The vaunted volunteers of Jacksonian myth provided manpower and enthusiasm, but they lacked this expertise.

The officer corps' claim to professional status and a role in its definition depended on civilian acceptance of its claim to authority over a distinct social role, especially the power to select and exclude aspirants to that role, in the face of challenges from the anti-standing army and militia ideals, from private and volunteer military units, and from frontier constituencies who acclaimed those ideals and created such units when they believed that the regular army was acting contrary to their interests, as was often the case in the confused welter of borderlands diplomacy. Despite widespread (though primarily Democratic, and very rarely Whig) criticism as aristocrats, martinets, dandies, and Indian sympathizers, the officers of the regular army secured a fundamental acceptance of their professional role in the federal government and among the gentry and middle classes who served in and identified with it. This acceptance permitted continued and in fact extraordinarily secure employment, making possible careers that lasted an average of more than two decades, and meant that the regulars ordinarily exercised senior-level command over volunteer and militia forces during wartime. The officer corps gained this acceptance through fiscally accountable administration, genteel interaction with the local and national civilian elites, the exercise through military command of an authority most civilian elites could only dream of, and the politically reliable performance of their duties negotiating, mediating, intimidating, and coercing non-citizens along the borders and frontiers. They also made cogent arguments for the value of experience and specialization in military tasks, arguments that gained increasing acceptance among nationalist Republicans, National Republicans, and Whigs, and they proved their capability during the war with Mexico.

The officer's performance of accountability was focused in three key relationships, two of them with civilians and all of them ultimately sociocultural and political rather than specifically or distinctively military in content. Officers exercised command over enlisted soldiers within the army; they engaged in international, cross-cultural relationships of diplomacy with and coercion against Native Americans, Mexicans, Britons, and others; and they had close social relationships with upper middle-class (or 'respectable') and elite American civilians (particularly congressmen and federal officials), from whose ranks most officers came.[3] After addressing the character and growth of officer accountability, this essay turns for one element of explanation to the process that linked and underpinned all these relationships: officers' socialization, meaning the compound of their scientific-technical education, military training, and habituation to duty. All these began at the Military Academy at West Point.

Much of the republican critique of standing armies was based on assumptions about the character of their enlisted men, who were believed to be mercenary, dependent hirelings, not much above slaves. American social and political leaders (including officers themselves) shared this assumption, which was reasonable, in republican terms, given the impoverished social origins of most enlisted men and the harsh discipline to which they submitted. But subordinates only appeared on elite radar screens when they resisted demands for obedience. Indeed, the hierarchical officer–enlisted relationship, whether seen as paternalistic or outrightly coercive, could serve as something of a model for class relationships for an increasingly conservative middle class in the decades of working-class formation after 1840. Day-to-day, ideology aside, civilian leaders thought of the army in terms of the genteel officer corps with whom they dealt on practical military issues. In particular, civilian leaders and officers were closely and concretely linked by the selection, commissioning, and assignment process, which often involved considerations of personal friendship and patronage, as a brief look at the papers of any senior officer, and of most junior officers and national politicians, shows.[4]

Most officers initially developed their professional ethos through the mental and physical disciplines of classroom, drill, administration, and command at the national Military Academy at West Point, the most conscious, comprehensive socialization they received. This intensive process significantly strengthened the officer's claim to sociopolitical reliability and military capability, and also to a form of republican virtue, occupationally distinct but akin to the classical ideal, in the forms of specialized expertise (duty), integrity (duty and honor), gentility (honor), and service to and association with the national center. The officer's expertise and connections to the national center also aligned him with liberal ideals of cosmopolitanism and science.[5] Though derided by Old Republicans and populist politicians, the republican virtue embodied in the regular officer's concept of duty was accepted by the executive branch and Congress as a whole: despite periodic pushes to cut costs, appropriations were maintained at economical but essentially consistent levels from 1821 to 1846. Republican fears of standing armies were based in large part on their subservience to government, but for those serving in government this subordination was a virtue. Republican 'independence' and social gentility were expected of officers as men of honor and integrity provided with sufficient compensation to preclude the necessity for additional part-time labor, but neither the nation nor the state sought military officers or a military force independent of their control. Indeed, a 'dependent' standing army of men beholden to the nation-state perfectly suited executive branch officials, whatever their party or ideological perspective, in need of a reliable force to back up the thinly spread, often locally oriented federal civil officials – customs collectors, district attorneys, and marshals – in the implementation of national policy and the enforcement of national law and sovereignty along the borders and frontiers. In fact, every Democratic president realized this and acted on it: Jefferson during the Embargo – when he tripled the size of the army he had reduced in 1802 – Madison during the War of 1812, Monroe in intimidating Spain to gain Florida, Jackson – who relied primarily on Regular Army forces as the general conducting that intimidation – during the Nullification Crisis and Indian removal, Van Buren during the Canadian border crises, Polk in the war with Mexico, Pierce in the violence in Bleeding Kansas, and Buchanan in Kansas and the expedition to assert U.S. sovereignty over the Mormons in Utah.

The Military Academy and Accountability

The most concrete example of civilian acceptance of military professionalism is the acceptance of an officer corps dominated by West Point graduates. At the end of the War of 1812 less than 3 percent of the officer corps had been commissioned through the Military Academy, but 92 of the 102 graduates still in the army in 1815 were retained when the army was reduced that June, making roughly a seventh of the new officer corps. (Only 20 percent of the total wartime force was retained in service that year.) This proportion was sustained prior to the 1821 reduction in force, but during the 1820s the officer corps was virtually closed to those who did not graduate from West Point, and Academy graduates made up a substantial majority of officers entering the army during the 1830s, 1840s, and 1850s. More than 93 percent of the serving graduates were retained in the army during the reduction in force of 1821, an emphatic sign of their acceptance both by senior military leaders, none of whom (given the army's system of promotion by seniority) had graduated from the Academy, and the executive, despite the sustained offensive against the military establishment by Old Republicans that had led to the reduction. Nor does there seem to have been any significant outcry, in Congress or the public prints, over the disproportionate percentage of West Pointers retained. Combined with the growing number of cadets graduating each year, the disproportionate discharge of nongraduates in 1821 led to a tripling in the proportion of West Pointers in the officer corps to about 40 percent by 1823. By 1830 nearly two-thirds of the officer corps were graduates of the Academy, and by 1860 fully three-quarters, despite periodic infusions of officers commissioned directly from civilian life in units raised after 1832.[6]

West Point training in mathematics, science, and engineering provided the basis for exploration and infrastructural development difficult for the untrained (because unfunded) private sector to undertake, and by the 1840s Academy socialization in the professional ethic of duty, honor, and country had fostered a nationally oriented commitment and institutional cohesion that made army officers more reliable public servants than ever before. As such, the Regular Army officer corps served as one of the few forces for cohesion and connection between center and periphery in the early to mid-nineteenth century American borderlands, displaying leadership far beyond narrowly military spheres while playing crucial roles in implementing federal policy far from the capital. Whether acting as peacekeepers or conquerors, the army of the 1820s, 1830s, and 1840s proved far more capable, and far more reliable, than that of the 1790s, 1800s, and 1810s, aiding the nation's population movement and economic development while maintaining national sovereignty and helping to avoid war with Britain through peace-keeping, law enforcement, and diplomacy during crises along the border with Canada.

Indeed, developing a republican officer corps, and through it reliable public servants, was one of the principal reasons Thomas Jefferson created the Military Academy in 1802.[7] Amid the surge of nationalism after the War of 1812, Presidents James Monroe, John Quincy Adams, and Andrew Jackson all applauded the Military Academy, and by implication the Regular Army and its officer corps, as a linchpin of the more cohesive national republic beginning to emerge. Indeed, a reliable officer corps was essential to the orderly expansion and cohesion (such as it was) of Thomas Jefferson's 'empire of liberty,' Adams's 'American System,' and Jackson's 'area of freedom.' Academy graduates played important roles shaping the implementation, and thus the reality, of each of these visions. President James Madison began the applause in 1815, affirming the value of a 'national seminary… as a central resort of youth and genius from every part of their country, diffusing on their return examples of those national feelings, those liberal sentiments, and those congenial manners which contribute cement to our Union and strength to the great political fabric of which that [union] is the foundation.' Seven years later, supporting Superintendent Sylvanus Thayer's disciplinary efforts as an essential part of the military reforms Madison had begun, Monroe emphasized 'the restraint of [cadet and officer] ardor' by 'a just subordination,' because 'the Military Academy forms the basis, in regard to science, on which the military establishment rests.' In his final annual message Monroe observed that 'the Military Academy, on which the Army essentially rests, and to which it is much indebted for [its] state of improvement, has attained… a high degree of perfection,' while John Quincy Adams, who labeled the Academy one of 'the great features' of Monroe's administration, commended the 'faithful accountability which has pervaded every part of the system,' meaning the army and the military establishment as well as the Academy. Jackson, who had commanded West Pointers for seven years as one of the two principal Regular Army generals, praised the Academy in his first annual message as 'one of the safest means of national defense,' which had 'exercised the happiest influence upon the moral and intellectual character of our army.'[8]

West Point training and education did three basic things for graduates, providing them with experience and aptitude in all the missions they were called on to perform. First, the lack of opportunities to learn tactics under fire meant that new lieutenants needed a school to learn the drill on which nineteenth-century tactics were based. Drill at West Point gave future officers firsthand experience of the limits and possibilities of contemporary tactics, from the school of the individual soldier up to the battalion and sometimes, albeit in miniature, the brigade, simulating exercises of several hundred to a thousand soldiers. This training, followed by smaller-scale drill in their companies and supplemented between the mid-1820s and the mid-1830s by assignment to the regiment-sized schools of infantry and artillery at Jefferson Barracks (outside St. Louis) and Fortress Monroe (at Hampton Roads), was the foundation of the officer's military competence. Supplemented by the discipline of unit drill and small-unit leadership experience in the Second Seminole War, this expertise helped give the United States tactical superiority in the war with Mexico, and won regular officers recognition as troop-trainers at the outset of the Civil War.[9]

Secondly, by 1820 engineer, ordnance, and artillery officers were learning far more of their trade at West Point than they had ever learned while training in their units before the War of 1812. By 1825 graduates in these branches made up about two-fifths of the officer corps, planning and directing the construction of the extensive coastal fortification system, one of the principal elements of American defense against European attack throughout the nineteenth century (however irrelevant in retrospect). Graduates led surveys of U.S. international boundaries throughout this era, and under the General Survey Act of 1824 uniformed graduates conducted canal and railroad surveys and oversaw some railroad construction until the act was reversed by the Democrats in 1838. (Many more graduates did so after leaving the army, and these men continued doing so into the 1850s and beyond.) West Point-trained ordnance officers supervised the testing, construction, and maintenance of weapons for the expansible skeleton army planned for in the 1821 reduction in force, eventually developing many of the firearms used in the Civil War. Such men urgently needed technical training of the sort unavailable at civilian colleges and universities, but increasingly emphasized at West Point after 1820.[10]

Third, technical training in mathematics, science, and engineering helped foster a mindset of instrumental rationality, or what officers labeled a sense of 'system and regularity.' Some modern scholars, like the Radical Republicans in the 1860s, have criticized this training, which was far more rigid than a modern liberal education, arguing that the Academy produced inflexible thinkers unable to adjust to the changing battlefields of the Civil War. Yet all Civil War commanders, volunteers as well as regulars, amateurs as well as professionals, faced problems in exercising effective battlefield and operational command due to the scale of the conflict – unprecedented in American experience – their lack of experience employing new technologies (the rifled musket, the railroad and telegraph) on such a scale, and their lack of opportunities to practice large-scale command in the small prewar army. The limits or absence of postgraduate or staff schools notwithstanding, most students of the antebellum era – both modern scholars and contemporaries like commanding generals Jacob Brown and Winfield Scott – saw the dispersion of troops into company-sized posts as the principal factor limiting training opportunities and command experience. This dispersion, which Brown and Scott tried to minimize by establishing central reserves and posts for brigade-level training, was dictated by the army's constabulary missions policing the borders and frontiers. Even if there had been staff schools, the army was far too small, given the limited threat from overseas, for officers to practice large-scale maneuvers of the sort they would conduct after 1861. Yet regular officers, mostly West Pointers, were more tactically and strategically effective than their volunteer counterparts (usually non-graduates), and civil society clearly accepted them as such, for Academy graduates held virtually all of the operational and strategic – army and theater-level – commands on both sides, as well as most of the larger unit ones (over corps and divisions). The Radical Republican critique ultimately proceeded from political concerns about the West Pointers' commitment to a more total war rather than defects in their military competence per se, and as the war went on West Pointers like U.S. Grant and Henry W. Halleck were able to replace amateur generals with West Point-trained ones in most senior commands.[11]

Modern indictments of Academy training and army staff work take the twentieth century as a baseline, a less historical approach than using the War of 1812, which the pre-Civil War army took as its own baseline, a perspective from which army logistics and administration must be recognized as among the most advanced, and most effective, in pre- and early industrial America. Academy training instilled the numeracy, detail-orientation, mental discipline, and precision necessary for surveying, building, and accounting. Buttressed by the disciplines of drill and inspections, the mathematical rationality instilled at West Point encouraged timeliness and a habituation to and integrity in reporting – the regularity, or more broadly the *accountability*, by which officers often judged one another and were judged by Congress. Though limited in abstraction and rarely very critical, this outlook did encourage officers to think about the ways their actions and their consequences in one sphere influenced actions and consequences in another. However primitive, this sense of perspective helped officers to think more systematically – and systemically – than most civilians, to recognize the interactions involved in complex systems and the interdependence of modern society.[12]

These qualities were an essential starting point not only for the army's technical branches but for the junior officers now tasked with supply duties, duties handled very inefficiently by civilian contractors before the establishment of a permanent staff structure within the army after the War of 1812. The inadequacy of American logistical support is a common theme in histories of the war with Mexico, an interpretation based largely on Lieutenant D. H. Hill's letters from Texas to the *Southern Quarterly Review*. Examining the operations of the Quartermaster Department throughout the war tells a different story, of comparative, in fact decisive, effectiveness amid very difficult circumstances. Even the most superficial comparison with the experience of the War of 1812, when the United States was never able to mount an effective offensive to Montreal, much less Quebec, shows a profound improvement in army supply. This improvement was due in part to the ability to move supplies by rail and sea to New Orleans, and by sea to Corpus Christi, the mouth of the Rio Grande, and Veracruz, but the supplies still had to be transported overland by animal power to the arid Mexican interior – a problem not unlike that of doing so through the wildernesses of upstate New York and Ohio in 1812 – or purchased locally in sufficient quantities by the West Point-educated commissary officers, now called on to supply regiments, brigades, and divisions rather than companies and posts of 200 men or less (their usual experience before the war). Indeed, the army's logistic capability, along with the discipline enforced by West Pointers against depredations on the local populace, was a prerequisite for the success of Winfield Scott's strategy of conciliating the Mexican people as he advanced upon Mexico City, in order to ease the peace process once he had won a military victory against the armed forces of the Mexican government. Similarly, it is impossible to imagine the army of 1812–1815 sending several thousand men thousands of miles across the plains, mountains and desert to Santa Fe, Chihuahua, California, and Oregon, as it did in 1846 and 1847.[13]

Like most complex historical developments, this professionalization took time, and proceeded unevenly across a number of fronts, something surprisingly few scholars have recognized amid their attempts to judge the army 'professional' once and for all at a certain point in time.[14] This unevenness, combined with the political smoke that obscured or distorted efforts at professionalization, meant that the army's improved capability was not immediately or obviously apparent to outside observers before the war with Mexico. Indeed, much of civil society, led by the Old Republicans between 1815 and 1828 and some – though not in fact all – Jacksonian Democrats afterwards, refused to accept the Military Academy as the primary officer commissioning source. During the late 1820s, West Point came under growing attack as a bastion of monopoly – true, since virtually every officer commissioned during the decade came from the Academy – and social aristocracy (in that appointments to the Academy were supposedly reserved for the sons of the elite). The critics, usually Democrats who acclaimed the virtues of the volunteer citizen-soldier, reinforced their attacks with references to a related set of cultural values, decrying the Academy as a place of sedentary, effeminate fashion and abstract, book-learned theory, out of touch with the practical needs of the American people.

The cry against West Point 'theory' was a product of Jacksonian anti-intellectualism and a rhetorical vehicle for the critique of aristocracy rather than a serious intellectual or pedagogical critique. Indeed, the Academy's curriculum was the most practical in American higher education at the time, and the practical utility of the mathematics focus, particularly that on civil engineering, introduced during the early 1820s helped win the support of nationally minded Republicans, many of whom became Whigs and effectively defended the Academy from Jacksonian attack during the 1830s and 1840s. A number of contemporary officers argued that Academy training and education were too theoretical, but this was an internal, professional critique, distinct in both motive and content from the Democratic political one that used 'theory' indiscriminately as a synonym for idleness and effeminacy. The critique from within was intended to improve the Academy curriculum and connect it more closely to the army's missions, but accepted Academy education as a prerequisite for developing professional expertise.[15]

There was more basis to the charge of aristocracy, but its roots ultimately lay in the operation of the incompletely democratized American social and political system rather than the decisions of the superintendent and the secretary of war, who began to consult congressmen on cadet nominations during the 1820s. Pre-Civil War officers came disproportionately from urban areas and 'respectable' (upper middle class) or elite backgrounds, and especially from professional and officeholding families, who can properly be considered elites due to their social and political connections. Attending West Point did serve as a means of social mobility for a number of poor youths, but many of these, especially those whose fathers had died, were from professional and officeholding families whose economic status had slipped but still hoped to employ their social and political connections to Washington to gain security and status for their sons through military commissions. Indeed, more than a quarter of the officers on the 1830 Army Register were related to men who had served or were serving in high offices, nearly four-fifths of them in civilian life.[16]

Congress and the Democratic Party, the home of most of the critics, had the power to democratize appointments to the Academy, but they did not use this power to the degree – or as accountably – as their rhetoric would suggest they intended. In fact, both Andrew Jackson and Martin Van Buren obtained nominations to West Point – which Old Hickory labeled 'the best school in the world' – for their kin, albeit before becoming president.[17] One could argue that the Jacksonians were trying to use the political system, per their majoritarian philosophy, to deny the National Republicans and Whigs the opportunity to appoint the sons of the elite, much as Jefferson had intended in founding the Academy. Yet the Democrats appointed their own children, and scholars have long shown that Democratic leaders were not substantially more 'ordinary' in socioeconomic status than the Whigs. The research has not yet been done to determine whether Democratic appointments were actually less elitist than those of the Whigs, and the belief that this was the case can only be regarded as an assumption in light of the historiography on Jacksonian politics.

Accountability in Logistics and Power Projection

The Jacksonian assault would have been stronger, and more convincing, had army administration remained as poor as it was before and during the War of 1812. The principal reasons for its new efficiency were the managerial reforms initiated by young but veteran senior officers, like Winfield Scott and Quartermaster General Thomas Sidney Jesup, both in their late twenties at the end of the war. Given the sluggishness of promotion, which was done by seniority without a system of mandatory retirement, within so small an army, no Academy graduate attained general officer rank before 1860. (It should be noted that impartiality, both toward and by officers, was a common argument in favor of the seniority system: a method we tend to view as an impediment to merit was widely accepted by contemporaries as a means of enhancing accountability, while the meaning of 'merit' remained in dispute.) Yet reform requires execution as well as command, and non-West Pointers like Scott and Jesup applauded the ability of Military Academy graduates to implement those reforms through timely, accurate reporting to their superiors, and through them to Congress. Accountability demands the ability to count, and few Americans possessed this ability to so great a degree as West Point graduates. In fact, most officers spent substantially more time filling out forms than drilling troops: with the possible exception of the navy, the army was by far the largest, farthest flung, most internally articulated, and most expensive full-time organization in the United States before 1877. It required more constant logistical maintenance than any other organization in the country; it disbursed more funds than any other organization, public or private; and it intermittently launched active operations to project power on a greater scale than any other organization in the continental United States. The fur companies were miniscule in comparison, and their employees supplied themselves with most necessities. Post Office employees fed themselves; the vast majority were part-time, and often short-term because of the partisan nature of their appointments. Following the postrevolutionary disestablishment, similar economic dynamics applied in most churches, particularly evangelical ones. The army required greater administrative rationality and managerial capability than any other organization in the nation, and, apart from the uncertainties of on-the-job training, education and socialization at West Point were the primary means of consciously developing this ability among its officers. Indeed, historians of American accounting have traced the origins of an accounting mindset to the Military Academy of this era, and President Jackson's seventh annual message to Congress suggests his agreement: the varied duties discharged by army officers 'embrace very heavy expenditures of public money and require fidelity, science, and business habits in their execution... That this object has been in a great measure attained by the Military Academy is shown by the... prompt accountability which has generally followed the necessary advances.'[18]

Accountability to national civilian authority was also a foreign policy issue, and socialization at West Point influenced change in this arena. Prior to 1820 it was not at all unheard of for officers, both junior and senior, to plan or engage in independent foreign policy initiatives – invasions of neighboring countries, unauthorized by Congress – contrary to their oaths to uphold the Constitution and the neutrality laws passed in the 1790s. The most significant of these were Andrew Jackson's invasions of Florida in 1814 and 1818. While Jackson may have been an individual aberration, a number of officers up to and including long-time commanding general James Wilkinson (who was an active western separatist before he joined the army in 1791, and secretly advised the Spanish on the security of their colonies during much of his tenure as commanding general) participated in Aaron Burr's plans and other plots against Mexico between 1804 and 1816. Junior officer interest in these illegal military ventures culminated in the resignation of Captain Augustus Magee – a West Pointer from Connecticut, rather than a frontiersman like Jackson or Wilkinson, who graduated before the Academy's reform by Sylvanus Thayer and was stationed in command at Natchitoches near the Texas border – in 1812. Magee then led the American filibusters invading Texas that year. Seven years later his successor in the Natchitoches command, Captain William Beard (commissioned directly from civilian life in 1812), warned against filibustering but did not act – or was not able to act, due to the reluctance of local civil officials – to prevent it, and in 1820 Brigadier General Eleazar Ripley (a Massachusetts state representative before his military appointment in 1812) resigned his commission and accepted the title of president of Texas from filibuster James Long. (Ripley later became a Jacksonian Democrat and was elected to Congress from Louisiana in 1834 and 1836.) Even leaders in the army's professionalization – not yet

West Pointers, given the ranks in question – showed some interest in such schemes: Winfield Scott provided the Spanish revolutionary Xavier Mina with a letter of introduction to assist his plans for filibustering in South America.[19]

The Transcontinental Treaty of 1821 was intended to settle the country's disputed boundaries and reduce potential security threats, but the permanence of this settlement depended on the army's efforts to stem privately organized military expeditions, and hence on the officer corps' allegiance to national priorities and policy, above all to centralized, national control by Congress and the executive over American foreign relations and the use of armed power. The decline in filibustering among officers after 1820, and among civilians between 1820 and 1835, may best be attributed to changing national and international context – the settlement of boundary disputes and the availability of land and opportunities within the United States and Texas during the boom years from the mid-1820s to the mid-1830s – while the resurgence of filibustering among American civilians after 1835 might well be attributed to the reappearance of boundary questions (with the Texas Revolution) and the lack of economic opportunities during the depression that followed the Panic of 1837. On the other hand, agency counts too, and the army officer corps, more than 70 percent of which had been educated at West Point by 1835, played a crucial, perhaps decisive role as the only national force available to stem the filibuster tide during the Canadian border crises between 1837 and 1842, very likely the most dangerous point in Anglo-American relations after 1815. Their reaction, which was initially sympathy for the Canadian rebels, quickly turned to distaste as lawless American citizens sought to invade Canada and entrap the United States in a potentially disastrous war with Britain. Would this reaction have been the same had the crisis occurred in 1821 or 1825, when the officer corps still consisted largely of men commissioned directly from civilian life, without some socialization in professional ethics?[20]

President Jackson chose not employ the army to enforce the neutrality laws by restraining Americans going to fight in Texas in 1835, but the occupation of Texas and the advance across the Nueces River to the Rio Grande that precipitated the war with Mexico a decade later provide significant examples of increasing military accountability to civilian control. The crisis with Mexico pitted the United States against a weaker power, widely disdained on ethnic and cultural grounds, that presented few of the dangers that would be risked in taking on Britain. Even so, many officers, up to and including Brigadier General Zachary Taylor, commander of the army sent to occupy Texas in 1845, felt qualms about U.S. policy toward Mexico. These doubts were often related to Whiggish political sentiments, and the Whig associations of officers like Taylor were widely known. Yet the Democratic president, James K. Polk, usually an intense partisan, chose Taylor rather than the more expansionist brigadier general Edmund P. Gaines, a frontiersman and Democrat from Tennessee who was actually senior and superior to Taylor in the army's chain of command, to press U.S. claims across the Nueces.[21]

It is noteworthy that Polk felt enough confidence in Taylor's competence and sense of duty to choose a known adherent of the rival Whigs to execute his policies. Gaines had been in the army a decade longer than Taylor and had temporarily but successfully commanded the army in Canada in 1814 when Jacob Brown and Winfield Scott were wounded. He had far more tactical and operational experience against European-style foes than Taylor, whose War of 1812 experience had been limited. Indeed, Taylor's lack of tactical sophistication appears as a truism in virtually every account of the war with Mexico, so much so that one might ask why a Democratic militia general, perhaps no more skillful militarily but of greater partisan value and reliability, was not brought in to command the army sent to intimidate Mexico. In fact, Taylor's retention in command suggests several things that helped the regular army to maintain its monopoly over the operational direction of peacekeeping, coercive diplomacy, and war: inertia, the perception of experience and expertise, and the dilemmas of partisan appointments. Taylor had been the commander on the spot since the late 1830s, and he had been hailed as the victor of the battle of Okeechobee against the Seminoles in 1837, after he had survived a backlash against his criticism of the Missouri volunteers from Democratic senators Thomas Hart Benton and Lewis F. Linn. He had come up with a reasonable campaign plan while commanding U.S. forces in Florida, and he had a reputation as a troop trainer and battlefield leader that few if any militia generals could match. Removing him would have raised questions about administration partisanship, providing an opening for critics of Polk's expansionist policy, while his presence in command could be exploited in efforts to gain Whig support for Polk's policy of intimidation. Any alternative commander had to be willing to wait in Texas for months to see whether war would occur. And when the war began, Taylor's victories at Palo Alto and Resaca de la Palma gave him such fame that he became immune to partisan removal.[22]

But Taylor's retention in command was ultimately a testament to his reliability: though a Whig, he would faithfully execute presidential orders; and, because a Whig, he would do so cautiously, without getting out in front of the administration's timetable and causing diplomatic or political difficulty. Gaines, on the other hand, rushed to raise a mass of volunteers – something he had been warned against several years before, when frontiersmen spread false rumors of a Cherokee war along the Arkansas border – and was summarily packed off to a harbor fortress in New York City, about as far as he could be sent from the frontier and active service. Taylor's judgment and reliability, already demonstrated when he had discounted the rumors and kept the peace on the Cherokee frontier, was mirrored by the reliability of his West Point-trained junior officers, none of whom are known to have resigned due to their qualms over the war, and by the discipline those officers enforced, however brutally, over U.S. troops that helped minimize popular resistance in Mexico, enabling the army to supply itself there. American history might have been very different had a substantial number of officers resigned or otherwise refused to execute Polk's policy, and historians should consider such possibilities rather than assuming reliable civil–military relations as a given.[23]

The new regiments raised for the war in 1846 and 1847 were almost entirely officered by Democrats commissioned directly from civilian life, without West Point training; yet all but one of these units were temporary, and the regulars retained their commissions after the war, while virtually all of the officers of the temporary regiments returned to civilian life. Although Polk appointed a number of Democratic politicians as generals, his efforts to replace the Whig Scott with Democratic senator Thomas Hart Benton were rebuffed, despite a Democratic majority in Congress, suggesting that he was unable to rally enough support to overcome Scott's claims to military expertise. Taylor was retained in command throughout the war, and if anything, his supercession by Scott in command of the advance to Mexico City was a victory for Scott's claims to superior military experience and expertise, despite being far more overtly partisan than Taylor. (Scott had been talked of, and had maneuvered for, the Whig presidential nomination in 1840.) Democratic enthusiasts of Manifest Destiny got their chance for adventure, glory, and future political capital, but the political generals and citizen-soldiers served under the command of Regular Army men, setting a precedent that has never been broken since, and Scott and Taylor relied on their experienced regular subordinates, many of them West Pointers, for the most important missions at every level.[24]

After a generation of Democrats had denounced standing armies and military aristocrats, the ultra-Jacksonian Polk relied on the professional standing army, so closely associated with the Military Academy and Whiggish centralism, rather than the militia or state volunteers to lead the execution of his policy. This gap between rhetoric and reality was not new. It had also been the case in the war to remove the Seminole Indians from Florida under the administrations of presidents Jackson and Van Buren during the 1830s. As the Whiggish advocates of standing armies had long recognized, the militia and volunteers were eager to gain the hard currency paid for military service but too impatient to get back to their businesses at home to sustain the effort necessary to conquer the Seminoles, much less police the borders and frontiers every day. (This assumes that policing involves more even-handedness than the vigilante lynch violence often undertaken by whites on the frontiers: given their land hunger and the Seminoles' distrust, any conciliation or pacification short of conquest was out of the question if white citizen-soldiers from the South were to take the lead.) In fact, Jackson responded to military complaints and took command of military operations in Florida from the territorial governor, Richard K. Call, a former protégé, and gave it to Brigadier General Jesup during the fall of 1836. (Jesup was loosely associated with the Democrats, but was only selected after Scott and Gaines had both failed in campaigns that spring.) Indeed, federal officials increasingly tried to limit or prevent militia and volunteer call-ups for service in Florida, due to their expense and limited effectiveness. Though thousands of militia and volunteers were mobilized across the South during the Seminole War, the fighting and dying needed to implement the Democratic removal policy was largely done by the Regular Army the Democrats professed to hate.[25]

Along with, and as a culmination of, the army's duties policing the borderlands, that war became a crucible forging military accountability to national civilian authority. Despite arguments that the army became a 'cultural mirror' for Manifest Destiny during the decade after the war with Mexico, that expansionist ideology never drew significant numbers from their allegiance to the sovereignty of the nation-state and the policies of the civil government. Though many officers were sympathetic to the triumphalist exceptionalism of expansion, very few left the army to join filibusters during the years after 1845 – or those between 1821 and 1845 – and dramatic usurpations of national policy like those undertaken by Andrew Jackson simply did not recur, or were quickly quashed by the army chain of command, after 1821. Indeed, the independent or loosely sanctioned foreign policy ventures fairly common among officers on the southern frontier prior to 1821 had few counterparts afterwards. For example, General Gaines acted on President Jackson's authority in advancing to Nacogdoches, Texas in 1836, whereas General Jackson far exceeded the limited 'hot pursuit' authorized by his orders from President Monroe in 1817. Some musings by prominent officers notwithstanding, officer participation in filibusters was virtually nonexistent after 1820, and was far outweighed by their efforts enforcing the neutrality laws against filibusters. Contrary to the received wisdom that filibusters operated unhindered by federal authority, the army and navy did break up or obstruct a number of filibuster expeditions, probably doing as much as could be expected given weak neutrality laws, pro-expansionist juries, and civil officials, from the local level up to presidents Franklin Pierce and James Buchanan, who were sympathetic to the filibusters.[26]

John C. Frémont's expeditions were the outstanding exception to this growing self-restraint. Yet Frémont was the exception who proves the rule, exceptional both in his political influence – he was a political appointee married to the daughter of Senator Benton – and his lack of West Point socialization, as shown by his dispute with Brigadier General Stephen W. Kearny in California and his court-martial conviction by West Point-educated officers in 1848. Like the officers temporarily commissioned from civilian life during the war, and those of the militia and volunteers in general, Frémont found politics more to his taste than military subordination. Able to escape that subordination as an explorer in the Corps of Topographical Engineers, he quickly left the army once his independence was curtailed by contact with more disciplined officers, even though his dismissal from the army by the court was remitted by the president. (Polk's approval of the verdict prior to remitting the sentence led to a permanent break with Senator Benton.)[27]

The army generally acted to restrain filibustering on the Mexican border, and the tacit support of officers for Texas Rangers crossing the Rio Grande during the 1850s should be understood in light of their perception of Juan Cortina as an outlaw violating American sovereignty, rather than a social bandit or 'resister' of Anglo aggression. The belligerence of Lieutenant George Pickett and Brigadier General William Harney, which precipitated the San Juan de la Fuca crisis with Britain when they landed troops on disputed islands in Vancouver Sound in 1859, must be balanced against commanding general Winfield Scott's role in resolving the crisis – the third time he had been sent by a Democratic administration as the government's point man to help avert war with Britain. (One can also add his informal service in conciliating South Carolinians while overseeing the reinforcement of Charleston during the Nullification Crisis, during the administration of a Democratic president who he had challenged to a duel – which Jackson refused – in the early 1820s.) Despite eagerness for the promotions and glory war would bring, few officers went on record, publicly or privately, in support of Pickett and Harney, aggressive southerners whose romantic expansionism was expressed with greater subordination and restraint elsewhere in the officer corps. Their rash acts raised the specter of insubordination and indiscipline, anathemas to a conservative officer corps that sought predictability and order through the hierarchies of legally sanctioned command. Thus, Scott and the army acted repeatedly to prevent war between Britain and the United States, while trying to keep the peace and maintain national sovereignty in Kansas and Utah and hindering the operations of proslavery expansionists seeking spoils in Mexico and Cuba. Once again, historians should consider how history might have been different had there been war between Britain and the United States in either 1838 or 1859, or had proslavery imperialists been able to operate unhindered against Mexico and Cuba.[28]

The Military Academy and Accountability: Institutional Reform and Officer Socialization

The essence of post-War of 1812 military reform, and the roots of American military professionalism, lay in imbuing cadets at the Military Academy with the principles later embodied in the motto 'Duty, Honor, Country.' Probing beyond the slogan, analysis suggests that these words articulated essential prerequisites for the creation of a capable military leadership accountable to national civilian authority. 'Duty' meant subordination and accepting tasks assigned by constitutionally authorized and delegated command; 'honor' meant performing one's duties with selfless integrity in the defense of law, rather than the belligerent defense of personal reputation regardless of right or wrong; and 'country' provided the focus of service to the nation – rather than self, class, or section – for graduates' efforts to perform their duties. After four years of consciously practicing these principles, working together toward a common goal under the mentorship of officers who had experienced the same process as cadets themselves, graduates had imbibed a strong sense of their duty to serve the nation responsibly and accountably – the moral and emotional basis for professional commitment.

This process began with the Academy's reform under the superintendency of Captain Sylvanus Thayer between 1817 and 1833. Before 1817 the Military Academy graduated few officers, and most of them left the army just as quickly as men commissioned directly from civilian life. Each of the first three superintendents – Colonel Jonathan Williams, Colonel Joseph G. Swift, and Captain Alden Partridge, who like Swift was a graduate from the Williams era – resigned for selfish personal reasons in disputes over command, setting examples of impatience and insubordination rather than dutiful, disinterested commitment to national service. Arriving at West Point after 15 years of inattention, confusion, and recurrent disorder there, Thayer believed that the purpose of American higher education was primarily the inculcation of mental discipline, an instrumental rationality particularly essential for what Swift labeled 'a corps of instructed administrative officers to serve as a nucleus upon which may be predicated any necessary force' – the expansible army established in the reduction in force of 1821.[29]

As superintendent Thayer buckled down to establishing, standardizing, and inculcating discipline and order, fostering an unprecedented uniformity and predictability in the Academy's operations and graduates. He immediately 'commenced a system of reformation,' 'to regulate and harmonize the whole machine of instruction' by enforcing admissions standards already on the books, vowing that he 'would persevere until

I produce that state of Military Discipline which is as indispensable in an institution of this sort as in a regular Army.' (It should be noted that neither Williams nor Partridge had seen active service in the Regular Army during the War of 1812; Thayer had served in a variety of capacities in the field throughout the war.) Thayer quickly divided the corps of cadets into four year groups based on their academic progress, and he defined and enforced both the academic year, refusing to accept cadets who arrived at West Point after the beginning of classes, and the daily schedule, demanding the promptitude required ever since. With funding from an equally reform-minded War Department, classes now continued through the winter months, and cadets were required to attend the Academy for the full four years demanded by the curriculum. Cadets were forbidden to leave post without permission, and furloughs were normally limited to the summer between the second and third year. The simple requirement to be physically present for duty began the long process of remolding the values and personae of independent-minded young gentlemen by habituating aspiring officers to practicing the principle of duty – the accountability – that gave focus and substance to their commitment to serving their country.[30]

Thayer's intent is often summarized as the creation of a school for civil engineers, but this explanation puts the cart before the horse. Thayer realized that no curriculum could possibly do all of the valuable things sought in all the proposals by his predecessors and the reports of the Boards of Visitors. He therefore chose to pursue depth, rather than a breadth he feared would degenerate into superficiality, almost regardless of subject. Thayer shared his predecessors' desire to sustain the Corps of Engineers as an elite intellectual cadre, and he sought to diffuse the knowledge of fortification design he had encountered at the French *Ecole Polytechnique*, but his first concern was to foster a military atmosphere of discipline, subordination, and habituation to duty. This, as much as any specific desire to teach engineering, was the reason for the curriculum's emphasis on mathematics and the physical sciences, and accounts for Thayer's initial resistance to incorporating civil engineering into a curriculum he felt was already overstretched. (He regarded French and English grammar as essential to understanding the art of fortification and communicating with others, and was required by law to maintain the course in history, geography, and ethics, despite its somewhat cursory character.) Yet, regardless of Thayer's intent, or who actually initiated the shift, the introduction of civil engineering into the curriculum – which did not occur until 1824 – was indispensable to the implementation of the General Survey Act of 1824, which provided dozens of government engineers for road, railroad, and canal surveys, and from the late 1820s to the design and construction of the Baltimore and Ohio and many other railroads.[31]

Thayer developed one of the early republic's most systematic efforts at shaping and transforming individuals, perhaps matched only by the penitentiaries. He systematized cadet ranks and responsibilities already on the books, creating an organizational hierarchy of cadet companies, with cadet officers and noncommissioned officers, analogous to that in the army in order to give graduates training in the processes of command and administration and the values of duty and subordination – the ancestor of the Cadet Leadership Development System in place today. He crafted and enforced a comprehensive system of regulations more rigorous than anywhere else in American higher education – or indeed in the army itself – and brought in experienced officers – the commandant and tactical officers, still present today – from the army's combat arms to serve as drill instructors, disciplinary officers, and mentors to the cadets. The tactical officers lived in the barracks with the cadets and inspected their rooms several times every day. Cadets were forbidden alcohol and tobacco, and were not permitted to gamble, spit, or swear. They had to get Thayer's permission to subscribe to newspapers or receive money, even from their parents. (It does not appear that Thayer inspected their letters very thoroughly, however, and many did receive money and other presents from home.) They slept on mattresses on the floor, and were supposed to remain in their rooms at all times unless in class, at meals or on drill. Offenses against regulations were punished by a standardized number of demerits, and receiving 200 demerits led to a cadet's dismissal. Indeed, many of the regulations carried the threat of dismissal, and Thayer did not hesitate to enforce them, whatever a cadet's social standing or political connections. Yet he also sought explanations and repentance for derelictions, and often rewarded the responsibility and integrity of well-intentioned cadets by remitting their punishments when they came forward. Thayer's willingness to take cadets at their word in order to encourage and reward personal responsibility was the product of genteel assumptions about honor and the root of the formal Honor Code that later demanded its practice; both the assumptions and the code were essential for men charged with the accountable expenditure of public funds.[32]

To stimulate the cadets' sense of duty and their habits of preparation, Thayer demanded that every cadet be responsible for his own learning. Classes proceeded by participation rather than lecture or recitation alone: the 'Thayer method' required – and still requires today – that every cadet be prepared to answer questions or solve problems in every class every day. Thayer encouraged cadets to channel their competitive energies through a merit system in which cadets were ranked weekly in each course. These rankings determined the specific section that cadets would attend in each course, and the rankings were posted in public in the hope of stimulating competition and learning – to encourage cadets to strive for sustained excellence in their duties. As cadets improved in a subject they advanced to sections in which instruction was accelerated, while the best qualified cadets often received added responsibilities and did double duty by serving as instructors to their peers. At the end of the academic year the names of the top five cadets in each subject were published in the annual *Army Register*, and at the end of four years a cadet's academic standing accounted for 70 percent of his class rank upon graduation. This class rank often determined the course of an officer's career, for it was used to decide what branch of the army a cadet could enter, and often (though indirectly) the unit and post where he would first be stationed. It also determined seniority in rank among the graduates of that year, and officers commissioned directly from civilian life on the same date were usually placed below West Pointers on the seniority list. All of these provisions still exist in some form today.

Thayer succeeded in reshaping the Academy and the officer corps because he was self-sacrificing enough to stick with the assignment for 16 years – an incredible amount of time to spend in one post, then or now – for eight of which he was supported by

Secretary of War John C. Calhoun, and for four by John Quincy Adams's secretaries of war, who shared Thayer's and Calhoun's commitment to reform. Prior to Calhoun's arrival, none of the secretaries of war took the time or had the ability to devote sustained attention to thorough-going military reform. Under Jefferson and Madison the executive branch generally adhered to a strict construction of the laws and their intent, and therefore deferred to Congress for substantive change at the Academy. President Monroe shared this concern, but the postwar move toward government reform and greater administrative capacity was most powerful in the military sphere, where Monroe permitted his activist secretary of war great latitude, congressional queries and investigations notwithstanding. The balance of initiative between legislative and executive action therefore shifted toward the latter, with Thayer and Calhoun initiating change and responding to congressional concerns, rather than remaining inactive while anticipating concerns that were never actually raised, as had been the case up to 1817.[33]

Disciplinary problems persisted, of course, but the institution of uniform standards, fairly enforced, and the gradual evolution of an honor code that encouraged personal accountability – rather than the self-righteousness of earlier officers like the superintendents before Thayer, who all resigned when they did not get their way on some issue – produced a balance of discipline and character development crucial to the professional military ethic of responsible service. Faced with higher standards, only one-third of the entering cadets graduated during the Thayer era (compared to half of those prior to his superintendency), but West Point gained a uniformity, regularity, and national recognition previously absent, and actually drew and graduated significantly more cadets than before. More than 1000 aspirants sought the 100 spaces available each year; during the 1820s there were five times more graduates than during the Academy's first decade; and during Thayer's 16 years as superintendent (1817–33) there were more than three times as many graduates as in the 16 years that preceded his appointment. Indeed, the government relied almost exclusively on West Point for officers from after the reduction in force of 1821 until 1836, by which time graduates composed more than 70 percent of the officer corps, nearly five times their proportion when Thayer arrived at West Point in 1817. As this statistic suggests, officers commissioned directly from civilian life became a distinct minority within the officer corps; there was sometimes friction between them and the West Pointers, but the tone of the officer corps was increasingly set by Academy graduates. Consequently, the junior officer corps became much more uniform in education, training, and socialization, reducing friction and disputes among officers, increasing predictability and capability in the performance of duty, and encouraging longer careers among men of similar habits and values. Despite the opportunities presented by a burgeoning economy, remarkably few officers – an average of less than 4 percent per year between 1821 and 1860 – left the army to enter civilian life. Most served their country dutifully, and accountably, for longer than ever before or since.[34]

This persistence should not be taken as a given. With civilian opportunities abounding, with few wars to fight and little glory to win against 'savage' Indians and Mexicans, the quasi-aristocratic motives of glory, reputation, and gentility inherited from the example of European officer corps were unlikely to hold restless, individualistic Americans under the constraints of military discipline long enough to develop professional commitment. Thus, while the officer corps attracted many cautious men, reluctant to chance the storms of life in a highly individualistic society, the short-lived surge in resignations during the mid-1830s, amid the country's biggest economic boom before the California Gold Rush, suggests that something more than personal psychological conservatism or the security of an army commission was responsible for the officer corps' unparalleled retention rate, about 90 percent per annum between 1821 and 1860. (More than half of the remaining 10 percent were involuntarily separated by death or, much more rarely, discharge or dismissal.) This rate of occupational and organizational persistence was unparalleled in any other institution, organization, occupation, or profession in the United States at that time, and probably exceeded that of most European officer corps as well.[35]

Even during the 1830s, when a wave of resignations totaled about a sixth of the officer corps between 1835 and 1837, the resignation rate for the decade actually averaged only 36 officers per annum, or 6 percent. (On average West Point graduated 44 cadets per year during this period.) This is a proportional jump of 50 percent from the 'normal' rate (4 percent per annum) between 1821 and 1860, but remains only 6 percent in absolute terms. In fact, only in 1836 – the peak of the economic boom, when officers' engineering skills were most in demand, and the year the second Seminole War began in Florida, promising arduous service in malarial swamps with little prospect of martial glory or public thanks – and 1837 did the resignation rate actually exceed 6 percent. Between 1839 and 1844 the rate was only 1.5 percent – less than half the normal percentage, even though the 'thankless,' 'inglorious war' in Florida continued until 1842, breeding increasing frustration, and even demoralization, in the officer corps. The 'resignation crisis' of the mid-1830s was a historical aberration. Concentrating on it, as most historians of the antebellum army have at some point done, leads to distortion. Such a focus does help provide us with a sense of the degree to which some officers – but, as the numbers show, a rather small percentage – saw their primary duty, their core competency, as civil engineering. Understanding this, historians should ask not only why there was a crisis but why it ended and why it was not repeated before 1860. Although many officers later famous in the Civil War left the army during the economic boom of the early to mid-1850s, they actually constituted a very small proportion of the officer corps as a whole. In effect, the surge in resignations between 1835 and 1837 was the exception that proved the rule of professional commitment and career persistence among West Point graduates and Regular Army officers.[36]

Professional commitment increased, and cadets submitted more willingly to institutional discipline, as the cadets began to develop a distinct professional identity and camaraderie as aspiring officers, with their own rituals and symbols as novitiates. Cadets began to speak, privately in letters and publicly in addresses to the cadet Dialectic Society – a debating club, established in 1826, indicative of the cadets' growing cohesion – of themselves as 'children of the Union' and of West Point as 'the National School,' 'the school of the Union,' a 'school for national feeling,' and a 'school of Union.' They contributed significant portions of their meager salaries to the construction of monuments to professional models like Thaddeus Kosciusko (the Polish military engineer who designed part of the West Point fortifications during the American Revolution) and the officers slain in Florida. They routinely referred to the Corps of Cadets, the officer corps, and the army as 'bands of brothers' sworn to serve the nation.[37]

This argument for graduates' nationalism may appear questionable in light of the resignation of so many West Pointers at the outset of the Civil War. About 43 percent of the prewar officer corps came from the South, a proportion somewhat higher than its total population, and substantially higher than its white population (about 30 percent of that in the United States as a whole), a result of the operation of the three-fifths clause upon congressional nominations to West Point and the efforts of Secretary of War Jefferson Davis commissioning southerners from civilian life to the regiments raised when the army was increased by about 25 percent in 1855. Yet, contrary to the contemporary perception that has shaped assessments ever since, only 25 percent of the officers who had graduated from West Point resigned, while 29 percent of the officers who had not graduated from the Military Academy joined the Confederacy. Despite – or perhaps because of – the conservatism of the officer corps, a remarkable 95 percent of northern-born officers remained in Union service to coerce the seceded states, as did two-thirds of those from the border states, more than one-third of those from the Upper South (including such Virginian luminaries as Winfield Scott and George H. Thomas), and nearly one-sixth of those from the Lower South. Indeed, the proportion of southern-born federal politicians and civil officials – who took oaths of office not unlike those sworn by soldiers – who went south was considerably higher than that of West Point graduates or the officer corps as a whole.[38]

Populist Myth, Professional Reality

Any occupational group dependent on others for its future will fear and resent criticism, and officers' laments have provided part of the basis for the historiographical tradition that the army was endangered by Jacksonian attack. This tradition is a testament to the power of perception, both contemporary and historiographical, for it is actually the product of two squeaky wheels: members of the officer corps at one end of the axle, and some – though hardly all – Democratic congressmen at the other end. Ideologues led both extremes, and Alden Partridge's *The Military Academy Unmasked* is often taken as a true reflection of popular, Democratic, or even congressional sentiment. Yet we actually know little beyond anecdotes about popular attitudes toward West Point and the Regular Army after the War of 1812, and much research, particularly on congressional roll call voting, needs to be done before historians can speak with confidence.[39]

Until then, historians must look to, and explain, outcomes as the measure of opposition and acceptance. The assault on military professionalism by Democratic radicals produced far more smoke than fire, smoke that continues to blind historians even today. The rigorous enforcement of academic standards under the Thayer system, under which rich and well-connected youths frequently flunked out and were refused reinstatement, plus the admission and graduation of a substantial number of cadets from middling or even impoverished backgrounds were such that, in the words of one otherwise critical historian, the Military Academy 'probably came closer to producing the aristocracy of talent espoused by Jefferson and John Adams than any other educational [or, it should be added, government] institution in the antebellum United States.' This meticulous, rigidly impersonal attention to assessment, encouraging future officers to strive for excellence in the performance of their duties, plus legislation in 1843 formalizing the congressionally apportioned system of nominating cadets – an informal practice since at least 1828 – enabled West Point to answer Jacksonian critics on their own terms of democracy, opportunity, and accountability as well as those of merit, specialization, and efficiency. Doing so helped to convince Congress to maintain the Academy as the army's principal source of officers and the Regular Army as the nation's *de facto* first line of defense on land.[40]

Readers swayed by the myth of Jacksonian egalitarianism, or those who see any criticism of the military as evidence of a persistently powerful ideological antagonism to standing or professional forces – a perspective often informed by the belief that 'republicanism is everywhere' that flourished among American historians in the 1970s and 80s – may question the argument that West Point, and by extension the regular army, was generally accepted in American political culture before 1846. Yet all the Jacksonian-era rhetoric and legislative proposals resulted in nothing more concrete than the discharge of a few officers in 1842 and the dismounting of the Second Dragoon Regiment as an economy measure between 1842 and 1844. Officers feared the retrenchment bills that appeared in Congress, pay did not keep up with inflation, and some standard expense allowances were cut or abolished, but pay was increased over time. The Jacksonians may have feared, resented, or disdained the standing army and military professionalism. But they accepted it with their tax dollars, in the Military Academy's dominance of officer selection and training, and in the dominance of long-service regular officers at all levels of command. In the process, the professional officer corps gained and maintained a *de facto* monopoly over the operational direction of constitutionally authorized American military force in civil and international war, while restraining the unauthorized projection of American force against neighboring countries in times of peace.[41]

Thayer resigned the superintendency in 1833 because of President Jackson's intervention (largely in reappointing cadets dismissed by Thayer) in the Academy's operation, but Thayer did not resign from the army, as all his predecessors had done, serving the United States for another quarter-century. Though the rigor of Thayer's system was reduced during the ensuing superintendency, the disciplinary standards Jackson had labeled undemocratic were reestablished, with Old Hickory's sanction, after only three years, though they were never again quite as severe. One of Thayer's protégés, Richard H. Delafield, assumed the superintendency in 1838, holding it until 1845 and returning from 1856 to 1861, the only officer (apart from Jonathan Williams, who had resigned the position) to hold the superintendency twice, and the officer who held it longest apart from Thayer.

To paraphrase historian Leonard White, Thayer's Military Academy fostered the first organized professional body in the nation's service. Indeed, since so many officers served as Indian agents, surveyors and railroad engineers, and the like after leaving the army, West Point and the Regular Army officer corps became the *de facto* basis for an informal national administrative cadre, in the Weberian sense of a body organized both hierarchically, to ensure subordination and accountability to control by national authority, and along lines of functional specialization, to ensure responsibility and effectiveness in the execution of specific missions and duties. At West Point merit was determined by constant, standardized and systematic – or in officers' words, 'regular' – evaluation, and competition under conditions of formal equal opportunity and clearly delineated lines of specialized expertise and authority – competition that habituated aspiring officers to functional specialization, subordination to legally constituted hierarchies of authority, and accountability to public values and expectations.[42]

Under Thayer West Point became one of the principal forces in the development of a distinctive professional ethos of disinterested public service, encouraging officers to view their posts as offices and their perquisites as privileges. Officers still disputed the perquisites and recognition due to specific ranks and offices, and they maintained a strong sense of their 'rights' as officers and gentlemen, but they increasingly demonstrated an understanding that these rights were derived from the duties of offices, not inherent in the individuals holding them. This sense of impersonal public service, open to public observation and political inquiry, was essential for effectiveness and accountability in public administration, and beyond that for responsibility to republican government and society. Allied with values of system, instrumental rationality, and order, specialization and organization became hallmarks of the officer corps, enhancing its engineering, logistical, and administrative aptitude while encouraging officers to respond to the demands of civilian supremacy with laudable accountability. Responding accountably to the pressures of politics and public opinion, the officers of the Regular Army became republicans as well as professionals – indeed they united republicanism and professionalism in their distinctive ethos of duty and service. Together, effectiveness and accountability enabled West Point, the officer corps, and the army to secure the institutional and occupational monopoly they sought, with far-reaching and ultimately positive consequences for the character of American expansion, foreign relations, and Union.

Notes

[1] Notable exceptions not mentioned below include Cress, *Citizens in Arms* and Kohn, *Eagle and Sword*.
[2] The generalizations about the officer corps in this essay are based on the research for Watson, 'Professionalism, Social Attitudes, and Civil–Military Accountability,' and Watson, *Federal Diplomats*. The most thorough source on the army officer corps as a social and occupational group is Skelton, *An American Profession of Arms*, an indispensable work for anyone interested in the subject. For a rather different perspective, rich in individual examples, see Coffman, *The Old Army*. For a concise summary of major trends in the army and its officer corps during this period, see Watson, 'The Growth of the Professional Army, 1815–1860.' I have enjoyed great benefits from discussions with and readings of my work by William Skelton, Ira Gruber, Gene A. Smith, John Boles, Michael Morrison, James Bradford, Theodore Crackel, Robert Wettemann, Donald Connelly, and Ethan Rafuse.

[3] Scholars should treat Grant's anecdote (reported at the end of ch. 2 in his *Memoirs*) about being harassed by a child more cautiously. If nothing else, the child probably couldn't recognize Grant's rank, and enlisted soldiers usually came from working-class, and often 'unrespectable,' backgrounds, which might help explain the child's derision. The reaction of a child is hardly the best evidence for national attitudes, nor are populist caricatures of militia musters very useful indicators of middle class or elite opinion toward the Regular Army. See Scott, ed. *Forgotten Valor*; Baker, ed. *The Websters*, to cite only sample published collections, for extensive evidence of very junior officers having genteel social relationships with both local elites and the highest civil officials. Coker, ed. *The News from Brownsville* and Thompson, ed. *Fifty Miles a Day and a Fight*, provide similar evidence from the borderlands. Perhaps the most representative evidence of attitudes toward the army provided by Grant's example is the way in which his West Point classmate introduced him to his future wife, the daughter of a planter.

[4] See, e.g., the edited works cited in note 3. This essay will not discuss the relationships between officers and enlisted soldiers; see Watson, 'Professionalism, Social Attitudes, and Civil–Military Accountability,' ch. 10, and Steinhauer, '"Sogers": Enlisted Men in the U.S. Army, 1815–1860.' See Myerly, *British Military Spectacle*, for an examination of the sociopolitical role played by the performance of command in Britain. The officer corps provided the long-term core of the army during the nineteenth century, because few noncommissioned officers equaled the officer's average of 20-plus years of service.

[5] See Watson, 'Professionalism, Social Attitudes, and Civil–Military Accountability,' ch. 3, for a thorough synthesis of the secondary literature on the Academy between 1817 and 1846. See Bullock, *Revolutionary Brotherhood*, particularly chs. 5 and 8, for a stimulating examination of the links between cosmopolitan learning, ambition, gentility, respectability, and nonsectarian nationalism among the Freemasons, links that were commonly present among officers. For another approach suggestive of officers' ability to secure public recognition and acceptance, see Nelson, *National Manhood*, especially ch. 3.

[6] Skelton, *An American Profession of Arms*, 138–9. Of the 89 men who had graduated from the academy before the declaration of war in 1812, more than 75 percent of those still available at the time of the 1815 reduction in force were retained. Of the 31 graduated during the war (one in 1813 and 30 the following year), 29 were retained, one was discharged and another declined retention in 1815, while all of the 30 cadets graduated in March 1815 were retained. Only two of the 102 declined to remain in the postwar establishment. Of the 111 cadets who graduated in the years between the reductions in force of 1815 and 1821, 13 (12 percent) left the army before the reduction (all by resignation or dismissal) but 94 of the remaining 95 were retained in 1821. Similar proportions prevailed among the graduates of earlier years who were still in the army: 15 of 18 of those graduated during the war and 21 of 23 of those trained before the war were retained (83 and 91 percent). In sum, 143 of 153 of those West Point graduates who remained in service in 1821 were retained. Calculations based on Cullum, *Biographical Register of the Officers and Graduates of the United States Military Academy at West Point*, vols. I–II, the basic source for graduates; Gardner, *A Dictionary of the Officers of the Army of the United States*; Hamersly, *Complete Army Register of the United States, for One Hundred Years*; Heitman, *Historical Registry and Dictionary of the United States Army*; and Gordon, *A Compilation of Registers of the Army of the United States*, which lists all the officers in their units.

[7] See Crackel, *Mr. Jefferson's Army*; Crackel, *A Bicentennial History of West Point*; and Crackel, 'Jefferson, Politics, and the Army: An Examination of the Military Peace Establishment Act of 1802': 21–38.

[8] Madison, 5 December 1815, Monroe, 3 December 1822, and 7 December 1824, Adams, 4 March and 6 December 1825, and Jackson, in Richardson, *Messages and Papers of the Presidents*, vol. II, 553, 757–8, 823–4, 863–4, 871–2, and vol. III, 1019. Jefferson did not mention the Academy in an annual or inaugural address; Madison did so in four annual messages (once implicitly), Monroe in three (1822–24) during his second term, and Adams in

three, including his inaugural, the only inaugural during this era to do so. Jackson praised the Regular Army in seven of his eight annual messages. The Academy was mentioned in nine of the 28 annual messages between 1801 and 1828. Indeed, West Point provides the only example of effective national support for higher education Daniel Walker Howe cites – or could have cited – in his 2001 Society for Historians of the Early Republic presidential address: Howe, 'Church, State, and Education in the Young American Republic,' 3.

[9] Skelton, *An American Profession of Arms*, 137–9. See Watson, 'Professionalism, Social Attitudes, and Civil–Military Accountability,' ch. 3, for a thorough treatment of military training at West Point before 1846. For a comprehensive assessment of the character, state, and evolution of Army troop training, drill, and combat readiness during this era, see ibid., chs. 5–7; see also Spiller, 'From Hero to Leader.' The contemporary perception, sometimes repeated today, that the Mexican army was equally or better-trained proved illusory, since that army lacked the leadership, discipline, and morale to maintain unit cohesion and execute its drills, however often practiced on the parade ground – and that frequency has been exaggerated by repetition of the observations made by a few travelers. See DePalo, *The Mexican National Army*, for the best treatment of its subject.

[10] For the fortification system, see Browning, *Two if by Sea*; Watson, 'Knowledge, Interest, and the Limits of Military Professionalism: The Discourse on American Coastal Defense, 1815–1860,' 280–307; and Price, 'American Coastal Defense.' Linn has argued the centrality of coastal defense to nineteenth-century officers' visions of American national security policy; see 'The American Way of War Revisited,' 508–9. For the ordnance, see Smith, *Harpers Ferry Armory and the New Technology*. For officers and exploration, see Goetzmann, *Army Exploration in the American West*; for officers and internal improvements, see Hill, *Roads, Rails, and Waterways*; Angevine, *The Railroad and the State*; and Wetteman, 'To the Public Prosperity.' For context, see Larson, *Internal Improvement*, and McCoy, *The Elusive Republic*.

[11] In 1865 all the army-level commanders (such as the commanders of the Army of the Potomac, the Army of the Tennessee, etc.) on both sides were graduates, as were nearly all corps commanders and the majority of division commanders. Every one of the 60 largest battles of the war was commanded by a graduate on at least one side, and in 54 cases by graduates on both sides. Crackel, *A Bicentennial History of West Point*, 135. See Polski, '"Mr. Lincoln's Army" Revisited: Partisanship, Institutional Position, and Union Army Command, 1861–1865,' 176–207, for the most thorough study of Union general officer appointment practices in print, and Goss, *The War Within the Union High Command*.

[12] Morrison, 'The Best School,' and Moten, *The Delafield Commission and the American Military Profession*. This critique has respectable antecedents from Edward M. Coffman to Russell F. Weigley, Samuel P. Huntington, Oliver Lyman Spaulding, and Emory Upton, but it is only with Skelton's *American Profession of Arms* that the evolution of American military professionalism has been viewed in a detailed historical light. See Hagerman, *The American Civil War and the Origins of Modern Warfare* for an analysis of the problems, organizational, tactical, operational, and logistical, American officers faced in that conflict, and their responses, which were much more innovative than the critics have concluded. See Watson, 'Knowledge, Interest, and the Limits of Military Professionalism,' for an elaboration of my argument here.

[13] Hill, 'The Army in Texas': 434–57, and 14 (July 1848): 183–97. For Scott's strategy, see especially Johnson, *Winfield Scott and the Quest for Military Glory*, which explicitly articulates this thesis; for the army's logistical structure, see Watson, 'Professionalism, Social Attitudes, and Civil–Military Accountability,' ch. 8; Risch, *Quartermaster Support of the Army*; Miller, 'The United States Army Logistics Complex, 1818–1845'; and Kieffer, *Maligned General*.

[14] See Watson, 'Knowledge, Interest, and the Limits of Military Professionalism,' and 'Professionalism, Social Attitudes, and Civil–Military Accountability,' chs. 3–6, for a critique of the uneven character, state, and evolution of the army's military expertise and capability during this period. Chapters 7–9 do the same for the army's combat readiness and internal cohesion,

while chapters 10, 11, and 14 do so for its often damaging impact on enlisted soldiers and Native Americans.

[15] Moten, *The Delafield Commission*; Morrison, 'The Best School'; and Watson, 'Professionalism, Social Attitudes, and Civil–Military Accountability,' ch. 3, address the limitations of the Academy curriculum. For West Point as a scientific or technical school, see Molloy, 'Technical Education and the Young Republic.'

[16] Only seven officers were commissioned between 1821 and 1831 without graduating from West Point, and three of those had left the Academy without graduating. See Skelton, *An American Profession of Arms*, Tables 9.4 and 9.5 (140–41 and 158–61) for comparisons with the civilian male population. The general group profile is much akin to that of the civil officers examined in Aronson, *Status and Kinship in the Higher Civil Service*.

[17] Bassett, ed. *Correspondence of Andrew Jackson*, 3: 190–91.

[18] Scott quoted in Croffut, ed. *Fifty Years in Camp and Field*, 310; Hoskin and Macve, 'The Genesis of Accountability: The West Point Connections,' 37–73; Jackson, 7 December 1835, quoted from Richardson, ed. *Messages and Papers of the Presidents*, vol. III, 1388–9. For the postal system, which underwent similar processes of rationalization, see John, *Spreading the News*; see Cohen, *A Calculating People*, ch. 4, for the role mathematics was expected to play in disciplining the minds of republican citizens, and ch. 5 for its role in early national state formation and public administration.

[19] Scott to Secretary of State James Monroe, 18 November 1815 and 19 March 1816, Winfield Scott Papers, U.S. Military Academy Library, West Point, New York (originals in the State Department Archives in Washington, D.C.), and Jefferson to Monroe, 4 February 1816, in Ford, ed. *The Writings of Thomas Jefferson*, 10: 19. For Beard, see Major General Andrew Jackson to Secretary of War John C. Calhoun, with enclosures, 24 July 1819, file J-55, Letters Received by the Secretary of War, Registered Series, Record Group 107, National Archives, and Watson, 'Professionalism, Social Attitudes, and Civil–Military Accountability,' 950–54. Among works on the Burr Conspiracy and other early national filibusters, see Crackel, *Mr. Jefferson's Army*, chs. 6 and 7; Owsley and Smith, *Filibusters and Expansionists*; and Watson, *Federal Diplomats*.

[20] The standard narrative history of the army during the early republic, Prucha's *The Sword of the Republic*, employs 'Agents of Empire' as the title for its chapter on the officer corps. Samuel J. Watson, 'The Uncertain Road to Manifest Destiny: Army Officers and the Course of American Territorial Expansionism, 1815–1846,' in *Manifest Destiny and Empire*, edited by Morris and Haynes, 68–114, and 'U.S. Army Officers Fight the 'Patriot War': Responses to Filibustering on the Canadian Border, 1837–1839,' 487–521, argue that officers were not especially bellicose – often less so than civilian expansionists, including the Jacksonian inheritors of Jefferson's mantle – but Prucha's label is certainly applicable to their work and its ultimate effects.

[21] For these qualms, see Watson, 'Manifest Destiny and Military Professionalism'. See Howe, *The Political Culture of the American Whigs*; Brown, *Politics and Statesmanship*; Kohl, *The Politics of Individualism*; and Holt, *The Rise and Fall of the American Whig Party* for Whig values, *mentalité*, and worldview, which generally suited officers more than those of the Jacksonians, though Skelton has pointed out that partisan affiliations were about equally divided among the officers whose allegiances could be discovered. See Skelton, *An American Profession of Arms*, ch. 15, for the most extensive treatment of officers and politics.

[22] Silver, *Edmund Pendleton Gaines*; Bauer, *Zachary Taylor*; Hamilton, *Zachary Taylor*; Watson, 'Professionalism, Social Attitudes, and Civil–Military Accountability,' 1200–1201.

[23] Ibid., 1288–1305, and ch. 15; Gaines to Sen. L.F. Linn and Rep. A.G. Harrison, 14 August 1837, in *The New American State Papers, 1789–1860: Military Affairs*, edited by Benjamin Franklin Cooling (19 vols., Wilmington, Del.: Scholarly Resources, 1979), 1: 288; Taylor to Adjutant General Jones, 23 December 1842 and 28 March 1843, cited in Brainerd Dyer, *Zachary Taylor*, 138–40. Gaines had become estranged from Jackson because of the

president's criticism of Gaines's advance to Nacogdoches in 1836, although Gaines was not in fact exceeding his instructions, nor had he violated direct orders, as Jackson had done in attacking Spanish posts in Florida in 1818. Yet Gaines clearly remained the army's leading 'frontier' general (in his eagerness for expansion) and its advocate of militia and volunteers par excellence, and he should have been the natural 'Jacksonian' choice. Foos, *A Short, Offhand, Killing Affair*, argues that the Mexican people rose up in arms against the atrocities committed by U.S. troops, especially the volunteers, but provides more evidence of the atrocities than of popular uprisings or effective guerrilla warfare. Scott was successful enough in maintaining discipline, or perhaps the Mexican populace was eager enough for U.S. currency, that the resistance that did develop was not sufficient to significantly hinder the attainment of U.S. national objectives.

[24] See Winders, *Mr. Polk's Army*, for a thorough examination of Polk's attitude toward the army that emphasizes his suspicion, but exaggerates its impact on the army's command and the postwar composition of the officer corps.

[25] An anonymous group proclaiming themselves 'Many Officers of the Army' had publicly appealed to the Attorney General against Call's unofficial appointment as theater commander in November 1836, on the legal grounds that Call was a civilian without either regular or militia rank. These regulars questioned whether Call's appointment was 'a *lawful* order,' and asked if he could 'be held amenable to any military tribunal' (i.e., a court-martial, like those in which Gaines and Scott were embroiled after the failure of their campaigns) if accused of misconduct. Call was relieved from his military post by President Jackson within the month and replaced by Jesup, who had been offered the command by Call in September while he was in Alabama commanding against the Creeks, but had chosen to serve under Call until the governor had had the chance to prove himself. 'Many Officers of the Army,' (reprinted from the *National Intelligencer* without date) *Army & Navy Chronicle* 3 (3 November 1836): 285, and Doherty, *Richard Keith Call, Southern Unionist*, ch. 7. In general, see Mahon, *History of the Second Seminole War*. Ultimately, only 55 of the 30,000 volunteers who served in the war were killed in action, as opposed to 328 out of 10,000 regulars (Mahon, *History of the Second Seminole War*, 325).

[26] May, 'Young American Males and Filibustering in the Age of Manifest Destiny'; May, *Manifest Destiny's Underworld*; Heidler and Heidler, *Old Hickory's War*; Chaffin, *Fatal Glory*; Ball, *Army Regulars on the Western Frontier*. Though Ball stresses the politicization of army operations during the growing sectional crisis, he does acknowledge the restraint of officers, in contrast to the prevalence of belligerent expansionism and exterminationist racism among civilians. Most of May's examples are of enlisted soldiers, who lacked the statist socialization and the social, cultural, and economic incentives of officers, or of officers' opinions rather than their actions. See Skelton, *An American Profession of Arms*, ch. 17, for examples of officers' support for Manifest Destiny. For a critique of these arguments, see Watson, 'The Uncertain Road to Manifest Destiny,' which encapsulates the argument that military accountability developed in the crucible of borderlands policing, where Military Academy principles of national service and subordination were put into practice and tested by the opposition of local whites.

[27] Rolle, *John Charles Frémont*; Chaffin, *Pathfinder*; Clarke, *Stephen Watts Kearny, Soldier of the West*. Even within the Corps of Topographical Engineers, which is often used to provide examples of expansionist sentiment within the army, only eight of 72 officers were not West Point graduates (and two of the eight were drop-outs). As Adrian Traas notes, 'of these eight [non-graduates], only Frémont seemed to resent West Point's apparent domination of the Army' (*From the Golden Gate to Mexico City*, 9). See also Volpe, 'The Origins of the Frémont Expeditions.'

[28] Thompson, ed. *Fifty Miles a Day and a Fight*; Ball, *Army Regulars on the Western Frontier*, chs. 6–9. See Skelton, *An American Profession of Arms*, Table 9.1 (155), for statistics on the proportion of southerners in the officer corps, which was substantially less than received wisdom

would have us believe. The independent ventures by French officers in North Africa from the 1840s to the 1960s should caution us against assuming military accountability to government foreign policy, even in a democracy.

[29] Chief Engineer Joseph G. Swift, diary, 10 March 1814, in Ellery, ed. *The Memoirs of General Joseph G. Swift*, 125.

[30] Thayer to Josiah Moulton, 17 October 1817, Thayer Papers, U.S. Military Academy Library, West Point, New York. See Crackel, *A Bicentennial History of West Point*, and Pappas, *To the Point* for the best general histories of the Academy; for a concise summary, see *The West Point Bicentennial, 1802–2002* (West Point, NY: United States Military Academy Association of Graduates, 2002), 1–23. For the Academy prior to Thayer's arrival, see Watson, 'Professionalism, Social Attitudes, and Civil–Military Accountability,' 228–50, and idem., 'Developing "Republican Machines": West Point and the Struggle to Render the Officer Corps Safe for America,' in McDonald, ed. *Thomas Jefferson's Military Academy*. See the *American State Papers: Documents, Legislative and Executive, of the Congress of the United States, Class V, Military Affairs*, 7 vols. covering the years 1794–1836 (Washington, D.C.: Gales and Seaton, 1832–1861) 2: 77–9 and 648–57, for the 1820 and 1824 regulations.

[31] Molloy, 'Technical Education and the Young Republic'; Kershner, 'Sylvanus Thayer'; Crackel, *A Bicentennial History of West Point*, 96–8. The mathematics, military engineering, and drawing taught before and after 1824 were certainly of use to future civil engineers, but Crackel shows that no course in civil engineering was taught until that year, when the combination of a new engineering professor interested in civil engineering and the imminent passage of the General Survey Act (along with associated political pressure, which had been mounting, against Thayer's resistance, since his appointment) led the Academic Board (the heads of the departments, and the Superintendent) to mandate its addition to the curriculum. See Adams, ed. *The West Point Thayer Papers, 1808–1872*, or at http://www.library.usma.edu/archives/special.asp, for Thayer's correspondence.

[32] See Howe, *Making the American Self* and Meyer, *The Instructed Conscience* for the philosophy and means of fostering self-discipline and restraint of passion (Scottish Common Sense moral philosophy) commonly accepted by nineteenth-century Americans. The role this philosophy played at West Point is discussed in Ethan S. Rafuse, '"Old Cobbon Sense" and Common Sense: Faculty Psychology, the Middle-Class Mind, and the West Point Experience of the 1840s' (unpublished ms. in the author's possession). The qualities this philosophy sought to inculcate are much like the calm and coolness under fire required of leaders in battle; see Watson, 'Professionalism, Social Attitudes, and Civil–Military Accountability,' 474–83, for an assessment of these qualities as they were praised in and by officers.

[33] Spiller, 'John C. Calhoun as Secretary of War'; and Smith, 'The United States War Department.' Superintendents normally serve five-year tours today.

[34] Statistics derived from sources cited in note 6 above. On average, 11 cadets were appointed each year between 1802 and 1812, 79 between 1813 and 1817 (which includes the unusual 156 appointed in 1814, without which the average would be 59), and 93 between 1818 and 1832, nearly double the 47 admitted on average during the immediate postwar years 1815–17. (See Adjutant General Roger Jones to Secretary of War Lewis Cass, 20 January 1835, in *The American State Papers: Military Affairs*, vol. VII, 51.) Skelton, *An American Profession of Arms*, Figure 11.1 and Tables 11.1–11.4 (216, 182–83, 194, and 213), provides extensive data on attrition, retention, and the growing length of officers' careers, despite very slow promotion. The army's basic structure remained unchanged between the reduction in force of 1821 and the Civil War, and its size actually quadrupled (from about 6000 to about 25,000) as new regiments and staff departments were added during that period, many between 1832 and 1838. The reduction in force after the war with Mexico affected few officers from the antebellum army; virtually all of those disbanded in the reduction were wartime appointees from civil life. Skelton argues that Military Academy socialization reduced friction within the officer corps; the persistence of some disputes was significant, and natural given the individualism of the

officers' parent society, but he convincingly demonstrates the overall trajectory of change. See Watson, 'Professionalism, Social Attitudes, and Civil–Military Accountability,' ch. 9, for further discussion and examples, both of the West Point socialization process and of continuing friction.

[35] Skelton, 'The Army Officer as Organization Man.' See Harries-Jenkins, *The Army in Victorian Society*; Spiers, *The Army and Society*; Porch, *Army and Revolution*; and Curtiss, *The Russian Army Under Nicholas I* for the British, French, and Russian officer corps. There is no adequate study in English of the Prussian officer corps as a social and professional body between 1815 and 1860.

[36] 'A Subaltern,' 'Florida War, No. 4,' *Army and Navy Chronicle* 8 (4 April 1839): 220 ('thankless'); 'Florida War,' *Army and Navy Chronicle* 7 (16 August 1838): 105; 'Quasi Major,' 'The Seminole War' [a public letter addressed to the Secretary of War], *Army and Navy Chronicle* 7 (18 October 1838): 249; 'A Subaltern of the 7th,' 'The Seventh Infantry,' *Army and Navy Chronicle* 9 (22 August 1839): 116. (The last three citations are all to 'inglorious.') Statistics derived from Gordon, comp., *A Compilation of Registers of the Army*, and the registers for years after 1837 published annually by the War Department. See Watson, 'Professionalism, Social Attitudes, and Civil–Military Accountability,' 552–5, for an exploration of the crisis and its antecedents, and "This thankless… unholy war': Army Officers and Civil–Military Relations in the Second Seminole War,' for a discussion of both the officer corps' demoralization and its tempering during this difficult period.

[37] Quotations from Cadet Joseph Ritner, *An Oration Delivered Before the Corps of Cadets of the United States Military Academy at West Point, on the Fifty-Third Anniversary of American Independence*, Newburgh, NY: Parmenter and Spaulding, 1829, and Cadet Benjamin Alvord, *Address Before the Dialectic Society of the Corps of Cadets, in Commemoration of the Gallant Conduct of the Nine Graduates of the Military Academy, and Other Officers of the United States Army, Who Fell in the Battles Which Took Place in Florida*, New York: Wiley & Putnam, 1839. The term 'band of brothers' was very common in officers' and cadets' correspondence.

[38] See Skelton, *An American Profession of Arms*, ch. 18 (statistics in Tables 9.1, 155, and 18.2, 356), for the most thorough analysis of this crisis in the army officer corps; see Morrison, 'The Best School,' 134, for further statistics. See Breeden, 'Rehearsal for Secession? The Return Home of Philadelphia Medical Students in 1859,' for comparison.

[39] 'Americanus' (Partridge), *The Military Academy Unmasked, or, Corruption and Military Despotism Exposed*, Washington, D.C.: n.p., 1830. Other significant documents in the debate over 'West Point aristocracy' include 'Exhibit No. 1, Register of Cadets to December 31, 1829,' communicated to the House of Representatives, March 15, 1830, *American State Papers: Military Affairs* IV: 308–31, which lists cadets who were the sons of federal officers and congressmen; *Letter to the Honorable Mr. Hawes, in Reply to His Strictures on the Graduates of the Military Academy*, New York: Wiley and Long, 1836, which provided a graduate's argument that the Academy was a meritocracy; and Report of the House Committee on Military Affairs, 1844, Twenty-eighth Congress, First Session, House Report no. 476, 15–16, which listed the occupations of cadets' fathers and argued (rather questionably) that they demonstrated a broad social background. See Cunliffe, *Soldiers and Civilians*, 105–111 and 162–66, and chs. 4, 5, and 8 in general, for a balanced view of both the limits of the Jacksonian critique (which shared many of the limits of Jacksonian democracy) and the persistence of a strong socially elite presence in the Corps of Cadets and the officer corps.

[40] Morrison, 'The Best School,' 152–53; Crackel, *West Point*, 115.

[41] As suggested during the 1970s and 1980s, and above, republicanism took on many forms in the nineteenth century, including the persistence of variants of classical republicanism among elites and those aspiring to claim gentility. For a 'long view' tracking change across the late colonial, Revolutionary, early national, and Jacksonian eras, see Wood, *The Radicalism of the American Revolution*. Using Wood's conceptualization, Jacksonian and pre-Civil War army officers fit the 'republican' mold of the eighteenth century better than the 'democratic' one of

the era they lived in. Perhaps more significant than social origins per se, scholars generally agree that West Point shaped aspiring officers as gentlemen on the European, or at least English, model; this analysis should be extended, as Cunliffe, *Soldiers and Civilians*, 171, implies, to suggest that West Pointers, and army officers in general, played a role in the 'aristocratic revival' of the 1850s described by Bushman in *The Refinement of America*, and the shift from 'boundlessness to consolidation' in American life observed by Higham, *From Boundlessness to Consolidation: the Transformation of American Culture, 1848–1860*. Important works on the relationship between the emergence of professionalism and class formation include Bledstein, *The Culture of Professionalism*; Blumin, *The Emergence of the Middle Class*; and Haber, *The Quest for Honor and Authority in the American Professions*. Like Crackel, Cawelti, *Apostles of the Self-made Man*, 26, maintains that Jefferson sought a new institutional framework to foster a disinterested element in society, one without allegiances to existing class (meaning gentry, or more specifically Federalist) interests, but Cawelti argues that this effort failed. West Point did create a new social-occupational formation; its disinterestedness depends on one's perspective. Given the European models for their professional role, officers felt fewer of the qualms some American civilian elites expressed over emulating, or being perceived to emulate, manners and mores patterned on the European aristocracy. See for comparison Kilbride, 'Cultivation, Conservatism, and the Early National Gentry.' See Hammond, *An Oration on the Duties and the Requirements of an American Officer*, 12, for an extended vision of officers as a social elite.

[42] White, *The Jeffersonians*, 259. For individual examples, see Smith, *Harpers Ferry Armory and the New Technology*, and Watson, 'Thomas Sidney Jesup' in *The Human Tradition in Antebellum America*, edited by Michael A. Morrison. For further context see Crenson, *The Federal Machine*, and Nelson, *Roots of American Bureaucracy*.

References

Adams, Cindy, ed. *The West Point Thayer Papers, 1808–1872*. West Point, NY: Association of Graduates, 1965; reprinted Brookhaven Press, 2001.

Angevine, Robert G. *The Railroad and the State: War, Politics, and Technology in Nineteenth-century America*. Stanford, CA: Stanford University Press, 2004.

Aronson, Sidney H. *Status and Kinship in the Higher Civil Service: Standards of Selection in the Administrations of John Adams, Thomas Jefferson, and Andrew Jackson*. Cambridge, MA: Harvard University Press, 1964.

Baker, Van R., ed. *The Websters: The Letters of an American Army Family in Peace & War, 1836–1853*. Kent, OH: Kent State University Press, 2000.

Ball, Durwood. *Army Regulars on the Western Frontier, 1848–1861*. Norman: University of Oklahoma Press, 2001.

Bassett, John Spencer, ed. *Correspondence of Andrew Jackson*. 7 vols. Washington, DC: Carnegie Institution of Washington, 1926–35.

Bauer, K. Jack. *Zachary Taylor: Soldier, Planter, and Statesman of the Old Southwest*. Baton Rouge: Louisiana State University Press, 1985.

Bledstein, Burton J. *The Culture of Professionalism: The Middle Class and the Development of Higher Education in America*. New York: W.W. Norton, 1976.

Blumin, Stuart. *The Emergence of the Middle Class: Social Experience in the American City, 1760–1900*. Cambridge, UK: Cambridge University Press, 1989.

Breeden, James O. 'Rehearsal for Secession? The Return Home of Philadelphia Medical Students in 1859.' In *His Soul Goes Marching On: Responses to John Brown and the Harpers Ferry Raid*, edited by Paul Finkelman. Charlottesville: University Press of Virginia, 1995: 174–210.

Brown, Thomas. *Politics and Statesmanship: Essays on the American Whig Party*. New York: Columbia University Press, 1985.

Browning, Robert S. *Two if by Sea: The Development of American Coastal Defense Policy.* Westport, CO: Greenwood Press, 1983.

Bullock, Steven C. *Revolutionary Brotherhood: Freemasonry and the Transformation of the American Social Order, 1730–1840.* Chapel Hill: University of North Carolina Press, 1996.

Bushman, Richard L. *The Refinement of America, 1750–1850: Persons, Houses, Cities.* New York: Knopf, 1993.

Cawelti, John G. *Apostles of the Self-made Man: Changing Concepts of Success in America.* Chicago: University of Chicago Press, 1965.

Chaffin, Tom. *Fatal Glory: Narciso Lopez and the First Clandestine U.S. War against Cuba.* Charlottesville: University Press of Virginia, 1996.

———. *Pathfinder: John Charles Frémont and the Course of American Empire.* New York: Hill & Wang, 2002.

Clarke, Dwight L. *Stephen Watts Kearny, Soldier of the West.* Norman: University of Oklahoma Press, 1961.

Coffman, Edward M. *The Old Army: A Portrait of the American Army in Peacetime, 1784–1898.* New York: Oxford University Press, 1986.

Cohen, Patricia Cline. *A Calculating People: The Spread of Numeracy in Early America.* Chicago: University of Chicago Press, 1982.

Coker, Caleb, ed. *The News from Brownsville: Helen Chapman's Letters from the Texas Military Frontier, 1848–1852.* Austin: Texas State Historical Association, 1992.

Crackel, Theodore J. 'Jefferson, Politics, and the Army: An Examination of the Military Peace Establishment Act of 1802.' *Journal of the Early Republic* 2 (Spring 1982): 21–38.

———. *Mr. Jefferson's Army: Political and Social Reform of the Military Establishment, 1801–1809.* New York: New York University Press, 1987.

Crackel, Theodore J. *A Bicentennial History of West Point.* Lawrence: University Press of Kansas, 2002.

Crenson, Matthew A. *The Federal Machine: The Beginnings of Bureaucracy in Jacksonian America.* Baltimore: Johns Hopkins University Press, 1975.

Cress, Lawrence Delbert. *Citizens in Arms: The Army and the Militia in American Society to the War of 1812.* Chapel Hill: University of North Carolina Press, 1982.

Croffut, W.A. ed. *Fifty Years in Camp and Field: The Diary of Major-General Ethan Allen Hitchcock, U.S.A.* New York: G.P. Putnam's Sons, 1909.

Cullum, George W., comp. *Biographical Register of the Officers and Graduates of the United States Military Academy at West Point, from Its Establishment, in 1802, to 1890.* Boston: Houghton Mifflin, 1891.

Cunliffe, Marcus. *Soldiers and Civilians: The Martial Spirit in America, 1776–1865.* 2nd ed. New York: The Free Press, 1973.

Curtiss, John Shelton. *The Russian Army Under Nicholas I, 1825–1855.* Durham, NC: Duke University Press, 1965.

DePalo, William A., Jr. *The Mexican National Army, 1822–1852.* College Station: Texas A&M University Press, 1997.

Doherty, Herbert J. *Richard Keith Call, Southern Unionist.* Gainesville: University of Florida Press, 1961.

Dyer, Brainerd. *Zachary Taylor.* Baton Rouge: Louisiana State University Press, 1946.

Ellery, Harrison, ed. *The Memoirs of General Joseph G. Swift, L.L.D., U.S. Army, with a Genealogy of His Family.* n.p., 1890.

Foos, Paul. *A Short, Offhand, Killing Affair: Soldiers and Social Conflict in the Mexican-American War.* Chapel Hill: University of North Carolina Press, 2002.

Ford, Paul L., ed. *The Writings of Thomas Jefferson.* 10 vols. New York: G.P. Putnam's Sons, 1892–99.

Gardner, Charles K. comp. *A Dictionary of the Officers of the Army of the United States.* New York: D. Van Nostrand, 1860.

Goetzmann, William H. *Army Exploration in the American West.* New Haven: Yale University Press, 1957.

Gordon, William A., comp. *A Compilation of Registers of the Army of the United States, from 1815 to 1837*. Washington, DC: James C. Dunn, 1837.
Goss, Thomas W. *The War Within the Union High Command: Politics and Generalship during the Civil War*. Lawrence: University Press of Kansas, 2003.
Haber, Samuel. *The Quest for Honor and Authority in the American Professions, 1750–1900*. Chicago: Chicago University Press, 1991.
Hagerman, Edward L. *The American Civil War and the Origins of Modern Warfare*. Bloomington: Indiana University Press, 1982.
Hamersly, Thomas H.S., comp. *Complete Army Register of the United States, for One Hundred Years (1779 to 1879)*. Washington, DC: T.H.S. Hamersly, 1880.
Hamilton, Holman. *Zachary Taylor: Soldier of the Republic*. Indianapolis: Bobbs-Merrill, 1941.
Hammond, M.C.M. *An Oration on the Duties and the Requirements of an American Officer, delivered before the Dialectic Society of the United States Military Academy*. New York: Baker, Godwin, 1852.
Harries-Jenkins, Gwyn. *The Army in Victorian Society*. London: Routledge & Kegan Paul, 1977.
Heidler, David S., and Jeanne T. Heidler, *Old Hickory's War: Andrew Jackson and the Quest for Empire*. Mechanicsburg, PA: Stackpole Books, 1996.
Heitman, Francis B., comp. *Historical Registry and Dictionary of the United States Army, from Its Organization, September 29, 1789 to March 2, 1903*, 2 vols. Washington, DC: Government Printing Office, 1903.
Higham, John. *From Boundlessness to Consolidation: the Transformation of American Culture, 1848–1860*. Ann Arbor: William L. Clements Library, 1969.
Hill, Daniel H. 'The Army in Texas' *Southern Quarterly Review* 9 (April 1846): 434–57, and 14 (July 1848): 183–97.
Hill, Forest G. *Roads, Rails, and Waterways: The Army Engineers and Early Transportation*. Norman: University of Oklahoma Press, 1957.
Holt, Michael F. *The Rise and Fall of the American Whig Party: Jacksonian Politics and the Coming of the Civil War*. New York: Oxford University Press, 1999.
Hoskin, Keith W., and Richard H. Macve. 'The Genesis of Accountability: The West Point Connections.' *Accounting, Organizations, and Society* 13 (1988): 37–73.
Howe, Daniel Walker *The Political Culture of the American Whigs*. Chicago: University of Chicago Press, 1979.
———. *Making the American Self: Jonathan Edwards to Abraham Lincoln*. Cambridge, MA: Harvard University Press, 1997.
———. 'Church, State, and Education in the Young American Republic.' *Journal of the Early Republic* 22 (Spring 2002).
John, Richard R. *Spreading the News: The American Postal System from Franklin to Morse*. Cambridge, MA: Harvard University Press, 1995.
Johnson, Timothy D. *Winfield Scott and the Quest for Military Glory*. Lawrence: University Press of Kansas, 1998.
Kieffer, Chester L. *Maligned General: A Biography of Thomas S. Jesup*. San Rafael, CA: Presidio Press, 1979.
Kershner, James W. 'Sylvanus Thayer: A Biography.' Ph.D. diss., University of West Virginia, 1975.
Kohl, Lawrence Frederick. *The Politics of Individualism: Parties and the American Character in the Jacksonian Era*. New York: Oxford University Press, 1989.
Kohn, Richard H. *Eagle and Sword: The Federalists and the Creation of the Military Establishment in America, 1783–1802*. New York: Free Press, 1975.
Kilbride, Daniel P. 'Cultivation, Conservatism, and the Early National Gentry: The Manigault Family and Their Circle.' *Journal of the Early Republic* 19 (Summer 1999): 221–56.
Larson, John Lauritz. *Internal Improvement: National Public Works and the Promise of Popular Government in the Early United States*. Chapel Hill: University of North Carolina Press, 2001.
Linn, Brian M. 'The American Way of War Revisited.' *Journal of Military History* 66 (April 2002).

Mahon, John K. *History of the Second Seminole War, 1835–1842*. Gainesville: University of Florida Press, 1967.

May, Robert E. 'Young American Males and Filibustering in the Age of Manifest Destiny: The United States Army as a Cultural Mirror.' *Journal of American History* 78 (December 1991): 857–86.

———. *Manifest Destiny's Underworld: Filibustering in Antebellum America*. Chapel Hill: University of North Carolina Press, 2002.

McCoy, Drew R. *The Elusive Republic: Political Economy in Jeffersonian America*. Chapel Hill: University of North Carolina Press, 1980.

McDonald, Robert M.S., ed. *Thomas Jefferson's Military Academy: Founding West Point*. Charlottesville: University Press of Virginia, 2004.

Meyer, Donald H. *The Instructed Conscience: The Shaping of the American National Ethic*. Philadelphia: University of Pennsylvania Press, 1972.

Miller, Cynthia Ann. 'The United States Army Logistics Complex, 1818–1845: A Case Study of the Northern Frontier.' Ph.D. diss., Syracuse University, 1991.

Molloy, Peter M. 'Technical Education and the Young Republic: West Point as America's Ecole Polytechnique, 1802–1833.' Ph.D. diss., Brown University, 1975.

Morrison, James L. *'The Best School': West Point, 1833–1866*. 2nd ed. Kent, OH: Kent State University Press, 1998.

Morrison, Michael A., ed. *The Human Tradition in Antebellum America*. Wilmington, DE: Scholarly Resources, 2000.

Moten, Matthew. *The Delafield Commission and the American Military Profession*. College Station: Texas A&M University Press, 2000.

Myerly, Scott Hughes. *British Military Spectacle: From the Napoleonic Wars through the Crimea*. Cambridge, MA: Harvard University Press, 1996.

Nelson, Dana D. *National Manhood: Capitalist Citizenship and the Imagined Fraternity of White Men*. Durham: Duke University Press, 1998.

Nelson, William E. *Roots of American Bureaucracy, 1830–1900*. Cambridge, MA: Havard University Press, 1982.

Owsley, Frank, Jr. and Gene A. Smith. *Filibusters and Expansionists: Jeffersonian Manifest Destiny, 1800–1821*. Tuscaloosa: University of Alabama, Press, 1997.

Pappas, George S. *To the Point: The United States Military Academy, 1802–1902*. Westport, CT: Praeger, 1993.

Polski, Andrew J. '"Mr. Lincoln's Army" Revisited: Partisanship, Institutional Position, and Union Army Command, 1861–1865.' *Studies in American Political Development* 16 (Fall 2002): 176–207.

Porch, Douglas. *Army and Revolution: France, 1815–1848*. London: Routledge & Kegan Paul, 1974.

Price, Russell Reed. 'American Coastal Defense: The Third System of Fortification, 1816–1864.' Ph.D. diss., Mississippi State University, 1999.

Prucha, Francis Paul. *The Sword of the Republic: The United States Army on the Frontier, 1783–1846*. New York: Macmillan, 1969.

Richardson, James D., ed. *Messages and Papers of the Presidents*. New York: Bureau of National Literature, 1897.

Risch, Erna. *Quartermaster Support of the Army, 1775–1939*. Rev. ed. Washington, DC: Center of Military History, 1988.

Rolle, Andrew. *John Charles Frémont: Character as Destiny*. Norman: University of Oklahoma Press, 1991.

Scott, Robert Garth, ed. *Forgotten Valor: The Memoirs, Journals, & Civil War Letters of Orlando B. Willcox*. Kent, OH: Kent State University Press, 1999.

Silver, James W. *Edmund Pendleton Gaines: Frontier General*. Baton Rouge: Louisiana State University Press, 1949.

Skelton, William B. 'The Army Officer as Organization Man.' In *Soldiers and Civilians: The U.S. Army and the American People*, edited by Garry D. Ryan and Timothy K. Nenninger. Washington, DC: National Archives and Records Administration, 1987.

———. *An American Profession of Arms: The Army Officer Corps, 1784–1861*. Lawrence: University Press of Kansas, 1992.

Smith, Carlton B. 'The United States War Department, 1815–1842.' Ph.D. diss., University of Virginia, 1967.

Smith, Merrit Roe. *Harpers Ferry Armory and the New Technology: The Challenge of Change*. Ithaca: Cornell University Press, 1977.

Spiers, Edward M. *The Army and Society, 1815–1914*. London: Longman, 1980.

Spiller, Roger. 'John C. Calhoun as Secretary of War, 1817–1825.' Ph.D. diss., Louisiana State University, 1977.

Spiller, Ronald. 'From Hero to Leader: The Development of Nineteenth Century American Military Leadership.' Ph.D. dissertation, Texas A&M University, 1993.

Steinhauer, Dale R. '"Sogers": Enlisted Men in the U.S. Army, 1815–1860.' Ph.D. diss., University of North Carolina, 1992.

Thompson, Jerry, ed. *Fifty Miles a Day and a Fight: Major Samuel P. Heintzelman's Journal of Texas and the Cortina War*. Austin: Texas State Historical Association, 1998.

Traas, Adrian. *From the Golden Gate to Mexico City: The U.S. Army Topographical Engineers in the Mexican War, 1846–1848*. Washington, DC: Center of Military History, 1993.

Volpe, Vernon L. 'The Origins of the Frémont Expeditions: John J. Abert and the Scientific Exploration of the Trans-Mississippi West.' *The Historian* 62 (Winter 2000): 244–63.

Watson, Samuel J. 'Professionalism, Social Attitudes, and Civil–Military Accountability: The U.S. Army Officer Corps, 1815–1846.' Ph.D. diss., Rice University, 1996.

———. 'Manifest Destiny and Military Professionalism: A New Perspective on Junior U.S. Army Officers' Attitudes Toward War With Mexico, 1844–1846.' *Southwestern Historical Quarterly* 99 (April 1996): 466–98.

———. 'The Uncertain Road to Manifest Destiny: Army Officers and the Course of American Territorial Expansionism, 1815–1846.' In *Manifest Destiny and Empire: Essays on Antebellum American Expansionism*, edited by Christopher Morris and Sam W. Haynes. College Station, Texas A&M University Press, 1997: 68–114.

———. 'U.S. Army Officers Fight the 'Patriot War': Responses to Filibustering on the Canadian Border, 1837–1839.' *Journal of the Early Republic* 18 (Fall 1998): 487–521.

———. 'Knowledge, Interest, and the Limits of Military Professionalism: The Discourse on American Coastal Defense, 1815–1860.' *War in History* 5 (Fall 1998): 280–307.

———. '"This thankless... unholy war": Army Officers and Civil–Military Relations in the Second Seminole War.' In *The Southern Albatross: Race and Ethnicity in the South*, edited by David Dillard and Randal Hall. Macon, GA: Mercer University Press, 1999: 9–49.

———. 'The Growth of the Professional Army, 1815–1860.' In *The Oxford Atlas of American Military History*, edited by James C. Bradford. New York: Oxford University Press, 2003.

———. ed. *The International Library of Essays in Military History: Warfare in the USA, 1784–1861*. Aldershot, UK: Ashgate Publishing, 2005.

———. *Federal Diplomats: The U.S. Army Officer Corps in the Borderlands of the Early Republic*. Lawrence: University Press of Kansas, forthcoming 2007.

Wetteman, Robert P. '"To the Public Prosperity": The U.S. Army and the Market Revolution, 1815–1844.' Ph.D. diss., Texas A&M University, 2001.

White, Leonard D. *The Jeffersonians: A Study in Administrative History, 1801–1829*. New York: Macmillan, 1959.

Winders, Richard Bruce. *Mr. Polk's Army: The American Military Experience in the Mexican War*. College Station: Texas A&M University Press, 1997.

Wood, Gordon S. *The Radicalism of the American Revolution*. New York: Knopf, 1992.

Leaders for Manifest Destiny: American Volunteer Colonels Serving in the U.S.-Mexican War

Joseph G. Dawson III

An examination of the role of citizen-colonels in the U.S.-Mexican War offers an opportunity to assess America's attitude toward military preparedness in the mid-nineteenth century, relationship of politics to military service, and the colonels' leadership in the war. Senior volunteer army officers made significant political and military contributions in the United States war against Mexico, 1846–48. Some of the volunteer generals, of course, became national figures, but less appreciated have been the colonels who helped to recruit and lead new state regiments formed for the war. Historian Richard Bruce Winders points out that *all* of the volunteer generals were Democrats.[1] Many of the 63 colonels were Democrats, but several Whig colonels also supported the war, indicating that the Whigs were not a monolithic antiwar party. Among the new colonels, about three-fourths of them had no significant military experience before 1846, confirming the concept that America called citizen-soldiers to the colors when war began. By the end of the war some colonels had established creditable battle records, but only a few were considered exceptional military officers. Furthermore, some colonels related their time in the army to politics, and the colonels' prewar and postwar public service also merits examination. Regardless of political party, the volunteer colonels' public support for the war helped to galvanize Americans' enthusiasm for Manifest Destiny as they aimed to acquire vast lands from Mexico.

A decade of antagonisms and the rising tide of American Manifest Destiny brought on the war in 1846, crowned by the controversial annexation of Texas by the United States in 1845. Still claiming that Texas was part of the Republic of Mexico, Mexican officials disputed the legitimacy of Texas annexation but also disagreed with the new state's boundaries, as announced by the United States. After U.S. and Mexican troops skirmished north of the Rio Grande, both nations declared war. While some Mexicans worried about going to war, the United States was not the 'colossus of the north.' Some knowledgeable Mexican politicians and newspaper editors discounted the threat posed by the United States. After all, during the War of 1812 militia regiments of several states had not only been ineffectual, they also became laughingstocks by refusing to go on campaign or disputing orders from superior officers to invade Canada. Likewise, some Regular U.S. Army officers, such as James Wilkinson, William Hull, and William Winder, were embarrassing failures during the War of 1812. Only the astounding result of the Battle of New Orleans seemed to reverse the course of the conflict, allowing Americans to claim victory over Great Britain.[2] Moreover, Mexican leaders were aware that after the Texas Revolution of 1836, Texans (some of them transplanted U.S. citizens) had tried and failed three times to capture Santa Fe, capital of Mexico's state of New Mexico.[3]

Anticipating the possibility of war between the United States and either Great Britain or Mexico in 1845, U.S. President James K. Polk contended in his annual message to Congress that in the event of war, Americans traditionally relied 'mainly on our citizen soldiers, who will be ready… to rush [to arms] with alacrity, at the call of their country.' Instead of repeating the disappointments of the militia from the War of 1812, Polk planned to enroll thousands of short-term citizen soldiers in newly recruited regiments to supplement the modest Regular Army on duty in addition to any more Regular units that Congress might approve.[4]

Many in the United States had employed belligerent rhetoric when addressing international controversies in the 1840s. Acquiring all of Oregon, obtaining California, and annexing Texas had been on the agenda of American expansionists, but the United States hardly seemed to be a militaristic nation in 1846, judging by the size of its army and navy or by the anemic condition of most state militias. The standing army totaled less than 8000 men for a population of 17 million.[5] The U.S. Regulars deserved respect, but state militias varied in quality and numbers across the nation. Many militia units were badly organized and indifferently equipped. They seldom trained and many of their officers had little or no military experience. Most militia officers played politics rather than paying attention to military matters.[6] It remained to be seen if Americans would muster military forces to equal their rhetorical bombast, and the new volunteer colonels were vital to developing America's military capability.

Some 73,000 American men served in volunteer units raised by the states during the war with Mexico. More than 1000 of those signed up only for three months, notably from Louisiana. Approximately 11,000 remained on duty for only six months; some of them got to Texas but not across the Rio Grande. Of the rest, about 18,000 enlisted for one year of service and 33,000 'for the duration of the war.' For most of the latter group that meant serving about 12 months. Many of the 33,000 serving 'for the duration' were not recruited until the important campaigns were ending. Some volunteers did not leave their state, and others drew assignments for garrison duty in Texas or in some part of Mexico occupied by U.S. forces. Although some of the volunteers and their colonels compiled controversial records, steps taken by several of the 63 regimental commanders to raise regiments to be sent into battle and deployed as occupation forces were instrumental in creating a wartime force that could carry out President Polk's policies and give the United States victory in the war.[7]

Colonels often set the example by enlisting and encouraging others to enlist, and they represented 20 of 29 states in the Union in 1846. States not raising volunteer regiments included Connecticut, Maine, New Hampshire, Rhode Island, Vermont, and Delaware. From the Midwest and South U.S. volunteers turned out in unexpectedly strong numbers in 1846, demonstrating that the wellsprings for war were much deeper than some Americans and many Mexicans could have predicted.[8] Although the urge for war was weak in New England and in Ohio's counties known as the Western Reserve,[9] volunteers surged forward from other states, providing more men than could be sworn in by federal authorities. States such as Texas, Tennessee, Missouri, Kentucky, Ohio, and Indiana quickly answered President Polk's call for troops.[10] Florida and New Jersey, however, enlisted only a few companies and therefore had no regimental colonels.[11] Iowa raised a volunteer regiment but bureaucratic snarls blocked its entry into federal service.[12] Louisianians pointed with pride to the seven Bayou State regiments, but six of them were three-month or six-month enlistees who rendered minimal service.[13] Colonel Lewis G. DeRussy's regiment was the only one from Louisiana to serve for a year or more. Five of Louisiana's colonels saw little or no combat. But, unlike the haphazard behavior of state militias of 1812–15, in 1846 the new state volunteer regiments pledged to go on campaign and invade Mexico.

Volunteers took different paths to obtain their status as colonels. State governors appointed 11 colonels, usually but not always picking men of the same political party. For instance, Kentucky's Whig governor, William Owsley, appointed the colonels for his state's regiments, and three of four were Whigs. Democratic governors of Michigan and New York, respectively, selected Thomas B. W. Stockton to command Michigan's only regiment and Jonathan D. Stevenson to lead a New York regiment to California. Robert T. Paine of North Carolina and John F. Hamtramck of Virginia gained their rank by appointments from Whig governors. In an unusual move, President Polk tapped George W. Hughes to be colonel of the regiment raised in the District of Columbia and Maryland.[14] In another step leading to command, a few men serving as regimental lieutenant colonels succeeded to command when the colonel was killed, resigned, or promoted.[15] But many colonels – 29 (40 percent) – were elected. The voting might be restricted to other regimental officers, such as company commanders holding the rank of captain, or the more widely used method, all soldiers in the regiment could vote for the man who would be colonel.[16]

To give a few examples, Archibald Yell drew upon his prewar political luster as a congressman and governor to win election to command the Arkansas regiment. Caleb Cushing, recognized by his soldiers after holding seats in the Massachusetts state legislature and the U.S. Congress, was elected colonel of the state's regiment. Henry R. Jackson gained election to command Georgia's regiment. Members of the Illinois legislature before the war, William H. Bissell and Ferris Foreman were elected colonels of two Illinois regiments. Soldiers from the Indiana regiments elected all five of their colonels.[17]

During the war, when officer vacancies occurred due to illness, wounds, resignation, or death, it almost was inevitable that another election would follow. For example, in September 1847 poor health forced Colonel Reuben Davis to resign from his Mississippi regiment, on garrison duty in northern Mexico. Getting into the spirit of things, sometimes potential colonels brought out liquor to sway the volunteers' votes. The division commander, General John Wool, a Regular officer, called a halt to the festivities and delayed the regiment's election for a month, demanding proceedings with more decorum. Wool chastised the Mississippians: 'It is with deep regret & mortification that the General Commanding this Division feels himself compelled to announce to his Command, that owing to the disgraceful & drunken scene... by members of the [Second] Mississippi Regiment the Election of Col[onel]... is postponed... Officers who could, by means of [giving away] intoxicating liquors... obtain votes for the high and dignified office of Colonel, are unworthy to hold that or any other office in the military service of the United States.'[18]

The Davis anecdote and the examples of electing colonels serve to highlight historian Marcus Cunliffe's play upon the oft-quoted maxim from Clausewitz. For Americans in the mid-nineteenth century, Cunliffe concludes, 'In a volunteer army, war was truly, though not in the sense Clausewitz intended, *"politics carried on by other means."*'[19]

Whether appointed or elected, America's 63 volunteer colonels of 1846–48 may be categorized or subdivided in a number of ways. One subdivision collects those men who had served in the Regular U.S. Army before the war. Other categories recognize the colonels by political party affiliation and prewar political offices. Some gained battlefield success. No matter if they were heroic, controversial, or unsuccessful as colonels, in the postwar years a number of them resumed or initiated political careers. (For aspects of prewar military experience, see Table 3.)

Clearly identifiable are the 15 men (almost 24 percent of the 63 colonels) who had held a commission in the Regular U.S. Army. Eleven of them had been graduated from the U.S. Military Academy at West Point, New York (hereafter abbreviated USMA), two had matriculated at the Academy but had not graduated, and two had received direct commissions into the Regular service from civilian life. Creating a pool of men who had been introduced to the military arts, former West Pointers could return to uniform during wartime, partly confirming President Thomas Jefferson's expectation for the

Military Academy when it was established in 1802. The 15 former Regulars provided high-profile leadership for America's citizen soldiers. Most of them made worthwhile contributions to the United States war effort, though a few were disappointments.

Some of the former Regulars became well known and highly respected colonels. Perhaps foremost among them was Jefferson Davis (USMA, Class of 1828), colonel of the First Mississippi Rifles, who received national acclaim for leading a successful counterattack at the Battle of Buena Vista.[20] Also touted for his heroic actions, Colonel William R. McKee (USMA 1829) led a Kentucky cavalry regiment and was killed in action at Buena Vista.[21] Other serving Regulars or former Regulars also were accorded high marks by their contemporaries. For instance, Albert Sidney Johnston (USMA 1826), elected colonel of a six-month Texas unit, was cited for gallant conduct at the Battle of Monterrey.[22] President Polk's appointee, George Hughes (USMA cadet 1823–27, but not a graduate), an officer with 20 years in uniform, commanded the regiment from Maryland and the District of Columbia, fought at Cerro Gordo, and was praised for gallantry. Hughes also acted as military governor of Jalapa, Mexico.[23] Ward B. Burnett (USMA 1832) held a Regular commission for four years before becoming a civil engineer. He gained command of one of the New York regiments, landed at Vera Cruz with General Winfield Scott's army, and was wounded at the Battle of Churubusco, near Mexico City.[24] George W. Morgan (USMA cadet 1841–43, but not a graduate) was an Ohio volunteer colonel 1846–47 before Polk appointed him to the Regulars as colonel of a new federal unit, the U.S. Fifteenth Infantry Regiment. Morgan distinguished himself in action at the battles of Contreras and Churubusco, earning a brevet of brigadier general for his leadership.[25]

Other former Regulars established creditable records. For example, a Louisianian, Lewis DeRussy, graduated from the Military Academy in 1814 and had made a career with the Regulars until 1842, rising to the rank of major. In 1846 he became colonel of one of the Louisiana infantry regiments and fought in the skirmish at Huamantla, Mexico, in 1847, northeast of Puebla. DeRussy also carried out military engineering projects at the Mexican coastal city of Tampico. Alexander M. Mitchell (USMA 1835) served on active duty only from 1835 to 1837. He led an Ohio regiment, was wounded in action at Monterrey, and subsequently held the post of military governor of that city from April to June 1847.[26]

Additional officers also had experience in the Regulars before serving as colonels in 1846–48, but their wartime assignments were unexceptional. Horatio Davis, a former captain, had campaigned during the War of 1812. As colonel of a Louisiana regiment, he served only six months in 1846. Samuel R. Curtis (USMA 1831) had left the army in 1832 to become a civil engineer. He commanded an Ohio volunteer regiment and handled administrative duties during the occupation of Camargo, in northern Mexico. Thomas Stockton (USMA 1827), credited with Regular service from 1827 to 1836, colonel of Michigan volunteers, and William Irvin (USMA 1839, served 1839–41), colonel of another Ohio outfit, had unremarkable records in the Mexican War.[27]

A few former Regulars fared poorly when they returned to uniform. Among them, Pierce M. Butler, a Regular infantry captain from 1819 to 1829, and later governor of South Carolina, was the tenuous colonel of the state's volunteers. Butler never seemed to have effective control over his regiment, though he became a martyr to Manifest

Destiny when he was killed in action at Churubusco.[28] Humphrey Marshall (USMA 1832), a Kentucky colonel, suffered through a controversy over the manner in which his regiment maneuvered and then retreated from the battlefield at Buena Vista.[29] John Hamtramck (USMA 1819) had returned to civilian life in 1822. As colonel of the Virginia volunteers, and even with the assistance of his lieutenant colonel,[30] Thomas B. Randolph (USMA 1812), Hamtramck could not prevent his men from rioting in camp with volunteers from North Carolina. Hamtramck did render some beneficial administrative service by being military governor of Saltillo.[31]

The 15 former Regulars returning to uniform were not evenly distributed in the volunteer regiments. Several states had no former Regulars among their colonels, including Alabama, Arkansas, Georgia, Illinois, Indiana, Massachusetts, Missouri, North Carolina, and Tennessee. Two states had modest Regular influence: Mississippi (one of three colonels had been a Regular), and Kentucky (one of four). Two others had minimal Regular representation: Louisiana (one of seven) and Texas (one of six). In six states, Regulars played a greater part. These were New York (one of two) and Ohio (three of five); and for Maryland, Michigan, South Carolina, and Virginia, each state had one colonel and each was a Regular or former Regular.

Some volunteer colonels had gained military experience during the War of 1812 or had been mobilized for frontier duty. Among those having the most military experience, Archibald Yell of Arkansas had served in the War of 1812. Two volunteer colonels, John Hardin of Illinois and James Drake of Indiana, had participated in the Black Hawk War of 1832. Veterans of the Seminole War in the 1830s included lawyer William T. Haskell and planter Richard Waterhouse from Tennessee, and state senator Samuel Marks of Louisiana. Three Texans, lawyer William C. Young and John Coffee Hays (both Texas Rangers), and Peter H. Bell (a veteran of the Texas Revolution), could point to duties that helped them prepare for formal military campaigning.[32]

By contrast with those who had been Regulars, most U.S. volunteer colonels in the Mexican War – 34 officers (54 percent) – were men who possessed little or no formal military background. Many Americans considered a standing army to be a potential threat to the wellbeing of the republic. They preferred to run the risks of relying on units called to serve only for the duration of the war rather than paying the high costs of maintaining a large professional peacetime army and expected that some men with little or no military experience would be junior officers as well leaders in the new regiments.[33]

Several of the new colonels had held appointments with a state militia. Much of this experience can be discounted. Most militia mustered occasionally and stressed ceremonial or social activities rather than giving military training a high priority. Whatever the quality of those units, if officers possessed a record of militia service it did not mean that their neighbors considered them knowledgeable in military evolutions.[34] For most officers, militia service turned out to be a social or political activity that might help some get appointed or elected to office, and several of the colonels drew upon their local or state recognition in roles such as officeholders, especially in the state legislature. Some turned the lack of formal military training into republican virtue and played upon the widespread antipathy toward perceptions of elitism among officers in the Regular Army[35] (see Table 3).

In a strike against military elitism, many Americans expected their country to produce some 'natural soldiers,' ones who would be equal to or better than the Regulars. Once assembled, the volunteer units usually elected their officers, and sometimes elevated candidates without much military experience over veterans or former Regulars. For instance, Alexander Doniphan, a lawyer and militia general having no combat record, was elected colonel by the soldiers of a Missouri regiment over John Price, a former volunteer regimental commander in the Seminole War, and over two former Regular officers, Charles Ruff (USMA 1838) and William Gilpin, a former Regular holding a direct commission who had served 1836–38. Other Southern colonels having militia experience included lawyer Humphrey Marshall and planter Stephen Ormsby of Kentucky, businessman James H. Walton and architect James H. Dakin from Louisiana, Judge Reuben Davis of Mississippi, Congressman Sterling Price and clerk of the state legislature John Ralls from Missouri, lawyer William B. Campbell and farmer Benjamin F. Cheatham of Tennessee. Northerners having served in the militia included state legislator Jonathan Stevenson of New York, newspaper owner Francis Wynkoop, businessman William B. Roberts, and civil engineer John White Geary from Pennsylvania, lawyer John J. Hardin and farmer William Weatherford of Illinois, merchant and judge James P. Drake of Indiana.[36]

As it turned out, several new colonels had no military experience, either on the frontier or even with a state militia. Nevertheless, for many Americans, the inexperienced officers of 1846–48 symbolically appeared to fulfill their expectations of Cincinnatus leaving the plow and drawing the sword.[37] Among those without substantive military experience from the slave states were businessman John R. Coffey of Alabama, former district attorney Henry Jackson of Georgia, Arkansas state legislator John Roane, two Kentuckians, Lieutenant Governor Manilus V. Thomson and lawyer John S. Williams, former Congressman Balie Peyton of Louisiana, planter Charles Clark of Mississippi, lawyer Robert Paine of North Carolina, and Tennesseans George R. McClelland and county sheriff Jonas E. Thomas. Northern colonels lacking military experience included from Illinois, state legislator William Bissell, former state legislator Ferris Foreman, Congressman Edward Baker, and merchant Edward Newby, most of the colonels from Indiana, state senator Joseph Lane, physician William A. Bowles, lawyer James H. Lane, businessman James Drake, and lawyer Willis A. Gorman, and former congressman Caleb Cushing of Massachusetts.[38]

Politics naturally was a significant aspect of nineteenth century America, and the colonels can also be categorized according to political party. Unlike the war's volunteer generals, all of whom were Democrats appointed by President Polk, the colonels represented both major parties, though not in equal measure. Democrats dominated the regimental commands, but party affiliations of a few of the 63 colonels remain unidentified.[39] Overall, 38 (60 percent) of colonels were Democrats or likely Democrats, and 18 of 25 Northern colonels (72 percent) were from Polk's party.[40] In some states, Democrats held all of the colonelcies (see Table 1).

Leading Northern Democrats included New Yorkers Ward Burnett (USMA 1832) and Jonathan Stevenson. Both promoted enlistment in volunteer regiments as a means of expanding the nation, especially Stevenson, whose 'California' regiment was trans-

Table 1 Political Party Affiliation by Region

	Whigs	Democrats	Unknown	Total
North	4	18	3	25
South	14	20	4	38
Total	18	38	7	63

ported by ship to San Francisco. All five of Indiana's colonels were Democrats. Polk promoted one of them, Joseph Lane, to brigadier general and made him leader of the Indiana Brigade. Pennsylvania's three colonels were Democrats. Scurrying to Washington only a few days after the Keystone State's governor called for troops, Francis Wynkoop met with Polk to gain approval for his regiment. Two other ardent Pennsylvania expansionists, William Roberts and his lieutenant colonel, John Geary, pushed for the creation of a second Pennsylvania regiment in late 1846.[41] Caleb Cushing was one of the Democratic colonels most outspoken in favor of Manifest Destiny. Commanding the Massachusetts regiment before gaining a brigadier's star from President Polk, Cushing was a noted Anglophobe determined to see the United States gain control of the Pacific coast as well as consolidate the annexation of Texas. As one Texan reported, 'Though [Cushing was] from the North, he was with us' on annexation. Within weeks of war being declared, Cushing lavishly spent $12,000 of his personal funds to raise a regiment to guarantee the Rio Grande boundary. Succeeding Cushing to command the Massachusetts regiment, Isaac Wright was a likely Democrat.[42] Other Democrats or likely Democrats helped to recruit volunteer regiments in the northern states, including Charles Morgan from Ohio and William Bissell and William Weatherford from Illinois. Ferris Foreman of Illinois, Thomas Stockton of Michigan, and William Brough of Ohio were probably Democrats.[43] Thus in the North, Democrats or likely Democrats dominated colonelcies in Indiana (five of five), Massachusetts (two of two), Michigan (one of one), New York (two of two), and Pennsylvania (three of three). They were influential in Illinois (three of six) and Ohio (two of five) (see Table 2).

From the slave states, Democrats appear to have held at least half of the colonelcies. Twenty of the 38 southern colonels were Democrats or likely Democrats, giving Polk's party about 53 percent of the South's colonels. Arkansas' former Democratic governor, Archibald Yell, pledged his support for bringing Texas into the Union. Yell left his seat in the U.S. House of Representatives to raise the state's only regiment for service in the war. Democrat John Roane replaced Yell as colonel. Democrats Jefferson Davis and Reuben Davis were strong expansionists from Mississippi. Democrat Henry Jackson commanded Georgia's regiment. From Missouri, Sterling Price was one of the state's leading Democrats, and John Ralls was probably a Democrat. Due to gallantry on the battlefield, Democrat John Williams gained an appointment from Kentucky. Tennesseans Richard Waterhouse, George McClelland, and Jonas Thomas were Democrats, and Benjamin Cheatham was a likely Democrat. From Louisiana, James Walton, Samuel Marks, and Horatio Davis were probable Democrats. Former governor Pierce Butler led the South Carolina regiment. President Polk selected George Hughes to lead

Table 2 Political Party Affiliation by State

	Whigs	Democrats	Unknown	Total
North				
Illinois	2	3	2	7
Indiana	–	5	–	5
Massachusetts	–	2	–	2
Michigan	–	1	–	1
New York	–	2	–	2
Ohio	2	2	1	5
Pennsylvania	–	3	–	3
South				
Alabama	–	–	1	1
Arkansas	–	2	–	2
Georgia	–	1	–	1
Kentucky	4	1	–	5
Louisiana	3	3	1	7
Maryland	–	1	–	1
Mississippi	1	2	–	3
Missouri	1	2	–	3
North Carolina	1	–	–	1
South Carolina	–	1	–	1
Tennessee	2	4	–	6
Texas	1	3	2	6
Virginia	1	–	–	1
TOTAL	18	38	7	63

the regiment from Maryland and the District of Columbia. From Texas, George Wood and Peter Bell were Democrats, and John Hays was a likely Democrat.[44] From the South, Democrats or likely Democrats dominated colonelcies in Arkansas (two of two), Georgia (one of one), Maryland (one of one), and South Carolina (one of one). Andrew Jackson's party held a high percentage in Mississippi (two of three), Missouri (two of three), Tennessee (four of six), and Texas (three of six). In Louisiana (three of seven) Democrats were also influential.

Across the United States, most leading Whig politicians opposed the war, but Whigs also contributed several volunteer colonels, demonstrating that support for the war was not limited to the Democratic party.[45] Fourteen regimental commanders were Whigs, and four others were probably Whigs, giving their party 28 percent of the regimental commanders, distinguished in quality, if not in quantity. The leading Whigs were Alexander Doniphan of Missouri, Tennesseans William Campbell and William Haskell, William McKee, Manilus Thomson and Humphrey Marshall of Kentucky, Texan Albert Sidney Johnston, Charles Clark of Mississippi, Balie Peyton and Lewis DeRussy of Louisiana, and Robert Paine of North Carolina. Likely Whigs included John Hamtramck of Virginia, Stephen Ormsby of Kentucky, and James Dakin of Louisiana. It is worth emphasizing that 14 of the 18 Whig colonels (77 percent) came from the slave states.[46] While few in number, northern Whigs included Congressman Edward Baker of Illinois, along with his Whig colleague, John Hardin. Two Ohioans were likely Whigs, Samuel Curtis, and Alexander Mitchell.[47] In summary, Whigs dominated colonelcies in only three states: North Carolina (one of one), Virginia (one of one), and Kentucky (four of five). Whig colonels were also a noticeable presence in regiments of Louisiana (three of seven), Ohio (two of five), Tennessee (two of six), and Illinois (two of six). Whigs also led troops from Mississippi (one of three), Missouri (one of three), and Texas (one of five).

Many Americans looked for colonels among politicians who had established records or showed military potential. Most of the colonels had an interest in politics before the war, with some having been prominent, such as in the state legislature, and others holding lesser offices. At least 21 colonels (33.3 percent) had been elected to a state legislature, ten from the North and 11 from the slave states. Southern legislators included Yell and Roane from Arkansas; Tennesseeans Haskell, Campbell, Waterhouse, and Thomas; Paine from North Carolina; Doniphan and Price from Missouri; Clark from Mississippi; and Marks of Louisiana. Northerners included Hardin, Bissell, Foreman, and Baker of Illinois; Joseph Lane, Bowles, and Gorman of Indiana; Cushing of Massachusetts; Stevenson of New York; and Brough of Ohio.[48]

Colonels also had held other political posts. Eight were sitting members of the U.S. House of Representatives in 1846 or previously had served in Congress, including northerners Cushing, Baker, and Hardin, and southerners Yell, Peyton, Price, Campbell, and Jefferson Davis. Two southerners (Yell and Butler) had been elected governor, and one southerner (Thomson) was a lieutenant governor. As for other offices, Reuben Davis had been a justice on the supreme court of Mississippi, Albert Sidney Johnston held the office of secretary of war for the Republic of Texas, and Thomas Stockton had been mayor of Michigan City, Indiana. Regardless of political party, most new colonels expected that their military roles would expire with the war's end but some logically would have expected that their military service could be a springboard to political office in the postwar years.[49]

In several instances, however, volunteer officers' military service proved to be disappointing or deficient. Performing like error-prone American officers in the War of 1812, some colonels embarrassed themselves and their states. Considering the feverish atmosphere of 1846, historian Joseph Chance points out, 'Many volunteer regiments, whose ranks were filled with first-rate men, failed in Mexico simply because they had elected unqualified officers.' Another historian, John Bloom, concludes: 'The most serious disadvantage was the selection frequently of men who had no military training or capacity whatever' as senior officers.[50]

Several factors can be used to evaluate the colonels. A good education can be considered an important attribute for a military officer. Knowing how to read and learning how to write effectively enhanced their capability to communicate with subordinates and superiors. The army expected the regiments to keep records and the colonels to submit reports. Thirty-two colonels (about 51 percent) attended or had been graduated from college in an age when only about one percent of Americans gained higher education. Of course, this group included those who had attended West Point. Two colonels matriculated at prestigious colleges – Henry Jackson of Georgia at Yale and Caleb Cushing at Harvard. Various colleges in Kentucky educated several colonels, including John Roane of Arkansas at Cumberland College, Alexander Doniphan of Missouri at Augusta College, and John Hardin of Illinois and Kentuckians Stephen Ormsby, Manilus Thomson, and Jefferson Davis at Transylvania. In Pennsylvania William Bissell of Illinois attended the Philadelphia Medical College, George Morgan enrolled at Washington & Jefferson College, John Geary of Pennsylvania at Jefferson College, and George McClelland of Tennessee at Washington College. Ferris Foreman graduated from Union College in New York. Willis Gorman attended Indiana University. John Williams of Kentucky matriculated at Miami University in Ohio. James Walton of Louisiana attended Louisiana College in Pineville and his colleague Horatio Davis graduated from St. Mary's College in Baltimore, Maryland. Missouri's Sterling Price attended Hampton-Sydney College in Virginia. Robert Paine of North Carolina attended Washington College (later Trinity College) in Connecticut. William Haskell of Tennessee attended the University of Nashville and John Hays of Texas went to Davidson Academy in the same city.[51]

Each of them had much to do with shaping his regiment, especially if he took his job seriously. The colonel's personality and energy could play a significant part in the regiment's development. A good-citizen colonel needed to instill some discipline but also be solicitous of his men.[52]

The best volunteer commanders knew when to be familiar with their soldiers. Citizen-colonels who held notable social, political, or economic positions in their states were known to their men before they began their military service and were naturally concerned about how their neighbors would perceive them after their service. William Campbell of Tennessee could have spoken for many colonels when he wrote: 'In the volunteer service the officers are constantly subjected to... public opinion even in camp... When the short term of service is over [an officer] goes back to a society composed in part of his [former] soldiers.'[53]

Therefore, regimental commanders had to be selective about when to stand on ceremony. Those attempting to puff their rank antagonized other volunteers, sometimes bringing hoots of derision. Colonel John Coffey of Alabama appeared to have difficulty instilling discipline in his regiment. An Alabama veteran, S. F. Nunnelle, contended that Coffey had 'no military gifts' and that the Alabama soldiers were 'disobedient' and only 'half drilled.'[54] Incidents of mutiny and altercations with other states' volunteers tarnished American military records during 1846–48. Such deplorable conduct appeared to support prewar notions of some Mexican observers and American critics that, like the militia outfits in the War of 1812, newly raised volunteer units of the 1840s would fail to provide useful service or fight well in battle. For instance, the only notation of 'combat' for the 900 men of the Georgia volunteers under Colonel Henry Jackson came during a mutinous free-for-all between two rival companies within the regiment. During the melee, the belligerent Georgians attacked Colonel Edward Baker and his Illinois volunteers who came to assist Jackson in trying to restore order.[55] Another disruptive incident indicated most volunteers' lack of discipline. On garrison duty in northern Mexico in August 1847, Colonel John Hamtramck's Virginians

Table 3 Pre-War Political and Military Experience

	Whigs	Democrats	Unknown	Total[1]
Northern Colonels				
Local[2]	–	2	–	2
State Legislature	2	8	–	10
State Executive[3]	–	–	–	0
State Other[4]	1	–	–	1
U.S. House	2	1	–	3
Other[5]	–	3	–	3
State Militia Member	2	6	1	9
Prior Military Experience[6]	3	5	2	10
Southern Colonels				
Local	–	–	–	0
State Legislature	5	6	–	11
State Executive	1	2	–	3
State Other[7]	–	4	–	4
U.S. House	2	3	–	5
Other	1	–	1	2
State Militia Member	6	5	1	12
Prior Military Experience	7	11	1	19

Notes

[1] Accumulated totals will not equal 63 as it includes those that held more than one post and excludes those with no pre-war political or military experience.

[2] This includes mayor, service on city council.

[3] This includes lieutenant governor and governor.

[4] This includes state adjutant general, judge, clerks, gubernatorial aide-de-camps and members of state constitutional convention.

[5] This includes federal agencies, Republic of Texas Constitutional Convention, Secretary of War for the Republic of Texas and executive aides. James P. Drake, a Hoosier Democrat, was a federal Land Office appointee and a federal receiver of public monies and is counted twice in this category.

[6] This includes West Point graduates, West Point cadets who did not graduate, service in the U.S. Army and service in wartime.

[7] John Ralls, a Missouri Democrat, was the state house clerk and aide-de-camp to Governor Boggs and is counted twice in this category.

ventured into the nearby camp of Colonel Robert Paine's North Carolina regiment, apparently to play a prank. The altercations got out of hand, leading to violence that some observers called a mutiny.[56]

Expecting that they were to be in uniform for only a matter of months, most colonels decided that they were better off if they avoided trying to enforce Regular Army rules on minor matters. On the other hand, measured doses of discipline, coupled with unpretentiousness and concern for the men's welfare, usually heightened a colonel's popularity. Volunteers wanted their leaders to set a personal example for bravery and most of them understood that some attention to organization and tactical drill was needed. But many usually bridled at former Regulars, and those volunteers who sought to emulate them, who intended to rigorously enforce army regulations,[57] especially when colonels recently had left their business, political office, or law practice.[58]

Successful volunteer colonels possessed certain traits often associated with good military leadership in any age. Among the most important of these was courage. Unappreciated factors for officers to possess included stamina and sound health. With diligence and practice, new officers could learn to evaluate terrain, assess enemy forces, and exercise some degree of command proficiency. One of the difficult matters was for new colonels to learn to make use of the advice of others who could impart professional military knowledge. These could include former Regulars serving as lieutenant colonels or Regular officers who offered advice with tactical drills or deployment. Effective colonels also used rhetoric to inspire soldiers.[59]

Even if they displayed or acquired some of these important traits, the colonels had to deal with subordinates. Captains leading companies usually were elected by those serving in them, and the colonel had to take what he got for his company commanders. Colonels also had to work with other regimental officers, such as the lieutenant colonel and the major, and in some cases those men had been rivals for the colonelcy. A few examples provide illustrations. Colonel Reuben Davis of Mississippi recalled that one of his captains, Benjamin Buckley, who had sought the colonelcy, was recalcitrant in his duties and vindictive forever after. Buckley later resigned from the regiment.[60] Alexander Doniphan lacked cordial relations with his lieutenant colonel, Charles Ruff, a former West Pointer.[61] Promoted to brigadier general, Joseph Lane maintained a proprietary interest in his old regiment and refused to let its new colonel, William Bowles, supervise its drill.[62]

Shaping their regiments and propelling them toward Mexico, several of the volunteer colonels compiled mediocre combat records and failed to demonstrate the attributes needed to be a 'good colonel.' According to army veteran Samuel Chamberlain, the 'material that these [volunteer] regiments were composed of was excellent – none could be better – …, but they had no discipline or confidence in their officers. Most of… [the officers] were wild reckless young fellows, with the most inflated ideas of their own personal prowess and a firm belief that their own State could whip the world and Mexico in particular.' Chamberlain pointed to Colonel Archibald Yell's Arkansans, contending that their indiscipline was 'fatal to their efficiency as soldiers.'[63] General John Wool agreed, noting the deficiency of the Arkansas Regiment: the soldiers were 'without any instruction. They do not appear to be under the control of their officers.'[64] Yell neglected to put his men through the evolutions of regimental tactical drill, and he and his subordinates seemed to delight in taunting the Regulars. Yell's regiment performed poorly at the Battle of Buena Vista, and the colonel was killed in action.[65] One Pennsylvania soldier called Colonel William Roberts 'an ignorant jackass' and related: 'Under such a colonel there is no danger that we will ever stand high as a regiment.'[66] In another example, trying to draw on his militia experience, John Hardin of Illinois failed to impress General John Wool, who labeled Illinois volunteer officers 'not worth a damn.' Chamberlain speculated that Hardin, hailed as a hero to Manifest Destiny, was so disliked in the regiment that he may have been killed by his own men during the Battle of Buena Vista.[67]

Only a few of the volunteer colonels earned high ratings. Alexander Doniphan of Missouri was probably the best colonel with no prior service in the Regulars, but he benefited from his close association with a Regular general, Stephen W. Kearny, commander of the First Dragoons. Kearny and his Regulars conducted basic training for Doniphan's regiment, and a few dragoons acted as advisers when the regiment defeated a Mexican force more than three times its size at the Sacramento River, near the provincial capital of Chihuahua City. Another Whig, Colonel William Campbell, devoted hours to studying Winfield Scott's manual of *Infantry Tactics* and was pleased by the gradual improvement of his Tennessee regiment. Nevertheless, after many days practicing the manual of arms and tactical drill he concluded that it was 'an impossible task to drill and discipline an army of volunteers like the Regular Army.' Campbell's regiment went on to fight well in the Battle of Monterrey. Inspirational and dedicated, William McKee of Kentucky, a West Pointer, was one of the most widely respected of all the volunteer officers. Albert Sidney Johnston of Texas also established a highly creditable record, helping him gain reappointment to the U.S. Army in 1849. Alexander Mitchell of Ohio was wounded at Monterrey and served as military governor of the city after the battle.[68] When coupled with the renown of triumphant Whig generals Zachary Taylor and Winfield Scott, Whig colonels gave their party an excellent wartime record, though it was overshadowed by the party's important political leaders who opposed 'Mr. Polk's War.'

Democrats also demonstrated exceptional military leadership as colonels. West Pointer Jefferson Davis of Mississippi gained a sterling reputation for his regiment's fighting in battles at Monterrey and Buena Vista, and Zachary Taylor complimented William Bissell of Illinois for his conduct at the latter battle. Ward Burnett of New York and John Williams of Kentucky stood out in the Mexico City campaign. Suppressing the Taos Revolt, Sterling Price of Missouri helped to solidify the conquest of New Mexico. Earning brevets for gallantry at Churubusco and Contreras, George Morgan of Ohio was made a brigadier general. George Hughes of Maryland won plaudits for gallant conduct at Cerro Gordo.[69]

Albert Sidney Johnston of Texas distinguished himself as a regimental commander, but other Texas troops, often collectively called 'Rangers,' generated controversies. Several Regular Army officers grudgingly acknowledged that Texans conducted timely reconnaissance and fought like mountain lions in combat. On the other hand, the record of Texas troops (and other volunteers as well) was stained with incidents of indiscipline and disorder, including violence against both Mexican civilians and Mexican prisoners of war. Texans under Colonel John Hays were involved in violent incidents against civilians. Colonel William Young's North Texas Mounted Regiment was mustered out after only a few weeks in federal service due to disciplinary problems. Although the Rangers gave America one of its national heroes during the war – Ben McCulloch – generals Taylor and Scott were displeased with the lack of discipline and behavior of most Texas regiments.[70]

Several former volunteer colonels drew upon their wartime service to seek or regain postwar political offices.[71] It was not always the most effective or heralded colonels who won elections or were appointed to the highest offices. But the number and types

Table 4 Postwar Political and Military Participation[1]

	Whigs	Democrats	Unknown	Total[1]
Northern Colonels				
Local[2]	–	1	–	1
State Legislature	–	3	–	3
State Executive[3]	–	5	–	5
State Other[4]	–	2	–	2
U.S. House	2	4	–	6
U.S. Senate	1	1	–	2
Federal Other[5]	1	5	–	6
Service in Postwar Army	–	–	1	1
Military Service in the Civil War	2	3	–	5
Southern Colonels				
Local	–	–	–	0
State Legislature	3	2	–	5
State Executive	1	5	–	6
State Other	–	3	–	3
U.S. House	3	2	–	5
U.S. Senate	–	1	–	1
Federal Other	2	1	–	3
Service in Postwar Army	1	1	–	2
Confederate Political Office[6]	1	1	–	2
Military Service in the Civil War[7]	4	8	1	13

Notes

[1] Archibald Yell, John Hardin, William McKee, and Pierce Butler were killed in action and William Roberts died of disease, reducing the number of former colonels to 58. Accumulated totals will not equal 58 as it includes those that held posts and excludes those with no postwar political or military participation.

[2] This includes a city mayor.

[3] This includes governors of states *and* territories, as well as James Lane, a lieutenant governor of Indiana.

[4] This includes state auditor, state adjutant general, state land surveyor and a judge.

[5] This includes a Vice Presidential candidate, U.S. diplomatic posts, attorney general, secretary of war, federal agencies, member of the Peace Convention of 1861 and federally-appointed territorial positions.

[6] This includes the Confederate Congress and Executive.

[7] Service encompasses all ranks, including two colonels, nine generals and one unknown rank. While most southern colonels from the Mexican War fought for the South in the Civil War, it should be noted that William B. Campbell, a Whig who commanded the 2nd Tennessee, was a general in the Union Army.

of offices held may be taken to indicate the overall quality and leadership potential of men who served as colonels. Of the 58 surviving veteran volunteer colonels, 30 held elective or appointive political offices between 1848 and 1865. Moreover, in the Civil War six of them served as Union generals, nine as Confederate generals, and other southerners served as lower ranking officers (see Table 4).

Several Democrats gained recognition as successful colonels and went on to gain political offices or military commissions. Distinguished on the battlefield, Jefferson Davis held high offices and achieved the most recognition. Davis was elected to the U.S. Senate, appointed secretary of war by President Franklin Pierce, and selected to be provisional president of the Confederate States by the Montgomery convention in 1861. Notable at the Battle of Buena Vista, William Bissell of Illinois was elected to the U.S. House of Representatives and later governor of the state. Wounded at Buena Vista, Willis Gorman of Indiana later served in the U.S. House, was appointed governor of Minnesota Territory by President Pierce, and was a Union general. John Williams of Kentucky later served as a Confederate general. Sterling Price continued his political career by being elected governor of Missouri and also was a Confederate general. After fighting at the Belen Gate outside Mexico City, John Geary was appointed governor of Kansas Territory, served as a Union general, and was twice elected governor of Pennsylvania. A veteran of Buena Vista as a company commander and also commanding volunteers for frontier defense of Texas during the war, Peter H. Bell was elected governor of Texas in 1849 and later served in Congress from 1853 to 1857.[72]

A few Democratic colonels made the most of modest accomplishments. John Roane was elected governor of Arkansas and served as a Confederate general. A veteran of Cerro Gordo, Ferris Foreman of the Illinois volunteers moved to California and served in the state legislature and as secretary of state. George Morgan of Ohio later gained an appointment from President James Buchanan as minister to Portugal, was a Union volunteer general, and served in the U.S. House of Representatives. George T. Wood returned home during the war and was elected governor of Texas in 1847. Benjamin Cheatham of Tennessee failed in his campaign for mayor of Nashville but later served as a Confederate general.[73]

Other Democratic colonels came out of the war with lackluster records but sought political rewards or military rank anyway. James Drake won a term in the Indiana state legislature. Samuel Marks held the office of Louisiana state auditor from 1850 to 1856. Horatio Davis of Louisiana served in the postwar as state adjutant general. Reuben Davis of Mississippi saw no combat during the Mexican War but went on to be a U.S. congressman and a Confederate general. Both a colonel and a general, Caleb Cushing served in the Massachusetts state legislature, on the state supreme court, and as U.S. attorney general under Franklin Pierce, among other postwar offices. Tennessee voters elected Richard Waterhouse to the state senate. His colleague, George McClelland, subsequently won a seat in the Tennessee legislature and later held the rank of colonel in the Confederate army.[74]

Despite having questionable or controversial war service, other Democrats still ventured into politics, and some reached high posts. Henry Jackson of Georgia served as a judge on the Georgia Supreme Court, U.S. minister to Austria, and a Confederate general. Joseph Lane, controversial colonel and also volunteer brigadier appointed by President Polk, went on to be governor of Indiana and U.S. senator from Oregon. Lane also ran as the vice presidential candidate on the ticket of Southern Democrat John C. Breckinridge in the presidential election of 1860. William Bowles of Indiana became a prominent 'Copperhead' during the Civil War. James Lane held the offices of lieutenant governor of Indiana and U.S. senator from Kansas.[75]

Some Whigs earned distinguished or commendable wartime records. Hero of Sacramento, Alexander Doniphan was elected to the Missouri state legislature and also served in the Peace Convention at Washington, D.C., in 1861, trying to forge a compromise to avoid a civil war. Edward Baker of Illinois, a veteran of Cerro Gordo, served as U.S. senator from both Oregon and California and was a Union general. After fighting at Monterrey, William Campbell of Tennessee was elected governor of Tennessee in 1851 and served as a Union general during the Civil War. Also a combat veteran of Cerro Gordo, Tennessee's William T. Haskell won a seat in the U.S. House of Representatives after the war. Lewis DeRussy held seats in the Louisiana legislature from 1851 to 1855. President Zachary Taylor appointed Alexander Mitchell of Ohio to be a U.S. marshal for Minnesota Territory.[76]

Whigs with lackluster records still gained rank or office in later years. Manilus Thomson of Kentucky served as a Confederate officer in the Civil War. Charles Clark became a Confederate general and governor of Mississippi from 1863 to 1865. Samuel Curtis moved from Ohio to Iowa, where voters elected him to the U.S. House and he later served as a Union general.[77]

Among the controversial Whig colonels, Humphrey Marshall of Kentucky was elected to the U.S. Congress, and during the Civil War he was a Confederate general and member of the Confederate congress. Robert Paine of North Carolina also won election to the U.S. Congress in 1854, running as a member of the American Party.[78]

Only three volunteer colonels sought postwar service with the Regular Army. Edward Newby of Illinois was in the army from 1855 to 1863, reaching the rank of major. George Hughes of Maryland completed a lengthy career as a Regular officer in 1851. Albert Sidney Johnston of Texas served in the Regular Army from 1849 to 1861. He then became one of the senior generals of the Confederacy, but was killed at the Battle of Shiloh in 1862.[79]

Collectively the former colonels' offices, ranks, and achievements after their war service of 1846–48 demonstrate they were capable individuals who continued to be influential. Of the surviving 58 former colonels, 15 (almost 26 percent) served as generals in the Civil War, nine with the Confederacy (Clark, Cheatham, Reuben Davis, Jackson, Johnston, Marshall, Price, Roane, and Williams) and six with the Union (Baker, Campbell, Curtis, Geary, Gorman, and Morgan). Fourteen (24 percent) were elected to the U.S. House or U.S. Senate, including Baker, Bell, Bissell, Curtis, Jefferson Davis, Reuben Davis, Gorman, Hardin, Haskell, James Lane, Joseph Lane, Marshall, Morgan, and Paine. Eleven (19 percent) went on to be governors of states or territories, including Bell, Bissell, Campbell, Clark, Geary, Gorman, Joseph Lane, Price, Roane, and Wood. Eight (14 percent) sat in state legislatures: Cushing, DeRussy, Reuben Davis, Doniphan, Drake, Foreman, McClelland, and Peyton. In some cases, notable and successful individuals held multiple offices.

In conclusion, the background of the volunteer colonels, including their lack of military education and training, reflected many Americans' impatience with military regimentation and disinterest in professional military knowledge. As a group, the colonels were uneven in quality, which follows from the uneven process of their election or appointment. Many colonels appear to have expected that one-year units, led mostly by military amateurs, would carry out America's war policies, reflecting the 'civilianized' wartime armies that prevailed throughout most of American history. Some American volunteer units helped win victories on the battlefields in Mexico but other volunteer expeditionary regiments lacked discipline and performed little better than American militia units serving in the War of 1812. Several regiments contributed by occupying Mexican lands during the war.

As was typical in the United States after a war, some writers and orators rushed to praise the volunteer soldiers of 1846–48. Giving a speech even before the war ended, Jefferson Davis emphasized that well-motivated and well-led volunteers could make notable contributions to the war effort, contending that some American volunteers were natural soldiers who rose to be heroes. He listed four regimental colonels (Clay, Hardin, McKee, and Yell, all killed in action) in this special category. Some of Davis's colleagues in Congress were more effusive. Many years later, John A. Logan wrote stressing the Civil War volunteer briefly and directly upheld the continuing ideal of the citizen-soldier as exemplified in the U.S.-Mexican War. Colonel Emory Upton, army reformer and staunch Regular officer, was an unlikely person to be complimenting volunteers, but even he acknowledged that U.S. volunteers in Mexico, despite their faults, also showed 'skill, fortitude, and courage.' Nay-sayers found it difficult to counter such praise, though Henry L. Scott, a Regular Army colonel, tried to undercut the inflated image of volunteers by reminding his readers that most volunteers had been poorly trained, indifferently armed, and unevenly led in the campaigns in Mexico. Scott's criticisms notwithstanding, it was the praise that carried over to the American wars of 1861–65 and 1898.[80]

The United States could not have prosecuted and won the war against Mexico without the inspiration and example set by the volunteer colonels. Covered with praise or trading upon their few months in uniform, they appeared to vindicate relying on the concept of citizen-soldiery. The exploits of the successful colonels and the heroic images in Currier and Ives prints of American volunteer regiments conquering Mexico discounted the role of the Regular Army in the war.[81] Lauding the volunteers also helped to reconfirm America's dependence on short-term units of citizen soldiers and meant that future Congresses and presidents did not have to fund a Regular Army commensurate with the expanded size of the nation after 1848. Although the army was boosted from about 8,000 to around 16,000, it was a modest army for a large nation.[82] In 1848 and for decades after, Americans acclaimed the colonels, several of whom became leaders in their states, in the Congress, and during the Civil War. Even after 1865, it was evident that the United States would be likely to depend in wartime on national volunteer regiments raised by the states. Therefore, the nation would be relying on volunteer colonels commanding such regiments for the rest of the nineteenth century.

Notes

[1] Winders, *Mr. Polk's Army*, 32–49, 66–87, especially 37–8, 75–6.
[2] See Hickey, *The War of 1812*, 80–87, 140, 144–6, 196–8, 206–14, 308–9, and Skeen, *Citizen Soldiers in the War of 1812*.
[3] Nance, *After San Jacinto: The Texas–Mexican Frontier*, 519.
[4] Richardson, ed. *Messages and Papers of the Presidents*, 4:413.
[5] Williams, *The History of American Wars*, 161.
[6] Cunliffe, *Soldiers and Civlians*, 179–212.
[7] Figures according to Winders, *Mr. Polk's Army*, 72.

[8] Wilcox, *History of the Mexican War*, 653–95. See Frazier, ed. *The United States and Mexico at War*, 495–7.
[9] See Morison, et al., *Dissent in Three American Wars*, 33–63; Paulhus, 'Rhode Island and the Mexican War,' 89–96; Michael, 'Ohio and the Mexican War: Public Response to the 1846–1848 Crisis,' 164–5.
[10] Michael, 'Ohio and the Mexican War,' 24–9, and Eubank, 'A Time of Enthusiasm,' 325–32.
[11] Davis, 'Florida's Part in the War with Mexico,' 235–59; Wilcox, *History of the Mexican War*, 656, 679.
[12] Three companies of Iowans signed on with a Regular outfit, the U.S. 15th Infantry Regiment. Williams, 'Forgetting Chapultepec,' 81–92; Wilcox, *History of the Mexican War*, 665.
[13] Wilcox, *History of the Mexican War*, 668–71; Gardner, *A Dictionary of All Officers*, 537–9; Germany, 'Patriotism and Protest: Louisiana and General Gaines,' 325–35; Kennedy, 'Louisiana in the Mexican War,' 40–49; Frazier, ed. *U.S. and Mexico at War*, 495–7.
[14] For officers in this paragraph: Kentucky: Kleber, *The Kentucky Encyclopedia*, 575, 610, 633, 956, Federal Writers Project/Works Progress Administration, *Military History of Kentucky*, 123, and Clift, ed. *Governors of Kentucky*, 182–3; Stockton: *American Biographical History of Eminent and Self-Made Men, Michigan Volume*, 65; Stevenson: Biggs, *Conquer and Colonize: Stevenson's Regiment and California*, 31; Paine: Wallace, 'Raising a Volunteer Regiment for Mexico, 1846–1847,' 20–22; Hamtramck: Wallace, 'The First Regiment of Virginia Volunteers, 1846–1848,' 46–77; Hughes: Trass, *From the Golden Gate to Mexico City*, 201.
[15] Lieutenant colonels succeeding to command included William Weatherford of Illinois, Isaac Wright of Massachusetts, and John Geary of Pennsylvania.
[16] Winders, *Mr. Polk's Army*, 78–84; Bauer, *The Mexican War, 1846–1848*, 69.
[17] For Yell: Hughes, *Archibald Yell*, 99; Cushing: Fuess, *The Life of Caleb Cushing*, 2:33, 36, 39; Jackson: Kurtz, 'The First Regiment of Georgia Volunteers in the Mexican War,' 301–23; Bissell: *Biographical Directory of the United States Congress, 1774–1989*, 625 (hereafter *Directory of Congress*); Foreman: *United States Biographical and Portrait Gallery, Illinois Volume*, 441–2; Perry, *Indiana in the Mexican War*.
[18] Wool, quoted in Bloom, 'With the American Army in Mexico,' 14. Liquor was provided at the time of other regimental elections. See Winders, *Mr. Polk's Army*, 83.
[19] Cunliffe, *Soldiers and Civilians*, 309.
[20] Chance, *Jefferson Davis's Mexican War Regiment*, 81–120.
[21] McKee's background is in Heitman, *Historical Register and Dictionary of the United States Army*, 1:671, and Cullum, *Biographical Register of the Officers and Graduates of the United States Military Academy at West Point, 1802–1867*, 1:343 (hereafter Cullum, *Officers and Graduates*). For McKee's heroic status, see Johannsen, *To the Halls of the Montezumas*, 97.
[22] Roland, *Albert Sidney Johnston*, 127–37, and Kreneck, 'From Enthusiasm to Disillusionment,' 366, 371.
[23] Trass, *Golden Gate to Mexico City*, 201; Heitman, *Historical Register*, 1:552.
[24] Cullum, *Officers and Graduates*, 1:405.
[25] Heitman, *Historical Register*, 1:725, Warner, *Generals in Blue*, 333–4, and Knepper, *Ohio and Its People*, 259.
[26] For DeRussy: Wilson, *Appleton's Cyclopedia of American Biography*, 2:149, and Cullum, *Officers and Graduates*, 1:134; for Mitchell: ibid., 1:480.
[27] For Horatio Davis: Heitman, *Historical Register*, 1:358; Curtis: Chance, *Mexico Under Fire*; Stockton: Cullum, *Officers and Graduates*, 1:314–15; Irvin: ibid., 1:585–6.
[28] Lander, *Reluctant Imperialists*, 88–9, 92, 94, 95, 96–7, 103, 105–6, 119–21, and Meyer, *South Carolina in the Mexican War*, 90.
[29] Cullum, *Officers and Graduates*, 1:417–18; Lavender, *Climax at Buena Vista*, 182–3, 188–9, 191, 197, 204; Salisbury, 'Kentuckians at the Battle of Buena Vista,' 40–42.
[30] Only six of more than 60 regimental lieutenant colonels (LTC) were former Regulars. Henry S. Burton (USMA 1839, on active duty when selected as LTC) served with Stevenson's New

York Regiment; see Cullum, *Officers and Graduates*, 1:577–8. Henry Clay, Jr. (USMA 1831, resigned 1831), son of U.S. Senator Henry Clay, served with the Second Kentucky Volunteer Cavalry; see ibid., 1:379–80. William H. Emory (USMA 1831, on active duty when selected as LTC) served with the Maryland and D.C. volunteers; see ibid., 1:386–8, and Norris, *William H. Emory, Soldier Scientist*, 6–65. Randolph (USMA 1812, resigned 1815) served with the Virginia volunteers; see Cullum, *Officers and Graduates*, 1:125. Jason Rogers (USMA 1821, resigned 1836) served with the First Kentucky Volunteer Infantry; see ibid., 1:219. Charles Ruff (USMA 1838, resigned 1843), served with the First Missouri Mounted Volunteers; see ibid., 1:570–71, and Dawson, *Doniphan's Epic March*, 55–8.

[31] Winders, "Will the Regiment Stand It,' 67–90. See also Wallace, 'Regiment of Virginia Volunteers,' 46–77, and McCaffrey, *Army of Manifest Destiny*, 115–17.

[32] Yell: Hughes, *Archibald Yell*, 22–3; Hardin: *Directory of Congress*, 1131; Haskell: ibid., 1149; Bell: ibid., 604; Drake: *Biographical History of Eminent and Self-Made Men of the State of Indiana*, 1:33–4; Waterhouse: McBride and Robinson, eds. *Biographical Directory of the Tennessee General Assembly*, 763–4; Marks: Conrad, ed. *Dictionary of Louisiana Biography*, 1:549; Hays: Greer, *Colonel Jack Hays: Texas Frontier Leader*, 22–114; Bell: Hendrickson, *Chief Executives of Texas*, 54.

[33] For example, see Watson, 'Congressional Attitudes Toward Military Preparedness, 1829–1835,' 611–36; Winders, *Mr. Polk's Army*, 73; Cunliffe, *Soldiers and Civilians*.

[34] Cooper, *The Rise of the National Guard*, 1–22, and Cunliffe, *Soldiers and Civilians*, 179–212.

[35] Johannsen, *Halls of the Montezumas*, 41; Cunliffe, *Soldiers and Civilians*, 102–10, 293–5.

[36] Doniphan: Connelley, *Doniphan's Expedition*, 128, 133. Ormsby: Eubank, 'A Time of Enthusiasm: Kentucky,' 334; Walton: Conrad, ed., *Dictionary of Louisiana Biography*, 2:823; Dakin: Arthur Scully, Jr., *James Dakin, Architect*, 118–22; Reuben Davis: Reuben Davis, *Recollections of Mississippi and Mississippians*, 211–21; Price: Shalhope, *Sterling Price, Portrait of a Southerner*, 55–60; Ralls: Conrad, ed. *Encyclopedia of the History of Missouri*, 5:292; Campbell: Sioussat, ed. 'Mexican War Letters of Col. William Bowen Campbell of Tennessee,' 129–39; Cheatham: Warner, *Generals in Gray*, 47; Stevenson: Biggs, *Conquer and Colonize*, 31; Wynkoop and Roberts: Hackenburg, *Pennsylvania in the War with Mexico*, 2, 5; Hardin: *Directory of Congress*, 1131; Weatherford: Ford, *A History of Illinois*, 2:230; Drake: Viola, 'Zachary Taylor and the Indiana Volunteers,' 336.

[37] For an explication of American attitudes see Richard, *The Founders and the Classics*, especially chapter 1.

[38] Coffey: Whitfield, 'Alabama and the Mexican War,' 21; Jackson: Edison, 'Henry Rootes Jackson,' 1:513–14; Roane: Donovan, et al., *Governors of Arkansas*, 20–22; Thomson: Clift, ed. *Governors of Kentucky*, 182–3; Williams: Eubank, 'Kentucky in the Mexican War: Public Responses, 1846–1848,' 46; Peyton: *Directory of Congress*, 1639–40; Clark: Warner, *Generals in Gray*, 51–2; Paine: Wallace, '[North Carolina] Volunteer Regiment,' 20–33; McClelland: McBride, ed. *Directory of the Tennessee Assembly*, 470; Thomas: ibid., 717; Bissell: *Directory of Congress*, 625; Baker: ibid., 565; Foreman: Bateman, ed. *Historical Encyclopedia of Illinois and History of Fayette County*, 751; Newby: Myers, 'Illinois Volunteers in New Mexico,' 5–10; Indiana: Perry, *Indiana in the Mexican War*; Cushing: Fuess, *Life of Caleb Cushing*, 2:33, 36, 39.

[39] Colonels lacking confirmed or likely political affiliations include Edward Newby and James Collins of Illinois, William Irvin of Ohio, John Coffey of Alabama, Edward Featherstone of Louisiana, and William Young of Texas.

[40] See also Winders, *Mr. Polk's Army*, 78–9.

[41] For Burnett and Stevenson, see Cullum, *Officers and Graduates*, 1:405, and Biggs, *Conquer and Colonize*, 31, 48, note 10. For Indiana: Viola, 'Taylor and the Indiana Volunteers,' 336–7; Kelly, *The Career of Joseph Lane, Frontier Politician*, 29–31, and Buley, 'Indiana in the Mexican War: The Indiana Volunteers,' 260–72. For Pennsylvania: Hackenburg, *Pennsylvania in the War with Mexico*, 2, 8, 14, and Tinkcom, *John White Geary, Soldier-Statesman*, 6–7.

[42] Cushing, a former Whig congressman turned Democrat, had a lengthy political career. See Belohlavek, 'Race, Progress, and Destiny,' 29–32, 37–8, quote on 37, and Fuess, *Life of Caleb Cushing*, 2:33, 36, 39–60, 75–7.

[43] For Morgan: *Directory of Congress*, 1531–2; Bissell: ibid., 704; Weatherford: Ford, *History of Illinois*, 2:230; Foreman: Bateman, ed. *Illinois and History of Fayette County*, 751; Stockton: *Eminent and Self-Made Men, Michigan*, 65; Brough: *History of Washington County, Ohio, 1881*, 416.

[44] Yell: Hughes, *Archibald Yell*, 80–82, 91–2; Roane: Donovan, *Governors of Arkansas*, 20–22; W. Davis, *Jefferson Davis*, 127–67; R. Davis: Davis, *Recollections of Mississippi*, and Bruce S. Allardice, *More Generals in Gray*, 72; Jackson: Edison, 'Henry Jackson,' in Coleman, ed. *Dictionary of Georgia Biography*, 1:513–14; Price: Shalhope, *Sterling Price*, and Warner, *Generals in Gray*, 149; Ralls: Conrad, ed. *History of Missouri*, 5:292. Williams: Kleber, ed. *Kentucky Encyclopedia*, 956, *Biographical Encyclopedia of Kentucky*, 1878, 177, and Eubank, 'Kentucky in the Mexican War,' 118–45; Waterhouse: Moore, *Tennessee, The Volunteer State*, 1:412, and McBride, ed. *Directory of the Tennessee Assembly*, 763–4; McClelland: ibid., 470; Thomas: ibid., 717; Cheatham: Losson, *Tennessee's Forgotten Warriors*, 23–5; Walton: Conrad, ed. *Dictionary of Louisiana Biography*, 2:823; H. Davis: ibid., 1217; Marks: Freeman, 'The Early Career of Pierre Soulé,'1039; Butler: Lander, *Reluctant Imperialists*, 36–37; Hughes: Trass, *Golden Gate to Mexico City*, 201; Wood: Hendrickson, *Chief Executives of Texas*, 50–53; Bell: ibid., 54–6; Hays: Greer, *Colonel Jack Hays*, 227; Young: *Biographical Directory of the Texan Conventions and Congresses*, 1941, 197.

[45] Schroeder, *Mr. Polk's War*, and Morison, et al., *Dissent in Three American Wars*, may leave the impression that Whigs were monolithic in opposing the war.

[46] For Doniphan: Dawson, *Doniphan's Epic March*, 8, 10, and Launius, *Alexander William Doniphan*; Campbell: Warner, *Generals in Blue*, 66; Haskell: *Directory of Congress*, 1149; Marshall: ibid., 1425; Peyton: ibid., 1639–40; Paine: ibid., 1606; McKee: Eubank, 'Kentucky in the Mexican War', 37–40; Thomson: Clift, ed. *Governors of Kentucky*, 182–3; Johnston: Roland, *Albert Sidney Johnston*, 124; Clark: Warner, *Generals in Gray*, 51; DeRussy: Wilson, ed., *Appleton's American Biography*, 2:149; Hamtramck: Wallace, 'Regiment of Virginia Volunteers'; Ormsby: Albert E. Pierce, comp., 'Ormsby Families of Louisville, Kentucky,' Family Files, Kentucky Historical Society, Frankfort, Ky.; Dakin: Arthur Scully Jr., 'James H. Dakin,' Garraty, ed. *American National Biography*, 6:16.

[47] Baker: *Directory of Congress*, 565; Hardin: ibid., 1131; Curtis: Warner, *Generals in Blue*, 108; Mitchell: Cullum, *Officers and Graduates*, 1:480.

[48] Yell and Roane: Donovan, *Governors of Arkansas*, 8–12, 20–22; Tennessee: McBride, ed. *Directory of the Tennessee Assembly*, 117–18, 342–43 470, 717, 763–64; Paine: *Directory of Congress*, 1606; Doniphan: Dawson, *Doniphan's Epic March*, 8; Price: Shalhope, *Sterling Price*, 22–6; J. Davis: *Directory of Congress*, 879–80; Marks: Conrad, ed. *Dictionary of Louisiana Biography*, 1:549; Hardin: *Directory of Congress*, 1131; Baker, ibid., 565; Bissell: ibid., 625; Clark: Warner, *Generals in Gray*, 51–2; Indiana colonels: *Directory of the Indiana Assembly*, 1:33, 55, 229; Cushing: Stevenson: Biggs, *Conquer and Colonize*, 31; Brough: *History of Washington County, Ohio*, 416.

[49] For Cushing: *Directory of Congress*, 861; Baker, ibid., 565; Hardin, ibid., 1131; Yell, ibid., 1639–40; Peyton, ibid., 1131; Price, ibid., 737; Campbell, ibid., 737; J. Davis, ibid., 879–80; R. Davis, ibid., 881–2; Butler: Meyer, *South Carolina in the Mexican War*, 31; Donovan, *Governors of Arkansas*, 8–12; Clift, ed. *Governors of Kentucky*, 182–3; Roland, *Albert Sidney Johnston*, 82–99; Stockton: *Eminent and Self-Made Men, Michigan*, 65.

[50] Chance, *Jefferson Davis's Regiment*, 12; Bloom, 'With the American Army into Mexico,' 15.

[51] Jackson: Edison, 'Jackson,' in Coleman, ed. *Dictionary of Georgia Biography*, 1:513; Cushing: *Directory of Congress*, 861; Roane: Donovan, *Governors of Arkansas*, 20–21; Doniphan: Dawson, *Doniphan's Epic March*, 6; Hardin: *Directory of Congress*, 1131; Ormsby: Pierce, comp., 'Ormsby Families of Louisville, Kentucky,' Family Files, Kentucky Historical Society;

Thomson: Clift, ed., *Governors of Kentucky*, 182; J. Davis: Cooper, *Jefferson Davis*, 23–6; Bissell: *Directory of Congress*, 625; Morgan, ibid., 1531–2; Geary: Warner, *Generals in Blue*, 169; McClelland: McBride, ed. *Directory of the Tennessee Assembly*, 470; Foreman: Bateman, ed. *Illinois and History of Fayette County*, 751; Gorman: *Directory of Congress*, 1079; Williams: Warner, *Generals in Gray*, 338; Walton: Conrad, ed. *Dictionary of Louisiana Biography*, 2:823; H. Davis: ibid., 1:217; Price: Shalhope, *Sterling Price*, 5–7; Paine: *Directory of Congress*, 1606; Haskell: ibid., 1149; Hays: Greer, *Colonel Jack Hays*, 19.

[52] On American volunteer colonels in the nineteenth century, see Williams, *Hayes of the Twenty-third*, 18–38. Williams' applicable chapter is entitled 'The Good Colonels.'
[53] Sioussat, ed. 'War Letters of Col. Campbell,' 151.
[54] S. F. Nunnelle, '[A Recollection of] Alabama in the Mexico [sic] War,' 417, 422.
[55] Kurtz, 'Regiment of Georgia Volunteers,' 314–17; Livingston-Little, ed. 'Mutiny During the Mexican War,' 340–45.
[56] Winders, 'Will the Regiment Stand It,' 67–90, Wallace, 'Raising a [North Carolina] Volunteer Regiment,' 65–8.
[57] Winders, *Mr. Polk's Army*, 80–81.
[58] Almost 40 percent of colonels had practiced law before 1846, including Yell, Roane, Jackson, Hardin, Bissell, Foreman, Baker, James Lane, Gorman, Marshall, McKee, Thomson, Williams, Peyton, Cushing, Reuben Davis, Doniphan, Price, Paine, Morgan, Irvin, Geary, Campbell, Haskell, and Young.
[59] Williams, *Hayes of the Twenty-third*, 18–38.
[60] Reuben Davis, *Recollections of Mississippi*, 222, 228, 232.
[61] Dawson, *Doniphan's Epic March*, 33, 35, 63, 89.
[62] The disagreements between Lane and Bowles contributed to poor performance of the Indiana Brigade at Buena Vista. Viola, 'Zachary Taylor and the Indiana Volunteers,' 337, 341.
[63] Chamberlain, *My Confession*, 89–91, quote on 89.
[64] Wool, quoted in Chance, *Jefferson Davis's Regiment*, 115.
[65] Hughes, *Archibald Yell*, 128–45; Bauer, *Mexican War*, 208.
[66] Peskin, ed. *Volunteers*, 126, 127.
[67] Wool, quoted in Bauer, *Mexican War*, 150; Chamberlain, *My Confession*, 131.
[68] Doniphan: Dawson, *Doniphan's Epic March*, 38–42, 103–19, 142–62; Campbell: Sioussat, ed. 'War Letters of Col. Campbell,' 139, 143–5, quotation on 151; McKee: Johannsen, *Halls of the Montezumas*, 97, 130; Johnston: Roland, *Albert Sidney Johnston*, 124, 127, 135; Mitchell: Cullum, *Officers and Graduates*, 1:480.
[69] Davis: Chance, *Jefferson Davis's Regiment*, 52–4, 94–5, 98–9, 102, 104; Bissell: Bauer, *Mexican War*, 214–15; Burnett: Bauer, *Mexican War*, 317, 352; Williams: Eubank, 'Kentucky in the Mexican War', 81, and Warner, *Generals in Gray*, 338. Williams earned his combat accolades as a captain commanding an independent company rather than as a colonel. His colonelcy came later in the war. Price: Shalhope, *Sterling Price*, 63–6, 71–4, 96–101; Morgan: Heitman, *Historical Register*, 1:725; Hughes: ibid., 1:552.
[70] For McCulloch, Cutrer, *Ben McCulloch and the Frontier Military Tradition*, 68–9, 73–4, 88–9. For Hays: Greer, *Colonel Jack Hays*, 129–63. See also Kreneck, 'The North Texas Regiment in the Mexican War,' 109–17, and Kreneck, 'The Neglected Regiment [of Colonel George Wood]: East Texas Horsemen with Zachary Taylor,' 22–31.
[71] Other colonels who may have sought office after 1848 died during the war. Killed in action were Democrats Archibald Yell and Pierce Butler, and Whigs John Hardin and William McKee. Democrat William Roberts died of typhus.
[72] J. Davis: Cooper, *Jefferson Davis, American*, 127–57; Bissell: *Directory of Congress*, 625; Gorman: ibid., 1079; Williams: Warner, *Generals in Gray*, 338; Price: Shalhope, *Sterling Price*; Geary: Tinkcom, *John White Geary*; Bell: Hendrickson, *Chief Executives of Texas*, 54–6; Cheatham: Losson, *Tennessee's Forgotten Warriors*.

[73] Roane: Donovan, et al., *Governors of Arkansas*, 20–22; Foreman: *Biographical and Portrait Gallery, Illinois*, 441–2; Morgan: *Directory of Congress*, 1531–2; Wood: Hendrickson, *Chief Executives of Texas*, 50–53; Cheatham: Losson, *Tennessee's Forgotten Warriors*.
[74] Drake: *Directory of the Indiana Assembly*, 1:105–106; Marks: Conrad, ed. *Dictionary of Louisiana Biography*, 1:549; H. Davis: ibid., 1:217; R. Davis: *Directory of Congress*, 881–2, and Allardice, *More Generals in Gray*, 72; Clark: Warner, *Generals in Gray*, 51–2; Cushing: Fuess, *Life of Caleb Cushing*; Waterhouse: McBride, ed., *Directory of the Tennessee Assembly*, 763–4; McClelland: ibid., 717.
[75] Jackson: Edison, 'Henry Jackson,' in Coleman, ed. *Dictionary of Georgia Biography*, 1:513–514; Joseph Lane: Kelly, *Career of Joseph Lane*, 25–60; Bowles: Klement, *Dark Lanterns*, 70, 155, 174, 184–5, 228; James Lane: Stephenson, *Political Career of General James H. Lane*.
[76] Doniphan: Dawson, *Doniphan's Epic March*, 208, 213–16; Baker: *Directory of Congress*, 565; Haskell: ibid., 1149; Campbell: Warner, *Generals in Blue*, 66–7; DeRussy: Wilson, ed. *Appleton's American Biography*, 2:149; Mitchell: Cullum, *Officers and Graduates*, 1:480.
[77] Thomson: Davis, *Breckinridge: Statesman, Soldier, Symbol*, 35; Clark: Warner, *Generals in Gray*, 51–52; Curtis: Warner, *Generals in Blue*, 108.
[78] Marshall: *Directory of Congress*, 1425; Paine, ibid., 1606.
[79] Newby: Heitman, *Historical Register*, 744; Hughes: ibid., 552; Johnston: Roland, *Albert Sidney Johnston*.
[80] Monroe et al., eds. *Papers of Jefferson Davis*, 3:182, and 261, notes 1–4; Logan, *The Volunteer Soldier of America*, 479, 550; Upton, *The Military Policy of the United States*, 222; Scott, *Military Dictionary*, 643–8.
[81] Johannsen, *Halls of the Montezumas*, 128, 226, 228; Dawson, *Doniphan's Epic March*, 154–5; Chance, *Jefferson Davis's Regiment*, illustration section.
[82] Nearly doubling the size of the modest pre-1845 army was enough for Congress and most Americans between 1849 and 1860. According to Weigley, *History of the United States Army*, 597–98, the Regular Army stood as a force of 10,744 in 1849, in contrast to a force of 8,500 in 1845, and was boosted to between 15,000 and 17,000 during the years 1855–60. From 1816 to 1845 the army had ranged in size from 6,000 to 12,000, but averaged between 7,000 and 8,000.

References

Allardice, Bruce S. *More Generals in Gray*. Baton Rouge: Louisiana State U. P., 1995.
American Biographical History of Eminent and Self-Made Men, Michigan Volume. Cincinnati, Ohio: Western Biographical Pub. Co., 1878.
Bateman, Newton, ed. *Historical Encyclopedia of Illinois and History of Fayette County*. Chicago: Munsell Pub. Co., 1910.
Bauer, K. Jack. *The Mexican War, 1846–1848*. New York: Macmillan, 1972.
Belohlavek, John. 'Race, Progress, and Destiny: Caleb Cushing and the Quest for American Empire.' In *Manifest Destiny and Empire: American Antebellum Expansion*, edited by Sam Haynes and Christopher Morris. College Station: Texas A&M U. P., 1997.
Biggs, Donald C. *Conquer and Colonize: Stevenson's Regiment and California*. San Rafael, CA: Presidio Press, 1977.
Biographical Directory of the Texan Conventions and Congresses. Austin: Book Exchange, 1941.
Biographical Directory of the United States Congress, 1774–1989. Washington, DC: US Government Printing Office, 1989.
Biographical Encyclopedia of Kentucky. Cincinnati, OH: Armstrong & Co., 1878.
Biographical History of Eminent and Self-Made Men of the State of Indiana. 2 vols. Cincinnati, Ohio: Western Biographical Pub. Co., 1880.
Bloom, John P. 'With the American Army in Mexico.' Ph.D. diss., Emory University, 1956.

Buley, Roscoe C. 'Indiana in the Mexican War: The Indiana Volunteers.' *Indiana Magazine of History* 15 (September 1919): 260–92.

Chamberlain, Samuel E. *My Confession: The Recollections of a Rogue.* New York: Harper, 1956.

Chance, Joseph E. *Jefferson Davis's Mexican War Regiment.* Jackson: U. P. of Mississippi, 1991.

Chance, Joseph E., ed. *Mexico Under Fire: Being the Diary of Samuel Ryan Curtis.* Fort Worth: Texas Christian U. P., 1994.

Clift, G. G., ed. *Governors of Kentucky.* Cythiana, KY: Hobson Press, 1942.

Coleman, Kenneth, and Charles S. Gurr, eds. *Dictionary of Georgia Biography.* 2 vols. Athens: University of Georgia Press, 1983.

Connelley, William. *Doniphan's Expedition.* Topeka, KS: by the author, 1907.

Conrad, Glenn, ed. *Dictionary of Louisiana Biography.* 2 vols. Lafayette, LA: Louisiana Historical Association, 1988.

Conrad, Howard L., ed. *Encyclopedia of the History of Missouri.* 6 vols. New York: Southern Pub. Co., 1901.

Cooper, Jerry. *The Rise of the National Guard: The Evolution of the American Militia, 1865–1920.* Lincoln: University of Nebraska Press, 1997.

Cooper, William J. *Jefferson Davis, American.* New York: Alfred A. Knopf, 2000.

Cullum, George W. *Biographical Register of the Officers and Graduates of the United States Military Academy at West Point, 1902–1867.* 2 vols. New York: Appleton, 1868.

Cunliffe, Marcus. *Soldiers and Civilians: The Martial Spirit in America, 1775–1865.* New York: Free Press, 1968.

Cutrer, Thomas W. *Ben McCulloch and the Frontier Military Tradition.* Chapel Hill: University of North Carolina Press, 1993.

Davis, Frederick. 'Florida's Part in the War with Mexico.' *Florida Historical Quarterly* 20 (January 1942): 235–59.

Davis, Reuben. *Recollections of Mississippi and Mississippians.* Boston: Houghton Mifflin, 1889.

Davis, William C. *Breckinridge: Statesman, Soldier, Symbol.* Baton Rouge: Louisiana State U. P., 1974.

———. *Jefferson Davis.* New York: HarperCollins, 1991.

Dawson, Joseph G. III. *Doniphan's Epic March: The 1st Missouri Volunteers in the Mexican War.* Lawrence: U. P. of Kansas, 1999.

Directory of the Indiana General Assembly. 2 vols. Indianapolis: Indiana Historical Bureau, 1980.

Donovan, Timothy P., et al. *Governors of Arkansas.* 2nd ed. Fayetteville: University of Arkansas Press, 1995.

Edison, John O. 'Henry Rootes Jackson.' In *Dictionary of Georgia Biography,* 2 vols., edited by Kenneth Coleman and Charles S. Gurr. Athens, GA: University of Georgia Press, 1983.

Eubank, Damon R. 'A Time of Enthusiasm: The Response of Kentucky to the Call for Troops in the Mexican War.' *Register of the Kentucky Historical Society* 90 (Autumn 1992): 323–44.

———. 'Kentucky in the Mexican War: Public Responses, 1846–1848.' Ph.D. diss., Mississippi State University, 1989.

Federal Writers Project. *Military History of Kentucky.* American Guide Series. Frankfort, KY: State Journal, 1939.

Ford, Thomas. *A History of Illinois.* 2 vols. Reprint, Chicago: Donnelley Co., 1945–46.

Francaviglia, Richard V., and Douglas W. Richmond, eds. *Dueling Eagles: Reinterpreting the US-Mexican War.* Fort Worth: Texas Christian U. P., 2000.

Frazier, Donald S., ed. *The United States and Mexico at War.* New York: Macmillan, 1998.

Freeman, Arthur. 'The Early Years of Pierre Soule.' *Louisiana Historical Quarterly* 25 (October 1942): 971–1127.

Fuess, Claude M. *The Life of Caleb Cushing.* 2 vols. New York: Harcourt Brace, 1925.

Gardner, Charles K. *A Dictionary of All Officers Who Have Been Commissioned, or Have Been Appointed and Served in the Army of the United States.* New York: Putnam's, 1853.

Garraty, John A., ed. *American National Biography.* 24 vols. New York: Oxford U. P., 1999.

Germany, Kent B. 'Patriotism and Protest: Louisiana and General Edmund P. Gaines's Army of Mexican-American War Volunteers.' *Louisiana History* 37 (Summer 1996): 325–35.
Greer, Jack K. *Colonel Jack Hays: Texas Frontier Leader.* New York: Dutton, 1952; College Station: Texas A&M U. P., 1987.
Hackenburg, Randy. *Pennsylvania in the War with Mexico.* Shippensburg, PA: White Mane Pub. Co., 1992.
Haynes, Sam, and Christopher Morris, eds. *Manifest Destiny and Empire: American Antebellum Expansion.* College Station: Texas A&M U. P., 1997.
Heitman, Francis B. *Historical Register and Dictionary of the United States Army.* 2 vols. Washington, DC: US Government Printing Office, 1903.
Hendrickson, Kenneth E. *Chief Executives of Texas.* College Station: Texas A&M University Press, 1995.
Hickey, Donald R. *The War of 1812.* Urbana: University of Illinois Press, 1989.
History of Washington County, Ohio. Cleveland, OH: H. Z. Williams & Bro., 1881.
Hughes, William W. *Archibald Yell.* Fayetteville: University of Arkansas Press, 1988.
Johannsen, Robert. *To the Halls of the Montezumas: The Mexican War in the American Imagination.* New York: Oxford U. P., 1985.
Kelly, M. Margaret Jean. *The Career of Joseph Lane, Frontier Politician.* Washington, DC: Catholic U. P., 1942.
Kennedy, Bertha B. 'Louisiana in the Mexican War.' MA thesis, Louisiana State University, 1930.
Kleber, John E. *The Kentucky Encyclopedia.* Lexington: University Press of Kentucky, 1992.
Klement, Frank L. *Dark Lanterns: Secret Political Societies, Conspiracies and Treason Trials in the Civil War.* Baton Rouge: Louisiana State U. P., 1984.
Knepper, George W. *Ohio and Its People.* Kent, Ohio: Kent State U. P., 1989.
Kreneck, Thomas H. 'From Enthusiasm to Disillusionment: The Texas Volunteer Infantry in the Mexican War.' *Texana* 12 (1974): 366–71.
———. 'The Neglected Regiment [of Colonel George Wood]: East Texas Horsemen with Zachary Taylor.' *East Texas Historical Journal* 12 (1974): 22–31.
———. 'The North Texas Regiment in the Mexican War.' *Military History of Texas and the Southwest* 12 (1975): 109–117.
Kurtz, Wilbur G., Jr. 'The First Regiment of Georgia Volunteers in the Mexican War.' *Georgia Historical Quarterly* 27 (December 1943): 301–23.
Lander, Ernest M., Jr. *Reluctant Imperialists: Calhoun, the South Carolinians, and the Mexican War.* Baton Rouge: Louisiana State U. P., 1980.
Launius, Roger D. *Alexander William Doniphan.* Columbia: University of Missouri Press, 1997.
Lavender, David. *Climax at Buena Vista.* Philadelphia: Lippincott, 1966.
Livingston-Little, D. E., ed. 'Mutiny During the Mexican War: An Incident on the Rio Grande.' *Journal of the West* 9 (July 1970): 340–45.
Logan, John A. *The Volunteer Soldier of America.* Chicago: Peale Co., 1887.
Losson, Christopher. *Tennessee's Forgotten Warriors: Frank Cheatham and His Confederate Division.* Knoxville: University of Tennessee Press, 1989.
McBride, Robert M., and Dan M. Robinson, eds. *Biographical Directory of the Tennessee General Assembly.* Nashville: Tennessee Historical Commission, 1975.
McCaffrey, James M. *Army of Manifest Destiny: The American Soldier in the Mexican War.* New York: New York U. P., 1992.
Meyer, John A. *South Carolina in the Mexican War: A History of the Palmeto Regiment of Volunteers.* Columbia: South Carolina Department of Archives and History, 1996.
Michael, Steven B. 'Ohio and the Mexican War.' Ph.D. diss., Ohio State University, 1985.
Monroe, Haskell M., Lynda L. Crist, et al., eds. *The Papers of Jefferson Davis.* 11 vols. Baton Rouge: Louisiana State U. P., 1971–2003.
Moore, John T. *Tennessee, The Volunteer State.* 3 vols. Chicago: Clarke Pub. Co., 1923.
Morison, Samuel E., et al. *Dissent in Three American Wars.* Cambridge, MA: Harvard U. P., 1970.

Myers, Lee. 'Illinois Volunteers in New Mexico, 1847–48.' *New Mexico Historical Review* 47 (January 1972): 5–31.

Nance, J. Milton. *After San Jacinto: The Texas-Mexican Frontier, 1836–1841.* Austin: University of Texas Press, 1963.

Norris, L. David, et al. *William H. Emory, Soldier Scientist.* Tucson, AZ: University of Arizona Press, 1998.

Nunnelle, S. F. '[A Recollection of] Alabama in the Mexico [sic] War.' *Alabama Historical Quarterly* 19 (Fall/Winter 1957): 417–22.

Paulhus, David L. 'Rhode Island and the Mexican War.' *Rhode Island History* 37 (August 1978): 89–96.

Perry, Oran. *Indiana in the Mexican War.* Indianapolis: Burford, 1908.

Peskin, Allan, ed. *Volunteers: The Mexican War Journals of Private Richard Coulter and Sergeant Thomas Barclay.* Kent, OH: Kent State U. P., 1991.

Richard, Carl J. *The Founders and the Classics: Greece, Rome, and the American Enlightenment.* Cambridge, MA: Harvard U. P., 1994.

Richardson, James D., ed. *Messages and Papers of the Presidents, 1789–1897.* 10 vols. Washington, DC: US Government Printing Office, 1897.

Roland, Charles. *Albert Sidney Johnston, Soldier of Three Republics.* Austin: University of Texas Press, 1964.

Salisbury, Richard B. 'Kentuckians at the Battle of Buena Vista.' *Filson Club Quarterly* 61 (January 1987): 34–53.

Schroeder, John H. *Mr. Polk's War: American Opposition and Dissent, 1846–1848.* Madison: University of Wisconsin Press, 1973.

Scott, Henry L. *Military Dictionary* [1861]. Reprint, New York: Greenwood Press, 1968.

Scully, Arthur, Jr. *James Dakin, Architect.* Baton Rouge: Louisiana State U. P., 1973.

Shalhope, Robert E. *Sterling Price, Portrait of a Southerner.* Columbia, MO: University of Missouri Press, 1971.

Sioussat, St. George L., ed. 'Mexican War Letters of Col. William Bowen Campbell of Tennessee.' *Tennessee Historical Quarterly* 1 (June 1915): 129–67.

Skeen, C. E. *Citizen Soldiers in the War of 1812.* Lexington: University of Kentucky Press, 1999.

Stephenson, W. H. *Political Career of General James H. Lane.* Topeka, KS: Kansas State Historical Society, 1930.

Tinkcom, Harry M. *John White Geary, Soldier-Statesman.* Philadelphia: University of Pennsylvania Press, 1940.

Trass, Adrian. *From the Golden Gate to Mexico City: US Army Topographical Engineers in the Mexican War.* Washington, DC: US Government Printing Office, 1992.

United States Biographical and Portrait Gallery, Illinois Volume. Chicago: American Biographical Co., 1876.

Upton, Emory. *The Military Policy of the United States.* Washington, DC: US Government Printing Office [1904]. Reprint, New York: Greenwood Press, 1968.

Viola, Herman J. 'Zachary Taylor and the Indiana Volunteers.' *Southwestern Historical Quarterly* 72 (January 1969): 335–46.

Wallace, Lee A. 'The First Regiment of Virginia Volunteers, 1846–1848.' *Virginia Magazine of History and Biography* 77 (January 1969): 46–77.

———. 'Raising a Volunteer Regiment for Mexico, 1846–1847.' *North Carolina Historical Review* 35 (January 1958): 20–33.

Warner, Ezra J. *Generals in Blue: Lives of the Union Commanders.* Baton Rouge: Louisiana State U. P., 1964.

———. *Generals in Gray: Lives of the Confederate Commanders.* Baton Rouge: Louisiana State U. P., 1959.

Watson, Richard L. 'Congressional Attitudes Toward Military Preparedness, 1829–1835.' *Mississippi Valley Historical Review* 34 (March 1948): 611–36.

Weigley, Russell F. *History of the United States Army.* Enlarged ed. Bloomington, IN: Indiana U. P., 1984.
Whitfield, Henry J., Jr. 'Alabama and the Mexican War.' MA thesis, Alabama Polytechnic Institute/Auburn Unversity, 1940.
Williams, Ora. 'Forgetting Chapultepec.' *Annals of Iowa* 28 (October 1946): 81–92.
Williams, T. Harry. *Hayes of the Twenty-third: The Civil War Volunteer Officer.* New York: Alfred A. Knopf, 1965.
Wilson, James G., ed. *Appleton's Cyclopedia of American Biography.* 7 vols. New York: Appleton's, 1888.
Wilcox, Cadmus M. *History of the Mexican War.* Washington, DC: Church News Pub. Co., 1892.
Winders, Richard B. *Mr. Polk's Army: The American Military Experience in the Mexican War.* College Station: Texas A&M University Press, 1997.
———. '"Will the Regiment Stand It": The First North Carolina Mutinies at Buena Vista.' In *Dueling Eagles: Reinterpreting the U.S.-Mexican War,* edited by Richard V. Francaviglia and Douglas W. Richmond. Forth Worth, TX: Texas Christian University Press, 2000.

Soldier of the Pen: The Literary Careers of Richard Taylor, John Bell Hood, and W. H. Tunnard

Glenn Robins

Although Lost Cause writers and their works are aspects of a complex literary genre, historians, for the most part, have failed to provide a sophisticated analysis of how Confederates explained their war experience.[1] Specifically, historians have generally ignored the philosophical and intellectual framework around which Southerners understood and assigned meaning to the Civil War. Some early studies placed Confederate writings in such basic categories as biography, autobiography or reminiscences, unit histories, and apologia; the later included among its number those who were engaged in postwar controversies over strategies and tactics.[2] More recent studies have attempted to establish a causal link between the white Southerner's understanding and remembrance of the Civil War and the attitude of massive resistance that pervaded the region during the Jim Crow and Civil Rights eras.[3] In neither instance has appropriate attention been given to the literary tools, techniques, and schools of thought that Southerners used to construct their memory of the Civil War.

A more thorough study of Lost Cause literature will improve our understanding of Southern history in two important ways. The first would focus much needed attention on the postwar literary careers of former Confederate soldiers. The second would suggest that early Lost Cause writings were not simply the byproduct of an extreme form of sentimentalism, nor were they solely a function of the racist political culture of the New South. For this purpose the works of three former Confederate soldiers will be re-examined: Richard Taylor's *Destruction and Reconstruction: Personal Experience of the Late War*, originally published in 1879; John Bell Hood's *Advance and Retreat: Personal Experiences in the United States and Confederate States Armies*, originally published in 1880; and Will Tunnard's *A Southern Record: The History of the Third Regiment Louisiana Infantry*, originally published in 1866.[4]

The analytical framework for this re-examination is based on a number of broadly-defined working definitions. Thomas L. Connelly and Barbara Bellows have suggested that the Lost Cause is best understood as a literary movement, one that utilized two distinct approaches. The National Lost Cause represented a conscious effort on the part of Southern writers to explain 'the place of the South within the nation' and 'the meaning of the Confederate experience to outsiders as well as to Southerners.' The Inner Lost Cause represented a particular 'mentality' based on the adherent's belief that the South remained superior to the North 'in all standards of individual character.' According to Connelly and Bellows, this central theme of the Inner Lost Cause created a 'lasting bond between Confederate memory and southern piety.'[5] These definitions allow the observer to consider Lost Cause writings as a convergence of history and memory. This historicized or described past, while possibly lacking 'objectivity,' can nevertheless be traced to a stable epistemological framework and does not have to be viewed as an emotional or simplistic process.

Such an approach based on this hypothesis or theory postulates that some of the first generation of Lost Cause writers understood the Civil War and assigned meaning to its significance through a philosophical and artistic framework that had discernable ties to the values and epistemologies of the Enlightenment and the Romantic Movement. The coexistence of these perspectives may seem inconsistent since Romanticism is often considered a reaction against the Age of Reason. Consequently, a careful, specific, perhaps limited, definition of each term is critical to the applicability of the over-arching hypothesis. Defining the Enlightenment is not a simple task. As Peter Gay argues, 'to treat the Enlightenment as a compact body of doctrine, an Age of reason... is to strip the Enlightenment of its wealth' and true meaning. Enlightenment historians, Gay contends, were committed to securing 'rational control of the world' by supplying 'a coherent account of the motive power both within and among epochs.' They hoped to liberate history from 'the parochialism of Christian scholars and from theological presuppositions.' In addition, they rejected 'progressive' and 'cyclical' views of history, pursuing instead an approach that would ensure the triumph of reason over religious or theological superstition. History, therefore, was a quest for a useable past, a type of moral exercise that reinforces a distinctive cultural identity. The revival or recovery of classical humanism was an important part of this process. The Enlightened Humanist celebrated the man who 'was confident of his worth' and who 'faced life with courageous skepticism.' This Enlightenment ideal man also controlled his own 'moral universe.'[6]

Romantics valued individual experience and intuition, which was compatible with Enlightenment Humanism, although they denied that reason was the sole path to truth or knowledge. When viewed as a whole, the Romantic Movement, according to Rollin Osterweis, 'was a European literary and artistic effort to create a new set of values, made necessary by the intellectual, social, and political revolutions of the eighteenth century.' He further states that Romanticism 'had manifested itself in ancient times and in the Renaissance. It became a surging, self-conscious movement during a period of about a hundred years between the approximate dates 1760 and 1860. Its dynamic quality derived from its restless conviction that man was both creative and limited, a doer, and a sufferer, infinite in spirit and finite in action.'[7] In assigning meaning to their experiences and the events of the Civil War, the first generation of Lost Cause writers borrowed from both the Enlightenment and the Romantic Movement because each of these perspectives shared an emphasis on human agency. It should be noted that a third perspective could be included. Some literary critics and intellectual historians contend that Victorianism represented the transitional phase between the Age of Reason and modernism. Rather than explore the differences between Romanticism and Victorianism a definition of Victorianism will be proposed that will allow the two perspectives to be used interchangeably. In writing on American Victorianism and the Civil War, Anne Rose maintains that 'the Victorians no longer found traditional Christian concepts of personal and common purpose compelling... Thus the Victorians were romantics, not only in their search for intense experience, but in the stricter sense that made them a generation whose members approached society with questions raised by problems with faith... It was the Civil War, conceived as a struggle over profound issues, that convinced them that human effort even without clear supernatural references still had value.' It is therefore permissible to use Romanticism and Victorianism interchangeably when dealing with the notion of human agency, and with these definitions in mind we can proceed with a new assessment of how Confederate soldiers understood and explained their war experiences.[8]

Richard Taylor and the Great Man Theory

Son of President Zachary Taylor, Richard Taylor, according to the Civil War biographer and historian Douglas Southall Freeman, was 'the one Confederate general who possessed literary art that approached first rank.' Seemingly, Freeman's adoration of Taylor knew no limits. In fact, he suggested that in terms of 'mental power' the former general 'was one of the ablest sons of American Presidents' and 'had the beam of fate been tipped in the opposite direction, he probably would have... given the Taylor line... the continuing distinction that the Adamses won.' What impressed Freeman most about *Destruction and Reconstruction* was Taylor's keen analysis of individual characters. 'No firmer, more accurate pictures are to be found in Confederate literature,' Freeman observed, than Taylor's portraits of such Southern icons as Stonewall Jackson, Richard Ewell, and Robert E. Lee as well as 'others less renowned.'[9] Notwithstanding the importance of Freeman's accolades, the truth is Taylor's contemporaries recognized his literary gifts. Indeed, the demand for Taylor's *Destruction and*

Reconstruction was so great that classified advertisements appeared in the widely-circulated *Confederate Veteran* 26 years after its publication, instructing interested parties to contact the magazine's editor if they had additional copies of the book to sell.[10] Louisiana school children often cited Taylor's *Destruction and Reconstruction* in their class reports, some recognized the diversity of his literary interests and talents, and at least one student claimed that he 'cared more for books than for politics.'[11] Even as late as 1928, the Ruston, Louisiana, chapter of the United Confederate Veterans deemed Taylor's *Destruction and Reconstruction* as one of the canonical works produced by 'Southern writers who served the Confederacy.'[12] Each of these endorsements testifies to the enduring appeal of Taylor's book.

Readers appreciated Taylor's book for a variety of reasons, but one of the principal reasons was the colorful and penetrating character sketches that filled his war narrative. If character sketches were Taylor's literary forte, then his portrait of Confederate Vice President Alexander Stephens warrants closer inspection. The Georgian, Taylor commented, 'has an acute intellect attached to a frail and meager body. As was said by the witty Canon of St. Paul's of Francis Jeffrey, his mind is in a state of indecent exposure.' Prior to the war, Stephens had served in the United States House of Representatives and his 'device' or political compass, according to Taylor, was '*Fiat justitia, ruat coelum.*' Some of Taylor's animosity was of a personal nature. During the December 1849 contest for speaker of the House, Stephens, a Whig congressman, refused to support his party's candidate. His decision, in Taylor's mind, handed the leadership position of the House to the rival Democrats, which was certainly an unfortunate political setback for his Whig father. But there were other incidents that caused Taylor to view Stephens with contempt. As the sectional crisis erupted, Taylor explained, 'Mr. Stephens held and avowed moderate opinions; but, swept along by the resistless torrent surrounding him, he discovered and proclaimed that slavery was the corner-stone of the confederacy,' and 'as the struggle progressed, Mr. Stephens, with all the impartiality of an equity judge, marked many of the virtues of the Government north of the Potomac, and all the vices of that on his own side of the river.'[13]

Taylor also identified Stephens as the leader of the Richmond politicos, a cabal who exacerbated the Confederacy's military burden by interfering in areas where they had no expertise. Taylor was particularly outraged by the vice president's interpretation of the proper conventions of military discipline. Stephens' position was simple. He believed 'the war was for principles and rights, and it was in defense of these, as well as of their property, that the people had taken up arms. They could always be relied on when a battle was imminent; but, when no fighting was to be done, they had best be at home attending to their families and interests. As their intelligence was equal to their patriotism, they were capable of judging of the necessity of their presence with the colors as the commanders of armies.' To this form of military discipline, Taylor caustically opined: 'It may be observed that such opinions are more comfortably cherished by political gentlemen, two hundred miles away, than by commanders immediately in front of the enemy.' After the war, when Taylor was in Washington lobbying to have President Jefferson Davis released from prison he called on Stephens for assistance. 'I sought and found him sitting near a fire (for he is of a chilly nature), smoking his pipe,'

Taylor remembered, 'he heard me in severe politeness, and, without unnecessary expenditure of enthusiasm, promised his assistance. Since the war Mr. Stephens has again found a seat in the Congress, where, unlike the rebel brigadiers, his presence is not a rock of offense to the loyal mind.'[14]

The preceding sketch of Stephens first appeared in an article in the *North American Review* and was included in *Destruction and Reconstruction*. Taylor, however, used the publication of his book as a final opportunity to assail the former vice president. In a footnote, Taylor wrote of Stephens' postwar efforts to defend his public reputation: 'Like other ills, feeble health has its compensations, especially for those who unite restless vanity and ambition to a feminine desire for sympathy. It has been much the habit of Mr. Stephens to date controversial epistles from a 'sick chamber,' as do ladies in a delicate situation. A diplomatist of the last century, the Chevalier D'Eon by usurping the privileges of the opposite sex, inspired grave doubts concerning his own.'[15]

The imaginative tone and acerbic wit of Taylor's prose might compel the casual reader to conclude that the profile of Stephens was simply a function of political partisanship, petty bickering, and personality clashes. However, the final attack, calling into question Stephens' manhood, coupled with the previous aspersions on the vice president's character can actually be traced to Taylor's humanist-oriented worldview and value system. Specifically, Taylor held a philosophy of history remarkably similar to the British historian and essayist, Thomas Carlyle. In *On Heroes, Hero-Worship, and the Heroic in History*, Carlyle had proposed that 'in all epochs of the world's history, we shall find the Great Man to have been the indispensable saviour of his epoch... the History of the World... [is] the Biography of Great Men... and what is notable, in no time whatever can they entirely eradicate out of living men's hearts a certain altogether peculiar reverence for Great Men.' To the question what distinguishes the Great Man, Carlyle responded: 'I should say *sincerity*, a deep, great, genuine sincerity, is the first characteristic of all men in any way heroic.' He defined sincerity as 'the exercise of private judgment, faithfully gone about' and added that 'insincerity, half-belief and untruth' produce 'anarchy.' Carlyle further argued that 'the believing man is the original man; whatsoever he believes, he believes it for himself, not for another. Every son of Adam can become a sincere man... in this sense.'[16] If Taylor shared Carlyle's view of history, then his criticism of Stephens was designed to show that the Georgian's fatal flaw was that he lacked sincerity. Stephens' lack of commitment to the Whig party during the Taylor presidency, the Confederate cause, and the ease with which he reconciled with the enemies of the South after the war, demonstrated that Stephens was a man who lacked sincerity.

To understand fully Taylor's adherence to Carlyle's Great Man theory, it is necessary to consider his assessment of Union Major General George B. McClellan. Taylor believed the Napoleonic era held the key to understanding the 'few and unchangeable' principles upon which 'the art of war is based.' He attached great significance to the organization of armies and the strategy and tactics introduced by these combatants during this pivotal moment in world history. Prior to 1861, the United States had never mobilized on a scale that matched the Napoleonic era. Interestingly, Taylor wrote: 'the entire [United States] force engaged in the war with Mexico would scarcely have made a respectable corps d' armie' [sic] in the epic struggle that consumed Europe in the early nineteenth century. This judgment is noteworthy because the Mexican War was the platform on which Taylor's father emerged as an American military-political hero. In the half-century that followed the Napoleonic wars, significant advances in weaponry had taken place, particularly in the areas of field artillery and breech-loading firearms. 'All this,' Taylor maintained, 'must be considered in determining the value of McClellan's work. Taking the raw material intrusted [sic] to him, he converted it into a great military machine, complete in all its parts, fitted for its intended purpose. Moreover, he resisted the natural impatience of his Government and people, and the follies of politicians and newspapers, and for months refused to put his machine at work before all its delicate adjustments were perfected.'

Taylor acknowledged that the performance of the Army of the Potomac in battle had proved a disappointment under McClellan's command. It had also suffered 'painful defeat[s]' in the hands of his successors. However, McClellan's army 'always recovered, showed itself a vital organism, and finally triumphed.' Taylor's praise of the maligned Union general was profound: 'McClellan organized victory for his section, and those who deem the preservation of the "Union" the first of earthly duties should not cease to do him reverence. I have here written of McClellan, not as a leader, but an organizer of armies; and as such he deserves to rank with the Von Moltkes, Scharnhorsts, and Louvois of history.' Yet Taylor seemed to have held a special appreciation for the personal integrity or *sincerity* exhibited by McClellan in the face of a 'constant struggle against the fatal interference of politicians with his military plans and duties.' And the defeated Confederate paid the conquering Yankee the ultimate tribute when he remarked: 'General McClellan is an upright, patriotic man, incapable of wrong-doing, and has a high standard of morality, to which, he lives more closely than most men do to a lower one... Above all, he and a gallant band of officers supporting him impressed a generous, chivalric spirit on the war, which soon faded away; and the future historian, in recounting some later operations, will doubt if he is dealing with campaigns of generals or expeditions of brigands.'[17]

The Alexander Stephens–George McClellan comparison is revealing, but what is conceivably the most compelling example of Taylor's commitment to a humanist epistemology and the Great Man theory is his discussion of the gunboat battles that occurred during the famed Vicksburg campaign of 1863. In chronicling the Confederate capture of the Union gunboat the *Queen of the West*, Taylor utilized the concepts of human agency, purposeful action, and sincerity to identify the obscure Confederate soldier as a sincere man.

In his prefatory remarks on the gunboat engagements, the general portrayed himself and the Confederate soldiers stationed along the Mississippi River as men convinced of man's superiority to machines. Conversely, he mocked those Southerners, civilian or otherwise, who trembled at the sight and sound of the Yankees' alleged mechanical ingenuity:

> It is curious to recall the ideas prevailing in the first years of the war about gunboats. To the wide-spread terror inspired by them may be ascribed the loss of Fort Donelson and New Orleans. *Omne ignotum pro magnifico*; and it was popularly believed that the destructive powers of these monsters were not to be resisted. Time proved that the

lighter class of boats, called 'tin-clads,' were helpless against field guns, while heavy iron-clads could be driven off by riflemen protected by the timber and levees along streams. To fire ten-inch guns at skirmishers, widely disposed and under cover, was very like snipe-shooting with twelve-pounders; and in narrow waters gunboats required troops on shore for their protection.

Taylor and his men had occasion to test the Louisianan's so-called theory of gunboat warfare in February 1863, when the Federal gunboat *Queen of the West* slipped past the batteries at Vicksburg, causing a great deal of concern amongst the city's residents.[18]

Taylor intended to use a Confederate tow-boat, the *Webb*, 'as a ram and attempt the destruction of the *Queen*.' However, the anticipated duel never occurred. Instead, a Confederate battery on the banks of the Red River at De Russy opened fire and hit the *Queen*. The damage was not extensive, a steam pipe and tiller rope were cut, but the crew did abandon ship, appearing to validate Taylor's maxims on 'snipe-shooting.' But, as Taylor recalled, 'we had barely time to congratulate ourselves on the capture of the *Queen* before the appearance of the *Indianola* deprived us again of the navigation of the great river, so vital to our cause. To attempt the destruction of such a vessel as the *Indianola* with our limited means seemed madness; yet volunteers for the work promptly offered themselves.' The first order of business was to repair the captured *Queen* so that it could enter Confederate service to face the new threat posed by the *Indianola*. Taylor recollected how quickly the Confederates made the necessary repairs and were prepared to go on the attack, with one notable exception. There was 'difficulty' securing stokers. According to Taylor:

> Some planters from the upper Red River had brought down their slaves to De Russy to labor on earthworks, but they positively refused to furnish stokers for the boats. It was a curious feature of the war that the Southern people would cheerfully send their sons to battle, but kept their slaves out of danger. Having exhausted his powers of persuasion to no purpose, Major Brent threw some men ashore, surrounded a gang of Negroes at work, captured the number necessary, and departed. A famous din was made by the planters, and continued until their Negroes were safely returned.

Taylor's criticism of the slaveholding elite owed nothing to class antagonism. During his early adulthood, Taylor managed his father's cotton plantation in Jefferson County, Mississippi and later inherited 'Fashion,' a large sugar plantation in St. Charles Parish, Louisiana, which possessed a labor force of nearly 200 slaves. Taylor's criticism was a by-product of his Enlightenment orientation and his commitment to the principles of eighteenth century military professionalism. In this specific instance, the lack of sincerity or commitment exhibited by the slaveholding elite would not deter Taylor and his charges from accomplishing their objective.[19]

On the night of 24 February, the Confederates spotted the *Indianola* in the vicinity of the mouth of the Red River. Under the cover of darkness, the *Queen* approached to a point approximately 150 yards away before opening fire on the *Indianola*. Then, in the most intense moment of the confrontation:

> the *Queen*, followed by the *Webb*, was driven with full head of steam directly upon her [*Indianola*]... The momentum of the *Queen* was so great as to cut through the coal barrage and indent the iron plates of the Indianola, disabling by the shock the

engine that worked her paddles. As the *Queen* backed out the *Webb* dashed in at full speed, and tore away the remaining coal barge... Returning to the charge, the *Queen* struck the Indianola abaft the paddle box, crushing her frame and loosening some plates of armor, but received the fire of the guns from the rear casemates... Again the *Webb* followed the *Queen*, struck near the same spot, pushing aside the iron plates and crushing timbers. Voices from the *Indianola* announced the surrender, and that she was sinking.

The Confederates did in fact capture and sabotage the *Indianola*. The combined success of this action coupled with the capture of the *Queen of the West* allowed the Confederates to retain, temporarily at least, control of the Mississippi River between Vicksburg and Port Hudson. In a bit of hyperbole, Taylor believed the bold and 'daring' efforts of the Confederates during this campaign would 'bare comparisons with any recorded of Nelson or Dundonald.' He regretted that 'succeeding events at Vicksburg and Gettysburg' had 'obscured' the heroic deeds of the men, especially the common soldiers, under his command, and thus 'in justice to the officers and men engaged' Taylor deemed it his personal 'duty to recount' their exploits.[20]

On the one hand, Taylor's comparison of the Confederate naval operations on the Mississippi River to those of Horatio Nelson and Thomas Cochrane, 10th Earl of Dundonald, could deservedly be characterized as the fanciful musings of an arrogant Southerner. After all, Nelson is often recognized as Great Britain's greatest naval hero. Dundonald too served with distinction during the Napoleonic wars, and then had a second career as a freedom fighter, serving most notably with the Chilean navy in their successful bid to win independence from Spain. Yet, Taylor's artistic imagination, or exaggeration, might legitimately be viewed as a byproduct of his humanist epistemology.

As a Lost Cause writer, Taylor's intention was to place the Southern struggle for independence within the broader context of world history. In so doing, he created a historicized past that associated greatness (and Great Men) with purposeful action in defense of a cause. One might argue that in terms of writing style and epistemology Taylor resembled the 'Victorian Sage' of the mid and late nineteenth century. This writer-philosopher was concerned with expressing 'notions about the world, man's situation in it, and how he should live.' To answer these 'ultimate questions,' they often derived their answers from 'imagination rather than logic.' As a Victorian Sage, Thomas Carlyle used language as an emotive force, and 'some of his arguments and assertions are less factual than verbal.' His desire was to provide answers that each individual could 'read' from their 'own heart, from a felt indubitable certainty of experience.' In addition, his purpose – as was the case with all the Victorian Sages – was to assert that 'conviction comes... essentially from modifying the readers perceptiveness, from stimulating him to notice something to which he was previously blind.' Here, meaning and knowledge became a 'mystic act' related to individual experience.[21] In the gunboat battles, Major J. L. Brent, Captain E. W. Fuller, their respective crews, and the members of assorted artillery companies emerged as Great Men of history. Taylor demonstrated that ordinary men Brent, 'the lawyer by profession,' and Fuller, the simple 'western steamboat man,' offered a stark contrast to the Southern politicians and large slaveholders who placed self-preservation and economic interests above the Confederate military effort.

Taylor, as would be expected, identified Robert E. Lee and Stonewall Jackson as two of the Confederacy's Great Men. But what is often overlooked in the Louisianan's writings was his willingness to identify the obscure, the neglected Confederate soldier, as a sincere man. In chronicling the Confederate capture of the Union gunboat the *Queen of the West*, Taylor drew attention to these lesser-known figures. His intention was to remind the reader of past experiences. Indeed, Taylor admitted that the Confederate failures at Gettysburg and Vicksburg were of greater strategic significance than the gunboat victories. But Taylor's ultimate desire was to alert Southerners to historical examples that would illustrate a life-philosophy based on resistance and endurance. Similarly, he used the examples of Alexander Stephens and George McClellan to illustrate the observable or 'lived' characteristics of the Great Man. The Confederate vice president, of course, actually served as a foil; his physical declension ('frail and meager body,' 'chilly nature,' 'feeble health,' 'feminine desire for sympathy') was a metaphor for his moral failings. Conversely, the unappreciated Union general embodied the same qualities (patriotic, gallant, chivalric, 'incapable of wrong doing') as the more easily identifiable and accessible Great Men, Lee, and Jackson. In typical Carlylean fashion, Taylor used the Stephens-McClellan juxtaposition – their respective profiles appear sequentially in *Destruction and Reconstruction*, as the transition from First Manassas to the Peninsular Campaign – as a type of paradox to distinguish between the 'real' and the 'sham,' the 'true' and the 'false' man.[22]

John Bell Hood and the Ethics of War

In terms of personal suffering and loss, few individual experiences of the Civil War era are more tragic than that of John Bell Hood. His military career began at the United States Military Academy where he graduated in 1853; his class of cadets included Philip Sheridan and John Schofield. After graduation he served in Missouri and California before joining the elite 2nd Cavalry Regiment in Texas. Like many Southerners and quite a few Kentuckians, Hood resigned from the U.S. Army in order to fight for the Confederacy. He rose steadily through the officer ranks and in time came to command one of the finest brigades in the Army of Northern Virginia. Tragedy first visited Hood at the Battle of Gettysburg where he received a serious wound in his left arm that required two months of convalescence and deprived him of full use of his arm. At the Battle of Chickamauga Hood was shot in the upper right thigh, an injury that forced doctors to amputate his leg. Despite the seriousness of his wounds, Hood was given command of the Army of Tennessee in July 1864. His first setback as commander came in September of that year when General William T. Sherman forced him to evacuate Atlanta; this was followed by two disastrous defeats in Tennessee, the first at Franklin and the second at Nashville in December 1864. When the war ended a few months later, Hood moved to New Orleans. There, he engaged in a number of commercial activities, and married Anna Marie Hennen, the eldest daughter of a prominent Crescent City family. Apparently Hood was well-suited to fatherhood; he and his wife had 11 children, including three sets of twins. Then, in August 1879, a yellow fever epidemic swept through New Orleans, first killing Hood's wife and eldest daughter and then the general himself. He left behind ten orphans, a vivid reminder of his own tragic life and that of the Confederacy.[23]

Just a few months before his death, Hood completed *Advance and Retreat*, the account of his military service in the United States and Confederate armies. Unlike Taylor's *Destruction and Reconstruction*, which used lessons and examples from history to present a life-philosophy rooted in sincerity and human agency, Hood's *Advance and Retreat* was part of an unfortunate category of Lost Cause writings known as *apologia*. In fact, Hood admitted that his purpose in writing *Advance and Retreat* was to refute the 'most unjust strictures, passed upon me by General [Joseph E.] Johnston.' Johnston had recently published his own memoirs in an attempt to recover his good name and in the process had cast dispersions on Hood. Except for the opening chapters where Hood actually demonstrates some literary talent, *Advance and Retreat* reads like a legal brief. Yet even in these sections, we are able to catch a glimpse of Hood's philosophical and intellectual frame of reference.

Perhaps the most useful section in this regard is his debate with William Sherman concerning the evacuation of Atlanta.[24] After negotiating the terms for the evacuation of Atlanta, Hood exchanged communiqués with his Yankee nemesis. These letters, printed in their entirety in *Advance and Retreat*, addressed the nature of the warfare Sherman was conducting, with a particular focus on the displacement of Southern civilians. With the aggressiveness that he normally demonstrated on the battlefield, Hood declared: 'the unprecedented measure you propose transcends, in studied and ingenious cruelty, all acts ever before brought to my attention in the dark history of war. In the name of God and humanity, I protest.'[25]

Hood's accusations enraged Sherman, and the Union general quickly demonstrated that he was not only the superior warrior but was also the superior wordsmith. 'In the name of common sense,' Sherman replied, 'I ask you not to appeal to a just God in such a sacrilegious manner. You who, in the midst of peace and prosperity, have plunged a nation into war – dark and cruel war.' The Yankee commander further charged that the South had 'dared and badgered' the North into battle, by insulting the U. S. flag, seizing federal arsenals and forts, and by making 'prisoners of war' out of the Federal garrisons assigned to protect Southerners from the 'Negroes and Indians.' Sherman then proposed: 'If we must be enemies, let us be men, and fight it out as we propose to do and not deal in such hypocritical appeals to God and humanity. God will judge us in due time, and he will pronounce whether it be more humane to fight with a town full of women and the families of a brave people at our back, or to remove them in time to places of safety among their friends and people.'

In the same letter, Sherman also provided a reasoned but passionate explanation of his actions. He contended that the measures were not 'unprecedented' or unparalleled in the history of warfare, or, for that matter, the current conflict between the North and South. 'General Johnston himself,' Sherman suggested, 'very wisely and properly removed families all the way from Dalton down, and I see no reason why Atlanta should be excepted.' Furthermore, the Union general accused Hood of defending

'Atlanta on a line so close to town that every cannon shot and many musket shots from our line of investment, that overshot their mark, went into the habitations of women and children. General [William J.] Hardee did the same at Jonesboro', and General Johnston did the same last summer in Jackson, Mississippi.' If necessary, Sherman believed that he could 'enumerate hundreds of others [cases], and challenge any fair man to judge which of us has the heart of pity for families of a brave people.'[26]

Hood was not persuaded by Sherman's arguments and in fact refuted them point by point. There was nothing, Hood maintained, that 'gives the least color to your unfounded aspersions upon his [Johnston's] conduct. He depopulated no villages nor towns, nor cities, either friendly or hostile.' Regarding Hardee and himself, Hood retorted, 'Hardee defended his position in front of Jonesboro' at the expense of injury to the houses; an ordinary, proper, and justifiable act of war. I defended Atlanta at the same risk and cost. If there was any fault, in either case, it was your own, in not giving notice, especially in the case of Atlanta, of your purpose to shell the town, which is usual in war among civilized nations.' With respect to the causes of the war, Hood contended 'The truth is, we sent commissioners to you, respectfully offering a peaceful separation, before the first gun was fired on either side.' To the charge of imprisoning Federal military personnel, Hood argued, 'the truth is, we, by force of arms drove out insolent intruders and took possession of our own forts and arsenals, to resist your claims to do minion over masters, slaves, and Indians, all of whom are to this day, with unanimity unexplained in the history of the world, warring against your attempts to become their masters.' The Confederate general then introduced a comparison of his own: '[General Benjamin F.] Butler only banished from New Orleans the registered enemies of his Government, and acknowledged that he did it as a punishment. You issue a sweeping edict, covering all the inhabitants of a city.' As for Sherman's challenge to 'fight it out like men,' Hood wrote, 'my reply is – for myself, and I believe for all the true men, ay, and women and children, in my country – we will fight you to death! Better die a thousand deaths than submit to live under you or your Government and your Negro allies!'[27]

Whereas Hood was not able to subdue Sherman on the field of battle, he did compel his nemesis to retreat from their rhetorical skirmish. In retiring, Sherman simply remarked: 'We have no "negro allies" in this Army' and 'I was not bound by the laws of war to give notice of the shelling of Atlanta, a "fortified town, with magazines, arsenals, foundries, and public stores": you were bound to take notice. See the books. This is the conclusion of our correspondence, which I did not begin, and terminate with satisfaction.'[28]

Following the war, Hood accepted Sherman's challenge to 'see the books' and when he published *Advance and Retreat* additional commentary appeared on this enduring controversy. It is in this postwar commentary that Hood revealed the philosophical underpinnings of his value system. Upon further reflection, Hood admitted that 'extreme war measures' would have been warranted if Atlanta had been a 'regularly fortified city.' According to Hood, fortifications were classified as either temporary or permanent. 'The latter,' he explained, 'are constructed of the best material, iron, and stone, with parapet, deep and wide ditch and glacis, similar to the fortifications on Governor's

Island, and those of Fortress Monroe.' Sherman during the war as well as in his postwar memoir claimed that Atlanta qualified as a fortified town with arsenals and machine shops and the capacity to endure a siege of at least a year, possibly longer. Hood disagreed. He insisted that Sherman was deluded if he believed the 'dilapidated foundry, near the Augusta road' was capable of sustaining the city during a siege. Moreover, Hood declared that 'extreme war measures were not a necessity' because he had abandoned the city as per their agreement. At this point in the narrative, Hood turned to such political and military theorists as Hugo Grotius, Sir William Napier, Union general Henry W. Halleck, and most notably the Swiss jurist Emerich de Vattel to validate his arguments.[29]

By selecting Grotius, Hood expressed a willingness to address the moral or ethical dimensions of his debate with Sherman. Grotius was an early eighteenth century Dutch humanist, principally known for his theories of natural law but was also recognized for his work on the international laws of war and issues of peace and justice. Generally speaking, Grotius rejected Calvinist theology that identified God and divine truth as the only governors of human activity. He believed that reason invested the conscience with the power to make ethical decisions.[30] Hood discovered in Grotius' works a maxim that he believed could be cited to counter Sherman's hard war policies: 'It is a just remark made by some theologians, that all Christian princes and rulers who wish to be found such in the sight of God, as well as that of men, will deem it a duty to interpose their authority to prevent or suppress all unnecessary violence in the taking of terms, for acts of rigor can never be carried to an extreme without involving great numbers of the innocent in ruin; and practices of that kind, beside being no way conducive to the termination of war, are totally repugnant to every principle of Christianity and justice.'[31] Ironically, Sherman would have agreed with the fundamentals of Grotius' theology. As one historian has explained, Sherman 'did not believe that God was molding events in response to human petition, conduct, or spiritual state. In his mind the war did not obey the participants; they obeyed it' as such 'war was a natural phenomenon, guided by nature's laws which God had created but which operated with the consistency of mathematics, not by God's mere fiat.'[32] However, it is highly unlikely that Hood's particular example would have resonated or had any meaningful impact on Sherman. Whether Hood realized this or not is somewhat immaterial because only one of his ten examples relied on the principles of the Christian-oriented just war theory.

In addition to the one quotation from Grotius, there were two from Napier, one from Halleck, but six from Vattel. Each of the references to Vattel carried the same basic message: 'Women, children, feeble old men, and sick persons, come under the description of enemies; and we have certain rights over them, inasmuch as they belong to the nation with whom we are at war, and as, between nation and nation, all rights and pretensions affect the body of society, together with all its members. But these are enemies who make no resistance; and consequently we have no right to maltreat their persons, or use any violence against them... This is so plain a maxim of justice and humanity that at present every nation, in the least degree civilized, acquiesces.'[33] What is significant about Hood's repeated use of Vattel is that it suggests Hood's understanding of the war was firmly rooted in the mentality of the Enlightenment. As military historian Christopher Duffy remarks 'Vattel not only synthesised the views of earlier writers on the subject... he spoke with the authentic voice of the Age of Reason concerning the ways in which war ought to be conducted,' and central to the Vattel conduct of war was the notion of honor.[34]

Generally speaking, the officer class during the Age of Reason 'was strongly influenced by the dictates of honour, which were often eccentric and selfish in the ways they were expressed, but furnished the officers with a code of values independently of the state.' Duffy further notes that 'honour was a principle which for many gentlemen stood in no firm relation to morality.' Hood had accused Sherman of lacking honor and of refusing to follow the ethical guidelines of warfare formulated by seventeenth and eighteenth century military theorists. In the specific case of siege warfare the accepted constraints were that the noncombatants were 'usually spared the final ordeal of seeing their town stormed and sacked by the besiegers.' Furthermore, once 'the besiegers had it in their power to storm into town' the two sides adopted 'the principle of 'exchange' [and] the outcome was a negotiated capitulation' and safeguards were often granted to the citizens so that a 'free evacuation' could transpire. Duffy's summary of the rules of siege warfare help to demonstrate that Hood attempted to build his case against Sherman by using a code of military professionalism drawn from the Enlightenment. It is true that Hood revisited the Atlanta issue in an effort to repair his public reputation, but his writings represent something more than the rantings of a humiliated soldier. Indeed, Hood, Richard Taylor, and W. H. Tunnard are examples of Southern writers who understood the Civil War and assigned meaning to its events and their experiences based on a philosophical or intellectual framework that was not tied directly to the political exigencies of the New South.

Will Tunnard and War Realism

Will Tunnard was the youngest son of a rather prominent artisan of Baton Rouge, Louisiana. His father's business success afforded him an excellent education. In fact, Tunnard graduated from Ohio's Kenyon College in 1856, but returned to Baton Rouge after graduating to work in his father's carriage business. Tunnard, his brothers, and his father were all original members of the Pelican Rifles, an East Baton Rouge militia company formed in the aftermath of John Brown's raid on Harper's Ferry, Virginia in 1859. Despite his impressive pedigree, Tunnard never exceeded the rank of sergeant. During the war, he served with Company K of the 3rd Louisiana Infantry. His wartime experiences began in 1861 with the capture of the Baton Rouge Arsenal and ended with the surrender of his unit in Shreveport in 1865. Just 15 months after the surrender at Shreveport, Tunnard completed *A Southern Record: The History of the Third Regiment Louisiana Infantry*. It is a unique book in that it is based on a meticulously maintained journal that Tunnard kept during the war. In certain sections, such as the rather lengthy section on the siege of Vicksburg, the text has the style and tone of a diary, which is a stark contrast to the fluid prose of other portions of the book. Finally, Tunnard became an active participant in the various activities and celebrations of the Lost Cause movement, highlighted by his election as major general of the Louisiana Division of the United Confederate Veterans in the 1890s.[35]

Tunnard provided a literary reference point for this war narrative by inserting a stanza from a Henry Wadsworth Longfellow poem on the cover page of his book:

> Let us then be up and doing,
> With a heart for every fate,
> Still achieving, still pursuing,
> Learn to labor and to wait.[36]

This is the ninth and final stanza of Longfellow's widely popular 'A Psalm of Life.' The poem is a simple, but poignant, reminder of both an individual's societal responsibility and the power of the human spirit. In a critique of the stanza quoted by Tunnard, Richard Ruland, and Malcolm Bradbury have remarked that 'here… Romanticism merges with sentimental optimism and moral uplift to give that familiar poem its striving, cautiously spiritual note… [the poem] intones a confident voice that distills the strenuous moral truths of an earlier time to touch the hearts of countless unsophisticated readers.'[37] Tunnard used Longfellow's wisdom as a way to recount, interpret, and assign meaning to the 'cherished memory of the revered dead, and the undaunted gallantry of the… officers and men, of the THIRD REGIMENT LOUISIANA INFANTRY.' As Tunnard embarks on this epistemological journey, two themes seem to mark his course: the level of commitment (sincerity) of the Confederate soldier and the horrors of war.[38]

'Creole and American, Celt and Gaul, old and young, rich and poor, all were ready for the fray,' Tunnard explained, 'thousands… went forth to peril life and limbs in defence of cherished principles.' We were 'an isolated regiment amid Arkansas and Missouri troops, each member felt as if in his individual person was concentrated the honor and fair name of Louisiana – a feeling which undoubtedly contributed largely to their subsequent deeds of valor and unconquerable determination never to yield to the foe.'[39] According to Tunnard, the Battle of Oak Hills in southwest Missouri [also known as the Battle of Wilson's Creek, 10 August 1861] was the 3rd Louisiana's 'first initiation into the scenes of the bloody drama of the war.' Tunnard was concerned that too many Southerners had 'viewed' the war 'from the standpoint of the peaceful home circle, with its surroundings of happy and loved faces, and comforts and conveniences of life.' As such, they had been shielded from 'that hideous deformity which environs [war's] dread reality.' The Kenyon College graduate felt compelled to provide a vivid portrait of the scenes that he encountered as a corrective to any false memory of the war:

> The battle of Oak Hills enlightened many ignorant minds as to the seriousness and fearful certainty of the contest. It did not, however, unnerve a single arm to strike a fresh blow, or dampen the ardor of a single heart. It proved thoroughly the dashing bravery of the Southern soldiers, contending under every disadvantage against almost inevitable defeat, and taught the enemy also a severe lesson of what the future contained. So sudden and unexpected the attack, so close, terrible and obstinate the contest, that numbers thought the day irretrievably lost and gave up in hopeless despair. Not so with the Louisianians, who *never for an instant felt that they were whipped*. Through the thickest and hottest of the fight, where shot and shell fell fastest, and the rifles poured their storm of leaden hail, the regiment forced its way charging the foe with loud cheers, and always driving them from their positions. For more than six hours the desperate conflict continued, beneath the cloudless sky and in the sultry atmosphere of an August day.

The tone here was momentarily sentimental, but Tunnard was not a sentimentalist and his literary technique was to use his post-battle reflections to convey the harsh realities of war:

> Early Sunday morning, [the day after the battle of Oak Hills] Sergt. W. H. Tunnard, of Co. K, was detailed as sergeant of a large force to finish the burial of the enemy's dead. Armed with shovel, pick-axe and spade, the detail proceeded to the principal point of the battle-field to complete this mournful task, which the enemy, unable to accomplish, had abandoned in despair. The ground was still thickly strewn with the ghastly and mangled forms. Fifty-three bodies were placed in a single grave, all gathered within the compass of one hundred yards. These were hastily covered with brush and stones, when the detail precipitately departed. The effluvia from the swollen, festering, blackened forms, already covered with worms was too horrible for human endurance. Hundreds unburied were left food for the worms, fowls, and beast of the earth. No conception of the imagination, no power of human language could do justice to such a horrible scene.[40]

At this point, one might easily associate the above passages – and several others, most notably Tunnard's discussion of the siege of Vicksburg – with two types of war writers of the late nineteenth and early twentieth centuries. The first would be the war realist, who did not avoid the savage, the grotesque, or glamour-less images of the war. His technique and style also resembled those used by some British veterans who had experienced in 1916 the horrors of the Somme. Indeed, the routine-ness of death, the mangled and butchered corpses, and the disregard for the dignity of a fallen warrior, at first glance seem representative of the modernist's memory of the Great War.[41]

There are some interesting parallels. In distinguishing between the 'home circle' and the battlefield, Tunnard seems to suggest that there were two different categories of experience and understanding, especially when it came to death.[42] Yet, unlike a number of British soldiers who entered the Great War with a Victorian value system only to jettison it as a function of their modernist disillusionment, Tunnard retained his ideological and philosophical bearings. Although Tunnard claimed that 'human language' was inadequate for describing the reality of war, his vivid prose was a serious attempt at explaining his experiences and comprehension of the war. In fact, he concluded *A Southern Record* by adapting Longfellow's wisdom to the Civil War and the Southern experience:

> Who and what were these men? Let us answer. The members of the Third Louisiana Infantry were principally men of high social standing at home; intelligent, refined, young, the fires of youth glowing in their stalwart forms. Voluntarily offering their services to their country, they were actuated by a firm conviction of the justice of their cause. From workshop and counter, from cottage and mansion, from the lordly plantation and the crowded city, they came, standing side by side in defence of a common cause. Look at them; the fire of a fixed determination glowing in their clear, bright eyes, the strength of a settled purpose evinced in their firm tread and upright carriage... They are neither despondent nor despairing, but work with alacrity and cheerfulness to repair the many ravages of the conflict. Such are the positions of men who gave fortunes, staked their lives on the issue of war. The heroism displayed in accepting defeat is not less praise-worthy than their undaunted bearing in the deadly battle-field.[43]

For Tunnard, war was part of the human experience, a testing ground for the Great Men of history, and in his mind, the South had produced men worthy of emulation. In this tribute, Tunnard had replicated an additional stanza (the seventh) from Longfellow's 'A Psalm of Life.' 'Lives of great men all remind us/We can make our lives sublime,/And, departing, leave behind us/Footsteps on the sands of time.'

Conclusion

The recent trend has been to explain Civil War memory as a type of cultural competition between three distinct visions: the reconciliationist view, the white supremacist view, and the emancipationist view. Southern writers have most often been depicted as having produced a history of the war that validated white supremacy, the content of which was of little concern to those who favored rapid, regional reconciliation.[44] Without question, the Jim Crow South was built on white supremacy. But are we to conclude that Lost Cause writers were the principal architects of these racist doctrines or should such 'isms' as radical agrarianism, Social Darwinism, and scientific racism be identified as the ideological underpinnings of the Jim Crow system? Moreover, the Soldiers of the Pen – Richard Taylor, John Bell Hood, and W. H. Tunnard – shared a common commitment to a humanist and Romantic perspective that celebrated the value of human effort and potential. Their philosophical and ideological framework was not tied directly to the political exigencies of the New South or the evangelical religious beliefs of the region. Theirs was grounded in the secular values of the Enlightenment. Accordingly, they believed that despite the disasters of the Civil War human effort could influence, even shape the course of history, in sharp contrast to Sigfried Sasson and Wilfred Owen. By studying the past, the Soldiers of the Pen had embarked on a type of moral exercise designed to discover higher truths. The lesson they learned, or at least the lesson that they wanted to pass on to subsequent generations, was that Confederates were *sincere* men who lived by a reasoned and ordered societal code which was not destroyed by defeat. Quite the contrary, when the Rebel yelled he shouted for a South that had survived the travails of an Athenian tragedy. For the disciples of the Lost Cause, the Confederacy had become a protagonist for the entire world to emulate. This historicized past may not be 'objective' history, but it was nevertheless constructed within epistemological frameworks.

Notes

[1] Wilson, *Baptized in Blood*; Gaines Foster, *Ghosts of the Confederacy*. Each of these works focuses heavily on monument building and public celebrations.
[2] Freeman, *The South to Posterity*.
[3] Bailey, 'The Textbooks of the 'Lost Cause': Censorship and the Creation of Southern History'; Bailey, 'Mildred Lewis Rutherford and the Patrician Cult of the Old South'; Cox, 'Women, the Lost Cause, and the New South.'
[4] Taylor, *Destruction and Reconstruction*; Hood, *Advance and Retreat*; Tunnard, *A Southern Record*.
[5] Connelly and Bellows, *God and General Longstreet*, 5, 21, 38.
[6] Gay, *The Enlightenment*, 33–7, 261.

[7] Osterweis, *Romanticism and Nationalism in the Old South*, 237.
[8] See Rose, *Victorian America and the Civil War*, 4–5
[9] Freeman, *The South to Posterity*, 85–7.
[10] *Confederate Veteran* 24 (August 1916): 382.
[11] Essay #151, essay #250, in United Daughters of the Confederacy Papers, Louisiana Historical Association Collection, Joseph Merrick Jones Hall, Tulane University, New Orleans.
[12] *Confederate Veteran* 36 (April 1928): 152.
[13] Taylor, *Destruction and Reconstruction*, 21–2; lower case 'c' in the original.
[14] Ibid., 22–3.
[15] Ibid., 23.
[16] Carlyle, *On Heroes, Hero-Worship and the Heroic in History*, 13–14, 45, 125–6.
[17] Ibid., 25–8.
[18] Taylor, *Destruction and Reconstruction*, 118.
[19] Ibid., 122–4.
[20] Ibid., 125.
[21] Holloway, *The Victorian Sage*, 1, 4, 41. Holloway's Victorian Sages included Thomas Carlyle, Benjamin Disraeli, George Eliot, John Henry Newman, and Thomas Hardy.
[22] For Carlyle's use of paradox and truism see ibid., 50–57.
[23] McMurry, *John Bell Hood and the War for Southern Independence*.
[24] Hood, *Advance and Retreat*, 69; Johnston, *Narrative of Military Operations*.
[25] John B. Hood to William T. Sherman, 9 September 1864, in ibid., 230.
[26] Sherman to Hood, 10 September 1864, in ibid., 231–2.
[27] Hood to Sherman, 12 September 1864, in ibid., 232–5.
[28] Sherman to Hood, 14 September 1864, in ibid., 235–6.
[29] Hood, *Advance and Retreat*, 236–7.
[30] Dumbauld, *The Life and Legal Writings of Hugo Grotius*.
[31] Hood, *Advance and Retreat*, 239.
[32] Royster, *The Destructive War*, 269–70.
[33] Hood, *Advance and Retreat*, 239.
[34] Duffy, *The Military Experience in the Age of Reason*, 297.
[35] Tunnard, *A Southern Record*, ix–xxviii.
[36] See cover page in ibid.
[37] Ruland and Bradbury, *From Puritanism to Postmodernism*, 108.
[38] See dedication page in ibid.
[39] Ibid., 4, 23.
[40] The Oak Hills quotations are in ibid., 37–9.
[41] I have in mind here comparisons with the works of Edmund Blunden, Robert Graves, Wilfred Owen, and Siegfried Sassoon. For an overview of their writings and relevant excerpts see Fussell, *The Great War and Modern Memory*.
[42] Booth, *Postcards from the Trenches*.
[43] Tunnard, *A Southern Record*, 313–14
[44] Blight, *Race and Reunion*.

References

Bailey, Fred Arthur. 'The Textbooks of the "Lost Cause": Censorship and the Creation of Southern History.' *Georgia Historical Quarterly* 75 Fall 1991: 507–33.
———. 'Mildred Lewis Rutherford and the Patrician Cult of the Old South.' *Georgia Historical Quarterly* 77 (Fall 1994): 509–35.
Blight, David. *Race and Reunion: The Civil War in American Memory*. Cambridge, MA: Harvard University Press, 2001.

Booth, Allyson. *Postcards from the Trenches: Negotiating Space between Modernism and the First World War.* New York: Oxford University Press, 1996.

Carlyle, Thomas. *On Heroes, Hero-Worship and the Heroic in History.* [1841] reprint New York: T. Y. Crowell, 1969.

Connelly, Thomas, and Barbara Bellows. *God and General Longstreet: The Lost Cause and the Southern Mind.* Baton Rouge: Louisiana State University Press, 1982.

Cox, Karen. 'Women, the Lost Cause, and the New South: The United Daughters of the Confederacy and the Transmission of Confederate Culture, 1894–1919.' Ph.D. diss., University of Southern Mississippi, 1997.

Duffy, Christopher. *The Military Experience in the Age of Reason.* New York: Atheneum, 1988.

Dumbauld, Edward. *The Life and Legal Writings of Hugo Grotius* Norman: University of Oklahoma Press, 1969.

Forster, Gaines. *Ghosts of the Confederacy: Defeat, The Lost Cause, and the Emergence of the New South, 1865 to 1912.* New York: Oxford University Press, 1987.

Freeman, Douglas Southall. *The South to Posterity: An Introduction to the Writing of Confederate History.* New York: Charles Schribner, 1951.

Holloway, John. *The Victorian Sage: Studies in Argument.* London: Archon Books, 1953.

Hood, John B. *Advance and Retreat: Personal Experiences in the United States and Confederate States Armies.* [1880] Bloomington, Indiana: reprint Da Capo Press, 1959.

Johnston, Joseph E. *Narrative of Military Operations, Directed, During the Late War Between the States.* New York: D. Appleton, 1874.

McMurry, Richard M. *John Bell Hood and the War for Southern Independence.* Lexington: University Press of Kentucky, 1982.

Osterweis, Rollin G. *Romanticism and Nationalism in the Old South.* New Haven: Yale University Press, 1949.

Rose, Anne C. *Victorian America and the Civil War.* New York: Cambridge University Press, 1992.

Royster, Charles. *The Destructive War: William Tecumseh Sherman, Stonewall Jackson, and the Americas.* New York: Vintage, 1993.

Rutland, Richard, and Malcolm Bradbury. *From Puritanism to Postmodernism: A History of American Literature.* New York: Penguin Books, 1991.

Taylor, Richard. *Destruction and Reconstruction: Personal Experience of the Late War.* [1879] reprint Nashville: J. S. Sanders, 1998.

Tunnard, W. H. *A Southern Record: The History of the Third Regiment Louisiana Infantry.* [1866] reprint, Fayetteville: University of Arkansas Press, 1997.

Wilson, Charles Reagan. *Baptized in Blood: The Religion of the Lost Cause, 1865–1920.* Athens: University of Georgia Press, 1980.

'Romantic, isn't it, Miss Dandridge?': Sources and Meanings of John Ford's Cavalry Trilogy

Frank J. Wetta and Martin A. Novelli

Frank Nugent, a Hollywood screenwriter and *New York Times* film critic, recalled a conversation he had with director John Ford in 1947: 'I dropped by to see him one day and he started talking about a picture he had in mind. "The Cavalry." In all westerns, the Cavalry rides in to the rescue of the beleaguered wagon train or whatever, and then it rides off again. I've been thinking about it – what it was like at a Cavalry post, remote, people with their own personal problems, over everything the threat of Indians, of death.'[1]

The conversation envisioned the first in what became a remarkable series of motion pictures often referred to as the Cavalry Trilogy[2]: *Fort Apache* (1948),[3] *She Wore a*

Yellow Ribbon (1949),[4] and *Rio Grande* (1950).[5] Through these movies, Ford became the principal chronicler of the Plains cavalry in film. In 1973, Robert Utley, the preeminent historian of the Plains Indian Wars, introduced his definitive chronicle of frontier Regulars with a comment on current trends in the historiography of the West with reference to the influence of the films of John Ford: 'Until recent years, the heroic stereotype of the frontier army dominated the collective memory of Americans. It found its most vivid expression in the motion pictures of John Ford and the characterizations of John Wayne. Today [1973], however, a nation increasingly troubled by its historic treatment of the Indians has substituted the ugly for the stereotype. In great quantities of popular literature, in television productions, and motion pictures such as *Little Big Man* and *Soldier Blue*, the frontier Regulars are depicted as the nineteenth-century humanitarians saw them.' In the post-Civil War period, Easterners such as Wendell Phillips and William Lloyd Garrison had 'assailed [the Regulars] as butchers, rampaging around the West gleefully slaughtering peaceable Indians and taking special delight in shooting down women and children.'[6]

By the 1970s, the heroic West of John Ford had, in the critic's eye, become a rehearsal for the killing grounds of American imperialism. Indeed, scholar Edward Countryman noted the attitude of 'irreparable loss' which 'underlies the "Indian" films of the Vietnam era, most notably Arthur Penn's *Little Big Man* and Ralph Nelson's *Soldier Blue* (both 1970). The one can be faulted for its unhappy mixture of sentiment towards the Indians and self-contempt towards white culture, the other for the gratuitous violence with which it closes.'[7] *Brassey's Guide to War Films*, for example, calls *Soldier Blue*: 'an important, if pretentious, allegory coming shortly after the Vietnam My Lai revelations.' Further, 'It brought into popular focus the position of the Indian in modern times, and may have been influential in the 1973 siege of Wounded Knee, where, protesting for better conditions, two members of the American Indian Movement were killed by FBI agents.'[8]

Film scholar and biographer David Thompson declared, without reservation, in his biographical dictionary of filmmakers and actors, that Ford had nothing to say that transcended cheap romantic sentimentality. Thompson found little to like in his art and nothing to respect in his historical vision, since Ford 'refused to contemplate history or responsibility.' 'The visual poetry so often attributed to Ford,' he remarked, ' seems to me claptrap in that it amounts to prettification of a lie... the lines of cavalry in so many films, the lone figure in Monument Valley... It is worth emphasizing how far [Arthur] Penn, Anthony Mann, [Sam] Fuller, Nicholas Ray, and [Sam] Peckinpah have disproved those rosy, statuesque images.' Peckinpah and the others opened our eyes to the true West – a frontier devoid of false romance and near-fascist adoration of men in uniforms. Ford may have been a 'natural storyteller' who composed 'lovely scenes,' Thompson argued, but there is no artistic integrity, no intellectual honesty, and certainly nothing of historical value – his cavalry films are mere 'endorsements' of the military and his vision blurred by 'the booze mythology of complacency and sentimentality.' Further, Thompson said with contempt, 'Ford's art was always that of a mythmaker, a wishful thinker, a man without stamina for reality... In an age of diminishing historical sense in America, but of regular crises that dramatize our need to ask what happened (with Watergate, Vietnam, Iran-Contra, etc.), I marvel that Ford's heady obscurantism has... defenders.' In the 2002 revised edition of his dictionary of Hollywood, Thompson reflected on his own earlier but still unrevised criticism of Ford: 'The above was written for the 1975 edition, when Ford was already dead, and before the author had spent any time in the American West, and before he had begun to consider the tangle that has been made between Hollywood and what Americans take for their history. I say that to deter the hopes of those who like Ford... and who anticipated some greater kindness toward the director. My dismay is deeper now; my case, it seems to me, the more damning.'[9]

Thompson was not alone in his contempt; other critics found Ford part of a tradition of lying about the American experience: In 'The Night John Wayne Danced with Shirley Temple,' Max Westbrook detected an 'insidious' subtext in *Fort Apache* that justifies 'the cover up of the Kennedy assassination, Vietnam, Watergate, and Contragate.' Paul Buhle and Dave Wagner, in their sympathetic history of the political left in Hollywood, simply pronounced *Fort Apache* and *She Wore a Yellow Ribbon* to be reactionary and 'distinctly conservative-patriotic (and racist).'[10] Garry Wills stated that the hostile reaction to *The Green Berets* by film critics, though not the public, revealed the 'dead end he [John Wayne] had reached in pursuing the imperial certitudes of the Ford cavalry pictures.' 'The sixties had shattered confidence in empire,' Wills concluded, 'even among those still trying to maintain an empire.'[11]

Questions about history, responsibility, relevancy, and imperial dreams are essential in considering the work of John Ford and, in this case, his image of the Plains cavalry. Ford loved the military, hungered for medals recognizing his service during World War II, and was, like the majority of his generation, an unashamed patriot.[12] His sensibilities were informed by an America experience unlike the one that shaped the anxieties of the 1960s and 1970s, or the skepticism and cynicism about America values and its foreign interventions characteristic of those years. As Joseph McBride concludes, Ford's 'identification with the military ethos and his growing sense of himself as a national poet made him turn his postwar filmmaking efforts largely to American history.' In *Fort Apache*, for example, Ford 'wanted to offer a rich and accurate depiction of life on a frontier military outpost in the post-Civil War era while using it as a microcosm of national values and virtues.'[13] These depictions of American values and virtues were hardly the reflections of the Age of Assassinations and Cover-ups.

Are these anti-Ford critics right? Is there little of value or truth in Ford's work? Is Ford irrelevant? Is there anything that gives validity or currency to his movies? George McDonald Fraser, author of the popular 'Flashman' series of comic but well-regarded historical novels, praised Ford for his ability to reconstruct the past. 'There is a popular belief,' Fraser judged in *The Hollywood History of the World*, 'that where history is concerned, Hollywood always gets it wrong – and sometimes it does. What is overlooked is the astonishing amount of history Hollywood has got right, and the immense unacknowledged debt which we owe to commercial cinema as an illustrator of the story of mankind. This although films have sometimes blundered and distorted and falsified, have botched great themes and belittled great men and women, have trivialized and caricatured and cheapened, have piled anachronism on solecism on downright lies – still, at their best, they have given a picture of the ages more vivid and memorable than anything in Tacitus or Gibbon or Macaulay';[14] or, in Ford's case, anything in Rudyard Kipling. Fraser applauded Ford for his authentic portrait of the American frontier and, in particular, the colonial frontier community in *Drums along the Mohawk* (1939). The film, he judged, is 'a beautifully observed study of frontier life. Ford can let his camera range over a room, picking up tiny details of furnishing, or over a church service... and tell more about a period than an hour-long lecture. It is a gentle, pastoral film for the most part, which makes its violent passages all the more telling, and at the end one begins to understand what it must have been like to try to make a home on the edge of the wilderness, and the price that had to be paid for survival.'[15] The observations that Ford brought to his work in *Drums Along the Mohawk* were also evident in the frontier military community of the Cavalry Trilogy. In truth, Ford's three cavalry films come closer to Robert Utley's summary of the complex history of the Plains Indian wars than any revisionist critique: 'Just as campaigning troopers sported black and white hats – or any other hue that suited their fancy – so a fair appraisal of the Indian-fighting army must acknowledge a mix of wisdom and stupidity, humanity and barbarism, selfless dedication and mindless indifference, achievement and failure, triumph and tragedy; but above all, as in most human institution, of contradictions and ambiguities.'[16]

Ford's Hollywood Raj

Before the Cavalry Trilogy, Ford had refined his ability to reconstruct the life of imperial soldiers in *The Black Watch* (1929),[17] based on the novel *King of the Khyber Rifles* by Talbot Mundy (John Wayne was an extra in the film); *The Lost Patrol* (1934),[18] in which a British unit is destroyed by Arabs in the Mesopotamian desert during World War I, and *Wee Willie Winkie* (1937),[19] a film depicting the Black Watch (Royal Highland) Regiment in fictional 'Raj Pore' on the North West Frontier of India in 1897. Originally intended as a routine vehicle starring Shirley Temple, the world's most famous child star, the film is only tangentially related to Rudyard Kipling's story. The movie, however, evokes the atmosphere of Kipling's army in ways that anticipate the Trilogy. The language, routine, rituals, and martial liturgy of an army within the isolation of a cantonment amidst a hostile native population provide the context through closely observed studies of frontier military life. In *Wee Willie Winkie*, Garry Wills noted, 'Ford seized upon a rainy day to improvise a stirring funeral, much as he later shot into a storm to capture the realistic climatic tension in an army patrol in *She Wore a Yellow Ribbon*.' Further, Wills noted, the subdued ending to the film anticipates 'the same dynamic that makes *She Wore a Yellow Ribbon* so unexpected.' In addition, Wills described *Fort Apache* as a 'reworking of material from *Wee Willie Winkie*.'[20]

There is a thematic connection then between Ford's depiction of the British soldiers on India's North West Frontier and the American cavalrymen on the southwestern Great Plains. The United States Cavalry on the western plains were as much agents of the imperialism of the 1870s as were the British in their campaigns against the Ashanti (1873–74), the Zulus (1879), or the Afghans (1878–80). Lieutenant Colonel George A.

Custer's defeat at the Little Big Horn in 1876 is analogous to British Colonel Anthony Durnford's last stand at Isandhlwana in 1879; the isolated cantonments of India's North West Frontier are analogous to the outposts of the American Southwest. Thus, Garry Wills observed; 'The "Seventh Cavalry" of John Ford's Westerns had the legionary spirit... But even more important, the America of Ford's time had the sense of imperial burden.' 'Ford preferred to accept history and even legend as it was written rather than revise it in a radical or derisive spirit,' Andrew Sarris states. 'Why are the Indians on the warpath from Fort Apache to Cheyenne Autumn [1964]? Not, according to Ford, because of American Imperialism or White Racism or Manifest Destiny, but because the derelictions of the Indian Ring, 'the most corrupt band of politicians in our nation's history, graft and corruption on the local level rather than greed and conquest on the national level.'[20]

The appearance of the great character actor Victor McLaglen provides a unique continuity among Ford's films: he is Captain King (*The Black Watch*), the Sergeant (*The Lost Patrol*), Sergeant Mac Duff (*Wee Willie Winkie*), Sergeant Mulcahy (*Fort Apache*), Sergeant Quincannon (*She Wore a Yellow Ribbon*), and Sergeant Major Quincannon (*Rio Grande*). There is a genuine believability about his performances – he had been a real imperial soldier. Born in London (his father became Bishop of Clermont, South Africa), he fought for the Empire in the Boer War (a 'boy soldier') and in the Great War (a captain with the Irish Fusiliers); he even served as provost marshal of occupied Baghdad. His ability to fight was no mere invention either: he once went six rounds with heavyweight champion Jack Johnson. McLaglen was ideal for Ford's giant 'tough-soft cavalry sergeant.'[21]

In *The Long Recessional: The Imperial Life of Rudyard Kipling*, David Gilmour notes the influence Kipling had on the British and American public and among British soldiers themselves: contemporaries 'praised the 'literally photographic' accuracy of Tommy's portrait in verse.'[22] According to one British general, 'the soldiers thought, and talked, and expressed themselves exactly like Rudyard Kipling had taught them in his stories... Kipling made the modern soldier.'[23] John Ford had a similar influence on what American filmgoers came to believe of the western cavalry. In time, many American officers and enlisted men came to model their behavior on what they had learned from watching John Wayne as Captain Brittles or Colonel Yorke, or his characterizations in his famous World War II movies. In its spirit and documentary quality, like Kipling's stories, the Cavalry Trilogy provides a sympathetic portrayal of frontier Regulars – America's own imperial frontier soldiers. Thus, according to Wills, Ford 'felt himself a vicarious participant' in the growth of [the American] empire.'[24] And Ford, like Kipling, always regretted not being a real soldier.

Backstories

During the pre-production process of filmmaking, researchers and screenwriters often create fictional 'backstories' that serve to reveal in direct or indirect ways the context of a screenplay. The purpose of such documents is to explain the real or imagined history and motivation of the characters. They do this in the film itself through flashbacks and dialogue, or merely through background information provided to the director and actors. The backstories for the Cavalry Trilogy came from three principal sources: the work of Frederic Remington and other western artists, the short stories of James Warner Bellah, and the findings of pre-production research assistants. These resources enabled Ford to create a remarkably accurate portrait of the Plains Cavalry and the late-nineteenth century American empire both in look and in spirit. Thomas Doherty, in a discussion of Hollywood and the artistic legacy of World War II, noted that the Trilogy emphasizes 'the force of tradition, the burden of command, and the rules of martial behavior.'[25] 'So here they are,' the trailer to *Yellow Ribbon* grandly announces, 'the dog-faced soldiers, the Regulars, the 50-cent-a-day professionals riding the outposts of a nation from Fort Reno to Fort Apache, from Sheridan to Starke. They were always the same – men in dirty-shirt blue and only a cold page in the history books to mark their passing. Nevertheless, whatever they fought for that place became the United States.' Perhaps the critics are right about the subtext of Cold War ideology or the need to believe in the myth of American history, but that does not explain the continued popularity of the three movies. The appeal of Ford's Trilogy (the three movies appear frequently on American television channels that feature classic films) lies in the continuing enduring attraction of John Wayne, Ford's ability to reconstruct the dirty-blue life of the frontier Cavalry, as well as compelling story lines.

The verisimilitude of the Cavalry Trilogy draws the viewers into the cavalrymen's experience in entirely believable ways. The backstory researchers were Major Phillip Kieffer (U.S. Army, retired) and Katherine Spaatz. The backstory for *Fort Apache*, for example, included references to Helen S. Griffin and Arthur Woodward's *Story of El Tejon* (1948), Lansing Bloom's series of articles in the *New Mexico Historical Review* on Captain John G. Bourke (1933–38), H. H. McConnell's *Five Years a Cavalryman* (1889), and Elizabeth Custer's *Boots and Saddles* (1885) and *Following the Guidon* (1890). Additionally, the researchers also interviewed the widow of a cavalry sergeant and another woman who had been married to a Seventh Cavalryman in Arizona in the 1880s.[26] From such sources and his own imagination, Ford created the seminal image of the horse soldiers in film.

It is no exaggeration to say that the Cavalry Trilogy formed the historical reality of the Plains Cavalry in the popular mind – as Frederic Remington, in his drawings and paintings had done for the Plains Cavalry before the invention of Hollywood. Critical to this image was Ford's sense of historical authenticity. Everything just looks right to the audience whether they have any real knowledge of the frontier or not. As the atmospheric films of British director David Lean made during the same period (*Great Expectations*, 1948 and *Oliver Twist*, 1949) evoked the Victorian world of Charles Dickens, so Ford evoked the Mid-Victorian American military frontier. In his enthusiastic review of *Yellow Ribbon* in *The New York Times* on 18 November 1949, Bosley Crowther wrote: 'For this big Technicolor Western, Mr. Ford has superbly achieved a vast and composite illustration of all the legends of the cavalrymen. He has got the bold and dashing courage, the stout masculine sentiment, the grandeur of rear-guard heroism, and the brash bravado of the barrack room brawl. And best of all, he has got the brilliant color and vivid detail of those legendary troops as they ranged through the silent "Indian country" and across the magnificent western plains.'[27]

In 1984, Jeffery Prater, then a student officer at the U.S. Army Command and General Staff College at Fort Leavenworth, Kansas, wrote the definitive scholarly 'backstory' for the Cavalry Trilogy. His comprehensive investigation of the 'vivid detail' in the three movies describes their relationship to the real Indian-fighting cavalry and confirms that Ford created an authentic if celluloid army. Prater's careful research reveals that in character, events, uniforms, accouterments, equipment, military professional and social life, music, forts, locations, and Indian fighting tactics, Ford, despite frequent inaccuracies and the inevitable dramatic inventions, reconstructed the world of the imperial cavalry with remarkable historical accuracy. In *Fort Apache* 'the shortcomings,' Prater concludes, 'err on the side of believability and are probably transparent to the average viewer; in this case, he has printed a legend based heavily on fact.'[28] 'His treatment of frontier army life [in *She Wore a Yellow Ribbon*] is historically correct and his strongest suit. The depiction of long careers with slow promotion rates is a good example. The music and bugle calls in the film are also noteworthy for their accuracy. Although Ford's 'grasp of history' in *Rio Grande* may 'be hazy' at times, nevertheless, 'the nature of Yorke's orders and subsequent raid into Mexico match those of Colonel Randall S. Mackenzie in 1873; the film's Second Cavalry is Mackenzie's Fourth.'[29]

Ford made the cavalry–Indian confrontations believable because he paid attention to the details as well as the spirit of the frontier soldiers. John Ford is the film poet of the reluctant imperialists through his recreation of a regiment of the U.S. Cavalry, its society, and its relationship with native insurgents on a distant frontier.

The Thin Blue Line

In a letter to James Warner Bellah in July 1948, Ford proposed making a movie in Technicolor that would bring to life the images of the U.S. Cavalry in the art of Fredric Remington, famed artist of the Plains Indian Wars: 'Jim, I think we can make a Remington canvas... broad shoulders... wide hats... narrow hips... yellow strips down the pants leg... war bonnets and eagle feathers trailing in the dust... the brassy sound of bugles in the morning... the long reaches of the prairie... the buttes and mesas in the distances and the buffalo.'[30] Critic and director Peter Bogdanovich asked Ford in an interview in 1966 which of the cavalry films was his favorite. 'I like *She Wore a Yellow Ribbon*,' he replied. 'I tried to copy the Remington style there – you can't copy him one hundred percent – but a least I tried to get his color and movement, and I think I succeeded partly.'[31]

It is not surprising that Ford found inspiration in Remington's work. The artist was a major influence in creating the image of the West in the popular mind. 'In his pictures of life on the plains, and of Indian fighting,' a commentator noted in 1892, 'he has almost created a new field in illustration, so fresh and novel are his characterizations... It is a fact that admits of no question that Eastern people have formed their conceptions of what the Far-Western life is like, more from what they have seen in Mr. Remington's pictures than from any other source.'[32] Remington produced some 400 illustrations for

Harper's Weekly, Harper's Monthly, Century, Scribner's Magazine and other publications by 1890, including the plates for *Tenting on the Plains*, Elizabeth Custer's memoir of frontier army life.[33] Like Ford, Remington waxed nostalgic about the end of the Plains Indian wars: 'The Indian suns himself before the door of his tepee, dreaming of the past,' Remington, wrote in 1899. 'For a long time now he has eaten of the white man's lotus – the bimonthly beef-issue. I looked on him and wondered at the new things. The buffalo, the warpath all gone. What of the cavalrymen… his Nemesis in the stirring days?'[34]

Nonetheless, Remington tempered his nostalgia or romanticism with close attention to authentic detail, personal observation and photographs of his subjects, and with an essential honesty about the real West. That detail revealed a tension in Remington's illustrations and paintings (as in Ford's Cavalry Trilogy) in which his imagination and his sympathy for the subject competed with his pragmatism. 'It was as a documentarian rather than as a moralist that Remington gained notice for his early paintings,' according to art critic Peter Hassrick. Thus, 'Remington had selected an exotic theme, the final act in the drama of the Far West, but he chose to portray this romantic theme in terms of a realist.' Further, his 'style of painting (like Ford's cavalry films)… remained distinctly narrative and overtly masculine.'[35] In addition, he painted with 'an abounding empathy for the army's "yellowlegs" who weathered the trials of plains life.' Ford did more than merely copy Remington's color and movement. It is this combination of romance and realism that characterizes both Ford's as well as Remington's views of the Plains Cavalry. In Remington's paintings, Edward Buscombe observes, in an essay on the influence of the artist on western film, 'soldiers are weary and dusty, their uniforms battered. Instead of the might of a huge army they deployed a thin blue line.'[36] He labels this view a 'variant of the Western myth which Remington and Ford represent founded upon a popularly constituted soldiery and upon glory attained in dignified defeat.'[37] Remington recalled seeing 'the blistered faces of the men, the gaunt horses dragging stiffly along to the cruel spurring, the dirty lack-luster of campaigning.'[38] *Fort Apache* ends in the massacre that recalls Custer's Last Stand. In *She Wore a Yellow Ribbon*, an officer is angered by his inability to prevent the murder of solders and civilians at a coach station that the army should have protected. In *Rio Grande*, the fort commander is constantly bedeviled by Apaches who raid across the Mexican border and evade capture. Ford's heroes, Geoffery O'Brien observed, 'patrol the perimeter of the encampment while the others – the innocents – feast, dance, live as they are meant to; live, that is, in the heart of a children's book. The soldiers are voluntary outsiders who sacrifice a normal life for the sake of those in their charge.'[39]

In all three cavalry films, there is no promise of final victory; the campaigns are portrayed as hard and, at best, limited victories. It is the spirit of this thin blue line, as the isolated agents of civilization, that animates Ford's trilogy and much of Remington's art. The scene of Colonel Thursday's defeat in *Fort Apache* evokes the composition of Remington's 'Last Stand.' *Rio Grande* begins 'with a cavalry column returning to the fort wounded and bedraggled.' In this matter, Joseph McBride explained, 'Remington's starkly beautiful paintings of cavalrymen, often tragic in tone, provided inspiration for the entire Cavalry Trilogy.'[40]

Ford also found inspiration in paintings, magazine illustrations, and images on book jackets created by other artists, including Harold von Schmidt's drawings for James Bellah's short stories in the *Saturday Evening Post*.[41] Joseph McBride noted the influence of the 'more romantic paintings of Charles Russell whose colorful landscapes and Indian scenes were imitated by Ford in his magnificent imagery of Indians on the march in *She Wore a Yellow Ribbon*.' Charles Schreyvogle ('Painter-Historian of the Indian Fighting Army') provided another source. Pat Ford said: 'My father kept a copy of a collection by Schreyvogle close to his bedside. He pored over it to dream up action sequences for his films.'[42] At least two scenes in *Yellow Ribbon*, for instance, seem inspired by Schreyvogle's 'Going for Reinforcements' (Trooper Tyree's ride) and 'Attack at Dawn' (the raid on the village to disperse the Indian ponies).[43] John Baxter, a screenwriter and film historian, concluded that Ford's movies 'express at their best a guarded sincerity, a skeptical satisfaction in the beauty of the American landscape, muted always by an understanding of the dangers implicit in the land, and a sense of the responsibility of all men to protect the common heritage.' Thus, 'he saw that we live in history, and that history embodies the lessons we must learn.'[44] The three films are not entirely 'celebrations' or false romances or adulations of the military ethos; rather, they are, in careful detail, 'revisionist' images of the guardians of empire – tragic in tone, guarded in sincerity, and skeptical in satisfaction.[45] During the long march in *She Wore a Yellow Ribbon* Lieutenant Flint Cohill asks of Olivia Dandridge, the love interest, 'Romantic, isn't it Miss Dandridge? Guidons gaily fluttering, bronze men lustily singing, horses prancing, bunions aching.'[46]

The American Kiplings

The short stories of James Warner Bellah appearing in the *Saturday Evening Post* were the principal literary source for the Cavalry Trilogy screenplays. In his biography of his grandfather, Dan Ford said of Bellah: 'He, more than John (though John Ford has been so named), was "The American Kipling." Bellah's novels and short stories echo in American terms Rudyard Kipling's call to empire. His work speaks of conquest and the white man's burden.'[47] Bellah was an American veteran of the Royal Air Force in World War I (1917–19). During World War II he served on the Southeast Asia Command staff under Lord Mountbatten and saw combat in Burma.[48] He assumed an imperial manner and accepted imperial honors – he was awarded the Imperial Russian Order of St. Nicholas. Later he became an international saber champion, and kept his British officer's swagger stick in a corner of his study. Thus, Bellah wrote stories attuned to the concept of Anglo-Saxon imperialism. But he had no illusions about the nature of his 'light fiction': 'My stories are better than pulp, but I know better than to think they are art.'[49] Bellah's *Saturday Evening Post* stories, 'Massacre' (22 February 1947),[50] 'Mission With No Record' (27 September 1947),[51] 'Big Hunt' (6 December 1948),[52] and 'War Party' (19 June 1948)[53], served as the basis for Ford's Calvary Trilogy. *Fort Apache* is 'derived' (there is no other word) from 'Massacre'; *She Wore A Yellow Ribbon* from 'War Party' and 'Big Hunt'; and *Rio Grande* from 'Mission With No Record.'

These stories are compressed, terse narratives that begin quickly, move ahead with dispatch, and end abruptly. The author's staccato approach fit well with Ford's style; however, there is little of the exposition evident in the films; nor any of Ford's customary Irish comic relief – the comic brawls that critics found distracting or self-indulgent. In an acerbic aside, James Agee said of Ford's sense of humor: 'There is enough Irish comedy (in *Fort Apache*) to make me wish Cromwell had done a more thorough job.' David Thompson was equally savage in his biographical sketch of Victor McLaglen. His character, Thompson stated, had become 'a punch-drunk clown, bursting out of his uniform and calling everyone "darlin."'[54] None of this is in "Mission No Record." The soldier fights in the short story are 'meticulous fury in performance. Quick animal fights in the bivouacs, put down quickly by harder fists.' The number of characters is kept to a minimum (no colorful Irishmen for Bellah); in particular, the women (and community) are practically non-existent, except as patient wives back at the fort or as victims of Indian savagery. In the latter case, Bellah would describe what could only be hinted at in the films – 'They found the burned-out wagon train and the dead wagoners, with one strapped face downward to the wagon shaft with his tongue cut out, but still alive to the horror of the writhing ants.'

If the films filter Bellah's cynical, anti-romantic tone, they, in turn, reflect Ford's own limited 'war experiences, his love of the military, and the sense of community he felt exists among fighting men and their families.'[55] 'The set pieces,' Andrew Sarris wrote of *Fort Apache* 'are among Ford's most memorable; the Grand March at the Enlisted Men's Ball; the women's farewell to the men going off to war; and the Apache massacre' of the cavalry.[56]

Fort Apache

'Massacre' illustrates perfectly Bellah's approach. Lieutenant Flintridge Cohill (a character who appears in *She Wore A Yellow Ribbon* but not in *Fort Apache*) is awakened at 3:45 a.m. by the arrival of Major Owen Thursday, no longer 'Major General Thursday of Clarke's Corps'; no longer 'Thursday of Cumberland Station and of Sudler's Mountain at twenty-six'– his glory days during the Civil War. Thursday is now just 'a major of cavalry at thirty-eight, back in the slow Army runway again, with the flame of glory burning low on the horizon.' Bellah is clear about the consequences of this fall from glory: 'for it is worse to go up and come back again than it ever is not to go up at all.' In a couple of sentences Bellah prepares the reader for the folly that Thursday will lead his men into, an ill-considered action that will cost the lives of 72 men in addition to Thursday's death.

The military community of the fort, real or imagined, is of little interest to Bellah – though of great interest to Ford.[57] In Bellah's narrative there is no Captain Kirby York trying to warn Thursday that his arrogance will lead to disaster. In the movie, Thursday says he saw a few Indians outside the fort and they didn't look dangerous. York replies, 'If you saw them, they weren't Apaches!' There is no cute Philadelphia Thursday – no daughter of the regiment (as played by Shirley Temple in the film) to attract the attention of newly minted lieutenant Michael O'Rourke. There is no

Sergeant-Major Michael O'Rourke and his staff of roughhouse Irish sergeants to welcome the young man back from West Point. And, there is no exchange where O'Rourke tells Thursday that his son had a Presidential Appointment to West Point and Thursday facetiously says: 'It was my impression that Presidential Appointments are only awarded to the sons of men who have won the Congressional Medal of Honor.' O'Rourke serenely replies: 'That was my impression as well, sir!' There is no dance at Bellah's Fort Apache (one of the truly authentic historical scenes in Ford's film) the night Thursday arrives. In fact, there is no 'Fort Apache'; in the short story, it is called Fort Starke.

There is actually no *later*. Almost immediately after arriving, Thursday leads a substantial portion of his troop into the field to teach Stone Buffalo a lesson. And, of course, Thursday's arrogance provokes a fatal error. For the expedition, Captain Joplyn orders 300 rounds of ammunition per man. Thursday countermands that order with: 'That is a lot of ammunition... for men who are supposed to be trained to shoot... One hundred rounds per man should be ample for any emergency.' Thursday is obviously digging his own grave and that of most of his men, as he does in the film. Bellah (Ford as well) has him compound his mistake: 'I have a few ideas of my own on how Indians should be dealt with. I shall want colors and a proper color guard, guidons and trumpeters. Have the men bring their polishing kits and button sticks and boot blacking. A little more military dignity and decorum out here and a little less cowboy manners and dress, will engender a lot more respect for the Army.'

What does Bellah think of all this pomp and circumstance? 'The sun in August is a molten saber blade. It will burn the neckline and the back of a hand to blistered uselessness as you watch it. It sears the lower lip into noisome sogginess while you stand still.' Despite these conditions, Thursday remains undaunted. He tells Cohill to 'Move down the column and have every man crease his hat fore and aft as a fedora... They look like scratch farmers on market day! The hat is a uniform, not a subject for individual whimsical expression!' (a bit of dialogue repeated in the film). And why is Thursday so arrogant? Bellah describes Thursday's psychological makeup: 'The major had fewer years left to live than he had lived already, and when that knowledge hits a man's mind, he can break easily. He must hurry then, for his time is shortening. He must seek short cuts. And, seeking them, he may destroy the worth of his decisions, the power of his judgment.'

The rest of the story can be read as a gloss on those comments. One of his officers warns against allowing Indians into the camp so they cannot gauge the strength of Thursday's force. Thursday snaps: 'When I want advice from my officers... I'll ask for it. Will you remember that please?' If Thursday is a fool, the Indians are mere savages, although clever savages as the case in 'Massacre' proves. Stone Buffalo *speaks* to Thursday for a *long* time. Cohill says: 'All he has said so far is that he is a very, very brave man.' Stone Buffalo 'talked on for many more minutes.' Cohill adds: ''He says now that he is also a great hunter – he and his whole tribe.' Cohill *also* tries to warn Thursday: 'I don't like any of it, sir. He's covering up for time. This is an insolent attempt at reconnaissance, I believe.' Ignoring Cohill's warning, Thursday seals his fate. 'They are recalcitrant swine. They must feel it.' Thursday then orders Cohill to command Stone Buffalo and the others to return to the reservation – or else: 'Tell them I find them without honor or manhood. Tell them it is written on sacred paper that they will remain on their reservation. That they have broken this promise puts them beneath fighting men's contempt, makes them turkey-eating women. Tell them the United States orders them to leave here at once. They will break camp at dawn and return to the reservation for I move in to their camp site at daylight.' (This confrontation also occurs in the movie – one of its most powerful scenes.)

In Bellah's treatment of the Indians, there is no New Age *Dances with Wolves* (1990) sentimentality' about 'Native Americans': 'the smell of an Indian is resinous and salty and rancid. It is the wood smoke of his tepee and the fetidity of his breath that comes of eating body hot animal entrails. It is his uncured tobacco and the sweat of his unwashed body. It is animal grease in his hair and old leather and fur, tanned with bird lime and handed down unclean from ancestral bodies long since gathered to the Happy Lands.' Bellah continues briefly: 'Major Thursday saw their impassive Judaic faces, their dignity, their reserve. He felt the quiet impact of their silence, but, being new to the game, he had no way of knowing that they drew all of it on as they drew on their trade goods blankets – to cover a childish curiosity and the excitability of terriers.' (In the movie, Ford's Indians are not portrayed in this manner. The director had a respectful if paternalistic affection for the Navahos, who played the hostiles in his films, regardless of the particular tribe identified in the Trilogy. This attitude is most evident in *Fort Apache*.)

After the Indians leave, Cohill and then other junior officers bemoan the position Thursday has put them in. Now Bellah foreshadows the conclusion: 'You have seen it so often in the Jonathan Hedfield print. The powder-blue trace of Crazy Man Creek against the burnt yellow grass on the rising ground behind. The dead of Company A stripped naked and scalped, their heads looking like faces screaming in beards. Major Thursday, empty gun in hand, dying gloriously with what is left of Company B, in an attempt to save the colors, but this is how it happened. This is *how it happened* (italics are Bellah's). 'And this is classic Bellah historicism: 'It's not always in the book. It's a hundred thousand years. It's heritage and a curse and the white man's burden. It's Cannae and Agincourt and Wagram and Princeton, and it's the shambles of Shiloh.'

Now comes the connection to the present: 'With Flint Cohill, it was thirty-one men on a hogback ridge and the thought in his angry mind that he'd never live now to be a general, but he'd die the best damned first lieutenant of cavalry that the world could find to do the job that morning!' 'All of his days the ghost of today had ridden with him, mocking his pride, pointing the finger of scorn at his personal ambition.' Thursday then rides back to his dying troopers and puts a bullet into his own brain. 'Glory is a jade in the street who can be bought for a price by anyone who wants her. Thursday wanted her, but his pockets were empty, so Cohill lent him the two dollars for posterity.' Cohill throws away Thursday's pistol and protects the legend that Thursday died gallantly with his troops. '"Major Thursday," he would say to those who asked, "was a very gallant officer. We found him dead with the little group that defended the colors... No man could have wished for more." But even when he was very old, Cohill always looked sharply at anyone who said, "for the good of the service," and he always said,

"What exactly does that mean to you, sir?"' Such is the hard, un-romanticized source for the film.

In the backstory created for the film, Owen Thursday has 'graduated West Point '55 ... second or third in his class... Remained in Washington until '69 and was sent as Military Observer to Europe. Saw the Prussian-Austrian War. Was present at Sadowa... great student of military affairs. A reputation as a brilliant Cavalry Tactician and a very strict soldier... He had been forcibly impressed with the Prussians.'[58] Seen from this perspective, *Fort Apache* is a perceptive study in outpost command that is well-grounded in post-Civil War military history. In the film, Owen Thursday (Henry Fonda) is assigned with the rank of lieutenant colonel, to command a dreary frontier outpost – an 'exile in the wilderness.' The dusty place is a constant reminder of a thwarted career, typical of officers like Custer or Nelson Miles. He had been a Brevet Major General, but now had accepted a lower rank to remain in the service. It is a superior performance by Fonda who, with his handsome goatee in the style of many Civil War officers, bears a close physical resemblance to General George B. McClellan, Abraham Lincoln's petulant commander of the Army of the Potomac. Film commentators often compare Thursday to George Custer mainly because of the tragic end to the film. In sharp contrast to the popular 'Little Mac,' however, Thursday's men hold no affection for their commander. He is elegant in appearance and attaches to his kepi a flap to protect the neck from the sun in the manner of Sir Henry Havelock (1795–1857), the British general who served in the Indian Mutiny. Thursday is impatient with the casual atmosphere of the encampment. When he arrives at the fort, he sets about alienating his officers and, through his arrogance, inadvertently insulting the regimental sergeant major and his wife. Worse, Thursday has no understanding or respect for the Apaches and their way of war.

Yet, the colonel is not without ability or a moral core. He is West Point-trained and has earned an enviable Civil War record. He is honest and courteous in speech, clear about his expectations for the regiment, and knowledgeable about military history and tactics. (Like McClellan, he has traveled in Europe and observed the armies of the continent.) In the film, Thursday, like the other soldiers at the fort, rightly holds the corrupt Indian agent assigned to the reservation in cold contempt. There is no question about his courage. Yet, in his desire to make the regiment into a well turned-out command, with his seeming focus on the Prussian formalities as opposed to the substance of military leadership, Thursday separates himself from those that can help him lead effectively. In the end, he tragically ignores the advice of Captain Kirby York, an experienced Indian fighter, and, expecting only the 'nit stings and flea bits of a few Digger Indians,' leads his command into an Apache ambush. Nevertheless, Thursday is a complex character and not without self-awareness; in response against the obvious resentment within his command, he protests, 'I am no martinet.' He even displays ability to outwit the Indians in a skirmish early in the movie. But, despite his talent for the military arts and sciences, his frustrations with an undistinguished frontier posting lead him to ruin.

Captain York, on the other hand, is fully a member of a democratic brotherhood of cavalrymen. He is, according to his backstory, 'the Washington to Thursday's

Braddock. He knows the country, He knows the Indians, York has a sense of humor. He loves and is perfectly satisfied with frontier life. He smokes cigars and drinks bourbon. A fair country-style poker player. A great horseman. Better yet, a great horse-trader.'[59]

The symbiotic relationship of Bellah's story and Ford's movie is complex. Ford retains dialogue and certain aspects of the short story, but the nuance of tone and vision are different. In his seminal work on the myth of the western frontier in American culture, Richard Slotkin argues that in *Fort Apache* 'most of the thematic and formal elements typical of the Victorian Empire formula are present: the regiment, the savage foe, the fanatic villain, the tyrant representing antidemocratic values, the border outpost, the dance scene, the massacre, the fatal cavalry charge. But in *Fort Apache* the meaning of the symbols is inverted; the colonel of the regiment is the fanatic and tyrant who breaks the warrior code of honor, women's values stand equal to men's, the Indians are victims and honorable fighters rather than savage rebels or aggressors, and the film's last stand is less a glorification of Western civilization than the culmination of a subtle critique of American democratic pretenses.' Ford achieved this, Slotkin contends, by transforming a traditional 'romantic' western into a 'gritty' combat film.[60]

She Wore a Yellow Ribbon

In his first detailed treatment of the screenplay for *She Wore A Yellow Ribbon*, Bellah wrote: 'This is a week in the life of Nathan Brittles, Capt., Cav., U.S.A. – The last week before his retirement at the Statutory Age of 64 – after 43 years of service. And at the same time – it is the story of his whole life, in cross section and of the routine of regimental life of C Troop – the garrison of Fort Starke. Fort Starke is a one troop post deliberately placed in a strategic position – between the western limits of the Plains Indian Country and the northern and eastern limits of the Apache Country. It is the story of American empire in the making – and a tiny regular army, operating always by small detachments, without thought of glory or gain or promotion, but by the heart of men alone, and the regimental pride… The time is 1–7 May, in the late 1870s.'[61]

She Wore a Yellow Ribbon emerged from a fusion of two Bellah stories – 'Big Hunt' and 'War Party.' More of the film is 'derived' from 'War Party' so that story will be discussed first. As always, Bellah makes no attempt to conceal his biases. The lead into the story's title reads: 'Forty weary cavalrymen were all that lay between the fort and the enemy's nine hundred – the savage, bloodthirsty *War Party*.' Captain Nathan Brittles (the character embodied by John Wayne in the film) is facing his final day of active duty. He is 64 years old; he has been in the army for 43 of them 'following the colors from Micanopy with the 2nd Dragoons against the Seminoles in '36, to this last reveille.' He is concerned about more than his retirement. Broken Wrist and his Comanches, along with Arapahoes and Kiowas have jumped the reservation, angry over broken treaties. Out on the Plains, observing their movements is Flintridge Cohill and C Company. Two other companies had left Fort Starke to go to Memphis for possible use in election riots. Fort Starke is dangerously under-garrisoned with only 70 people – including women and children – in residence.

Again Bellah swiftly moves his narrative forward from initial incident to conclusion. Besides Flintridge Cohill there is a young lieutenant, Ross Pennell, but there is no time for romantic rivalry in Bellah's West. There is no Olivia Dandridge to set the two friends against each other by flirting. Mrs. Allshard, a major figure in the film, is barely mentioned in the story – Brittles plans to give her his horse, Joker. (In the story, Pennel makes a *joke* about Brittles and Joker, saying to a visiting congressman: '*Total age of horse and rider, eighty-five years.*') There are, however, no bouts of Irish humor led by Sergeant Quincannon and his comrades. There is no Sergeant Quincannon in the story and certainly no Irish humor. There is a Sergeant Tyree but he is just another cavalryman, not the former Captain in the Confederate States Army as in the film. It is Tyree who presents to Brittles at the beginning of the story a silver watch and chain as a token of the men's respect.

As in the film, Brittles visits the fort's graveyard, not to *talk* to his dead wife, a sin the film indulges – Bellah would never succumb to that sentimentality – but just to visit his family for one last time: 'Mary Cutting Brittles, Nathan Cutting Brittles, and their dates. George Brittles, February–June, and his poor little date.' This last death Brittles feels with particular bitterness: 'Soft hands touched him for a moment, and an agony he had denied himself for years came back in all its lost terror. The noon heat was the red fever of smallpox again – the blasphemous fire in a soul that would not accept. So the madness had come upon him and for months he had traded that agony for whiskey, until he was no good for his grief, no good for his job.'

Brittles leaves Fort Starke, not to head West into retirement, as his comrades think, but to find, as in the film, Flintridge Cohill. Brittles has a personal investment in the young man. 'Cohill was his own handiwork, from the ground up. Like his own son in some ways. '*Never apologize, Mr. Cohill; it's a mark of weakness.*' '(That phrase becomes Wayne's mantra in the film.) Brittles finds Cohill, who is furious that he can do nothing to stop Broken Wrist and his followers. Brittles insists that he is not on duty but Cohill reminds him: 'You are still the senior officer present, sir.' 'Until midnight,' Brittles replies. Cohill reveals that Broken Wrist and his 900 warriors are moving slowly toward Fort Starke and its 'two low-strength companies.' Just to make everything 'official' – in case they survive and in case there is a court-martial – and to protect Cohill, Brittles relieves Cohill of command. Brittles has a plan, but first the saddle-weary troops must rest and refresh themselves.

This pause gives Bellah a chance for one of his hymns to the ordinary soldier (and America's imperial burden): 'Sulphur and sweat-soaked leather. Horse nitrogen and stale body grime in the soaking wool. Gun oil and the sweet brown spice of chewed Burley sweepings. Fifty cents a day to point the *march of empire* [italics ours]. Forty men on the rim of a nation, carrying the police power in their carbine boots, with a thousand savage warriors a few miles north of their bivouac. Dead soldiers, bloating and bursting their filthy shirts along the lone miles of the prairie. Scalped settlers and mutilated women and half-breeds born of white girls.' (A foreshadowing of the theme of Ford's *The Searchers*, seven years later.)

Brittles knows he must act quickly to prevent the Arapahoes and Kiowas from being drawn into the Broken Wrist uprising. 'The ends sometime justify any means,' Bellah judges of Brittles' actions, 'when the odds are twenty-three to one and *an empire hangs in the balance* [our italics].' As in the film, the cavalrymen stampede the Indian ponies but *unlike the film*, the stampede is only the beginning. Here is what Bellah says on the killing of the Indian mounts that Ford could not show to a movie audience of the 1940s: 'C Company... tore a wide pathway through, riding only for the ponies, pistoling them off their thrashing feet, stampeding them through the camp... driving them... in a panic of horse fear, circling and... firing into them, flaying them until the last of the bunched herd went down in torn agony. Then Brittles hauled the company off to high ground... and in the bright wash of the moon had them pick off the straggling ponies with carbine fire, until no one could see another one, nothing but the moiling outraged pandemonium of dismounted Kiowas and Arapahoes and Comanches, howling in lost dignity, bitten with the rage of crushed pride.' Bellah seems to exult in the humiliation of the Indians: 'Broken Wrist and his dismounted braves walked with squaws and in the dust on foot, with dogs and children at their ragged heels. And Kiowa spoke not to Comanche, and Arapahoe frowned in sullen silence.' (In the film, however, Wayne orders his troopers to follow the Indians at a distance so as not to humiliate the warriors as they walk back to the reservation.)

Turning to 'Big Hunt,' we find a story used as part of the larger picture included in *She Wore a Yellow Ribbon*. Brittles, Cohill, and Pennel discover the Comanche agent – Karl Rynders – is secretly selling rifles to the Indians. In the story, the agent is suspected by Captain Allshard and Lieutenant Pennell of gun-running and are furious about the deaths that have resulted, including that of the pay agent who had been bringing a payroll to Fort Starke where the soldiers had not been paid in two months. As usual, Bellah includes details about murdered and scalped settlers: 'The Comanche had crawled off into the rocks to die of his wounds. He had a towheaded scalp on him with braided pigtails and a pink hair ribbon. They scalped Coleman's entire family.' Allshard must also deal with the arrival of a U.S. Senator – Brome Chadbourne – who has come to Fort Starke to 'hunt buffalo.' Such things are only hinted at in the films.

Both Lieutenant Cohill and Sergeant Tyree are once again part of the action. Cohill is out on patrol trying to find the Comanche rifle caches. While accompanying the patrol, Senator Chadbourne gets more of a taste of the West that he ever imagined, with the discovery of several dead soldiers. In fact, the Senator is so infuriated that he demands that Rynders be arrested and sent back East for trial; suddenly he fires his pistol several times which causes a buffalo stampede. And where do these buffalo 'roam'? Right over the cliff and into the canyon below where they crush everything in their path, including Rynders. Although Ford removed much of the Bellah's darker tones from the film versions of the various stories, *She Wore a Yellow Ribbon* does contain a scene in which Brittles, Tyree, and Cohill, with a subdued horror and fascination, secretly watch while the Indians torture the gunrunners to death off-screen.

Rio Grande

The last of the Cavalry Trilogy, *Rio Grande*, was adapted from a single source, 'Mission With No Record,' published in *The Saturday Evening Post* on 27 September 1947. In *Rio*

Grande, John Wayne makes his second appearance as Kirby Yorke (for some reason the 'York' of *Fort Apache* is spelled 'Yorke' in the *Rio Grande* screenplay), now commanding officer of Fort Apache. In *Fort Apache*, there was no mention of Yorke having a family; yet in *Rio Grande*, he has an estranged wife, Kathleen, back East as well as an estranged son, Jeff, who has just flunked out of West Point, joined the cavalry, and has been assigned to Fort Apache. The arrival of, first Jeff Yorke, and later, of Kathleen Yorke, helps to romanticize the plot of *Rio Grande* in ways that Bellah would never permit in his stories. The arrival of Kathleen Yorke interjects the possibility of reconciliation between husband and wife.[62] This also allows Ford to indulge in his often annoying Irish sentimentality. It seems the Southern-born Mrs. Yorke has a long-standing (though somewhat good-natured) grudge against Sergeant Qunicannon because he burned her home in the Shenandoah Valley during the Civil War. Ford also uses Mrs. Yorke's presence for musical interludes, including 'Kathleen' by the Sons of the Pioneers, as the regimental singers (reflecting an authentic aspect of army life).

This kind of sentimentality, real or not, holds no interest for Bellah. *His* commanding officer is Colonel D.L. Massarene who lives, at Fort Starke, 'in Capuchin solitude, with one chair, one cot, one table. Ruling the West and the regiment with it, with the iron hand of duty. Never a meal with another officer. Never a word of praise or a word for laughter. Alone there and friendless (like Ford's Owen Thursday), with the grisly sobbing of his violin to lift the lost years from his soul and give him surcease.' If Thursday had lived, he probably would have ended up posted at Fort Starke, as Massarene does. (Though it is clear that Ford would not have John Wayne playing the violin.)

Unexpectedly, General Philip H. Sheridan himself arrives at Fort Starke with a 'mission' for Massarenes, the 'mission with no record' of the title, for this one will be 'off the books' in modern parlance. 'Massarene, I'm bringing you an order, giving it to you personally. I'm sending you across the Rio Grande after the Lipans, Kickapoos [no Hollywood cavalry ever fought 'Kickapoos,' as the Army did in reality – the audience would have laughed out loud] and the Apaches. I'm tired of hit and run, and… hide and seek. Cross the border… and to high hell with the War Department.' Massarene knows full well what is being asked of him. He says to Topliff, one of his officers, who hears what the General has said: 'You didn't hear… except officially. Which is not hearing at all.' There will be no written order for the mission. Sheridan: 'Grant and I will take personal responsibility in Washington but we want no official paper record to exist. My job is to protect Texas. You cross the Rio Grande and smash 'em.' (As noted above, Jeffery Prater states that the story is based, in part, on a real American retaliatory raid across the international border.)

It is at this point that Sheridan informs Massarene that his son was dismissed from West Point two months earlier. Massarene's reply is instructive: 'I have had no news of my son, general, since he was three years old. And I never expect to hear anything about him again.' But, of course, that is not the case. As Massarene completes his sentence, the names of the new arrivals are being called out and one of them is 'Massarene.' Within hours the whole fort is abuzz with: 'One of the new recruits from Jefferson is the Old Man's son! He failed in mathematics and they kicked him out of the Academy. He enlisted the same day.' But Massarene is certainly no beloved commander like Kirby

Yorke. 'They [the soldiers] hated Colonel Massarene because he hewed so close to the line that no humanity ever got between, only an immaculate military justice that was machine-made and as icy as the fingers of death. They hated him because he was ever right, and they hated him because they knew they could never love him.'

Before setting out, Massarene has a brief conversation with his son about the hard nature of imperial service: 'I shall give you my concept of you. It is not pleasant. Your... concept ... is a concept of plumes, parades, and band music... I put it to you flatly, that the royal flush of glory never comes up in life and that only fools hope for it.'

Young Massarene ends up in Flintridge Cohill's company and they depart on their off-the-books-mission into Mexico. As always, Bellah has no qualms about depicting, in the starkest terms, what the men find along the way: 'Women were dead in the yards, and there was a twelve year old girl with her mind gone completely and forever to her torn nakedness... And nothing is worse than burying women the Apaches have worked over; nothing is worse than an insane girl digging down again to her mother's dead face in the starlight.' (The 'insane' girl appears again in Ford's *The Searchers*, 1956 as well as traumatized children in *Yellow Ribbon*.)

For days, the troop trails the Lipans, Kickapoos, and Apaches until Massarene is ready to go into Mexico after them. Then he acts decisively. 'I'm burning out everything in my path – everything Kickapoo, Lipan and Apache and anything else that the darkness fails to distinguish. I'm going through like a scourge... so that the next five hours will be remembered for twenty years to come... You will leave your dead, shoot wounded horses and lash your wounded in their saddles.' Bellah enumerates the consequences of Massarene's mission and of his orders: 'There it is. No easy commitment, no racing flight in daylight across your own terrain with reserves behind you and surgeons to stop your bone-broken screaming... If your mount goes down on this, you're done to get back, unless you catch a free mount... If you're hit, you're done, unless a Bunkie ties you on. If you break, Cohill will shoot you like a dog. And if you are a hero, no one will see it in the darkness for a cheap reward.'

The raids in Bellah's stories are savage and intense. (In the film the only raid has the sole purpose of rescuing the captive children.) Yet, Massarene burns out seven villages with his men: 'Coming down like an avalanche from the darkness, leaving nothing behind but the wail of savage women.' In the blood and dust of the final raid, Colonel Massarene's son picks up a fallen soldier, only to have his mount, in turn, fall. His father secures a new mount and brings it through a hail of gunfire to his son and the other soldier. At that point a bullet strikes Massarene 'like a rock hurled into mud.' And 'it was also that he saw young Massarene's shoulder and upper arm torn clean open to the white bones.'

Now Bellah does something unexpected. He allows a change of heart in Massarene (and one that oddly foreshadows the sudden change of heart in the climatic scene of *The Searchers* that turns John Wayne's hatred of his niece to love). In *Rio Grande*, wounded father confronts wounded son and the wounds of years are healed: 'You're hurt...' says the father. 'That doesn't matter, does it, sir?' replies the son. Bellah ended the story with this line: 'The years they had lost were forgotten and the debt was paid in full.' Both film and story end on the same note of reconciliation, err on the side of believability, and are probably transparent to the average viewer.[63]

With Brittles on the Frontier

In *Empire: The Rise and Demise of the British World Order and the Lessons of Global Power* (2003), historian Niall Ferguson reflects on 'America's informal empire – the empire of multinational corporations, of Hollywood movies, and even TV evangelists' and the role of the United States as the hesitant successor to Great Britain. He reminds us of Kipling's appeal to Americans to 'Take up the White Man's Burden.' However, 'no one,' he judges, 'would dare use such politically incorrect language today.' Ferguson concludes that, 'The reality is nevertheless that the United States has – whether it admits it or not – taken up some kind of global burden, just as Kipling urged.' Later, in *Colossus: The Price of American Empire* (2004), Ferguson quotes journalist Max Boot's article in 'The Case for American Empire' in *The Weekly Standard*: 'Afghanistan and other troubled lands today cry out for the sort of enlightened foreign administration once provided by self-confident Englishmen in jodhpurs and pith helmets.'[64]

Recently in America, there has been a renewed interest in the works of the late-nineteenth century imperial writer G. A. Henty (1837–1902), 'the Boy's Own Historian.' He wrote over 140 historical adventures aimed at young boys, among them: *With Clive in India*, *The Dash for Kartoum: A Tale of the Nile Expedition*, *With Kitchener in the Soudan, A Story of Atbara and Omdurman*, *The March of Magdala: A Chronicle of the Abyssinian Campaign*, *At the Point of the Bayonet: A Tale of the Mahratta War*, *With Lee in Virginia*, and *Redskin and Cowboy: A Tale of the Western Plains*. His books (the series reprinted for the Unites States market) have become popular with the increasing numbers of American conservative home-schoolers attracted to stories for their children that celebrate sturdy character, patriotism, military service, and national destiny.

Ford's homage to America's imperial frontier cavalry, resonates today as the American Army seeks to pacify the old imperial frontiers of Afghanistan, Iraq, and other remote regions of the world, much as the British regiments had done earlier to protect their empire's commercial and strategic interests, even to American soldiers in Baghdad serving alongside a unit of Gurkhas, Britain's old imperial mercenaries. In *She Wore a Yellow Ribbon*, Captain Brittles is 'fated to wield the sword of destiny,' proclaims the film's narrator. Today, 'We don't know what division will go to the frontier of freedom,' a lieutenant colonel at West Point said to his cadets (in 2001), 'But I can guarantee you this: this class *will* move out, will go into the ranks of the Army. And somewhere, in some disputed barricade along the frontier, you will meet your destiny.'[65]

Notes

[1] Quoted in Anderson, *About John Ford*, 242.
[2] All three films deal with similar subjects, characters, themes, and locations; however, the series is not a trilogy proper since the stories are not directly connected or told in sequence. 'It is common to refer to Ford's cavalry trilogy as if each film was a piece of a planned whole, but in

truth he never planned to make three John Wayne cavalry films. It was more of a case of demand creating product.' In Roberts and Olson, *John Wayne: American*, 321–2.

[3] *Fort Apache*. 127 m, b/w. Argosy Pictures–RKO Radio. Director: John Ford. Producers: John Ford, Merian C. Cooper. Screenplay: Frank S. Nugent. Story Author: James Warner Bellah. Based on the short story 'Massacre' by James Warner Bellah. Camera: Archie Stout and Louis Clyde Stouman. Music Score: Richard Hageman. Research Editor: Catherine Cliffton. Technical Advisors: Major Phillip Kieffer, U.S. Army, retired, and Katherine Spaatz,. Costume Research: D.R.O. Hatswell. Locations: Corrigan Ranch, Simi Valley, California; Monument Valley, Arizona; Mexican Hat, Gooseneck, Utah, and RKO soundstages. Argosy Pictures–RKO Radio. Filmed, June–July 1947. Released: 9 November 1948.

[4] *She Wore a Yellow Ribbon*. 103m. color. Director: John Ford. Producers: John Ford, Merian C. Cooper. Screenplay: Frank S. Nugent, Laurence Stallings. Camera: Winton C. Hoch, Charles P. Boyle. Art Director: James Basevi. Narrator: Irving Pichel. Based on the short stories 'War Party' and 'Big Hunt' by James Warner Bellah. Music: Richard Hegeman. Technical Advisors: Major Phillip Kieffer, US Army, retired, Cliff Lyons. Costume Research: D.R.O. Hatswell,. Locations: Monument Valley, Arizona and Mexican Hat, Utah. Argosy Pictures-RKO Radio. Filmed, November–December, 1948. Released: 22 October 1949.

[5] *Rio Grande*. 105m. b/w. Director: John Ford. Producers: John Ford, Merian C. Cooper. Screenplay: James K. McGuinness. Camera: Bert Glennon and Archie Stout. Music Score: Victor Young. Songwriters: Dale Evans, Stan Jones, Tex Owens. Based on the short story 'Mission with No Record' by James Warner Bellah. Technical Advisor: Phillip Kieffer, US Army, retired. Uniforms: D.R.O. Hatswell. Locations: Moab, Utah at White's Rock, Professor Valley, Onion Creek Narrows. Argosy Pictures-Republic. Released: 15 November, 1950.

[6] Utley, *Frontier Regulars*, xiv.

[7] Countryman, 'Westerns in United States History,' 21.

[8] Evans, *Brassey's Guide to War Films*, 172.

[9] Thompson, *The New Biographical Dictionary of Film*, 304–5.

[10] Westerbrook, 'The Night John Wayne Danced with Shirley Temple;' Buhle and Wagner, *Radical Hollywood*, 138. One critic even sought to connect Ford to the issue of global nuclear proliferation. See Nolly, 'Printing the Legend in the Age of MX,' 82–8.

[11] Wills, *John Wayne's America*, 287.

[12] Ibid.

[13] McBride, *Searching for John Ford*, 447.

[14] Fraser, *The Hollywood History of the World*, xi–xii. His 'Flashman' series combines wit and rousing action within an accurate historical context.

[15] Ibid., 179.

[16] Utley, *Frontier Regulars*, xiv.

[17] *The Black Watch*. 93 m, b/w. Director: John Ford. Co-Director ('staged by'), Lumsden Hare. Screenplay: James Kevin McGuinness and John Stone from the novel *King of the Khyber Rifles* by Talbot Mundy. Camera: Joseph E. August. Fox. Released: 8 May 1929.

[18] *The Lost Patrol*. 74 minutes, b/w. Director: John Ford. Executive Producer: Merian C. Cooper. From the story 'Patrol' by Philip McDonald. Camera: Harold Wendstrom. Music: Max Steiner. RKO Radio Pictures. Location: Yuma, Arizona desert. Released: 16 February 1934.

[19] *Wee Willie Winkie*. 99–105 m, b/w. Director: John Ford. Producer: Darryl F. Zanuck. Screenplay: Ernest Pacal, Julian Josephson, Howard Ellis Smith, Mordaunt Shairp. From the story by Rudyard Kipling. Camera: Arthur Miller. Music: Alfred Newman. Location: Chatsworth, 40 miles from Los Angeles, California. 20th Century Fox. Released: 25 June 1937.

[20] Wills, *John Wayne's America*, 169.

[21] Sarris, *The John Ford Movie Mystery*, 128.

[22] Ephraim Katz, 'McLaglan, Victor,' in *The Film Encyclopedia*, New York: Thomas Y. Crowell, 1979.

[23] Quoted in Gilmore, *The Long Recessional*, 50.

[24] Wills, *John Wayne's America*, 24.
[25] Doherty, *Projections of War*, 270.
[26] Prater, 'John Ford's Cavalry Trilogy: Myth and Reality,' 28.
[27] Bosley Crowther, review of *She Wore a Yellow Ribbon* in *The New York Times Guide to the Best 1,000 Movies Ever Made*: Vincent Canby, Janet Maslin and the Film Critics of The New York Times, edited by Peter M. Nichols, New York, Three Rivers Press, 1999, 771.
[28] Prater, 'John Ford's Cavalry Trilogy,' 81.
[29] Ibid., 136.
[30] Quoted in Eyman, *Print the Legend*, 350. Ellipses are in the original quotation. Ford's letter is among the documents relating to *She Wore a Yellow Ribbon* (1949) in the John Ford Papers, Lilly Library, Indiana University.
[31] Bogdanovich, *John Ford*, 87.
[32] Quoted in Dipple, *Remington & Russell*, 3.
[33] Hassrick, *Frederic Remington*, 19.
[34] Frederic Remington, *Crooked Trails*, 63. (Page citation is to the reprint edition.)
[35] Hassrick, *Remington*, 24.
[36] Buscombe, 'Painting the Legend: Frederic Remington and the Western,' 163.
[37] Ibid., 165.
[38] Remington, *Crooked Trails*, 63.
[39] O'Brien, *Castaways of the Image Planet*, 20.
[40] McBride, *Searching for John Ford*, 448.
[41] Prater, 'John Ford's Cavalry Trilogy,' 15.
[42] Quoted in McBride, *Searching for John Ford*, 448.
[43] Horan, *The Life and Art of Charles Schreyvogle*, 5.
[44] Baxter, 'John Ford,' 176.
[45] McBride, *Searching for John Ford*, 457.
[46] For a discussion of romantic myth and cynicism in the film, see Dautelbaum, 'The Narrative Structure of *She Wore a Yellow Ribbon*,' 60–70.
[47] Ford, *Pappy: The Life of John Ford*, 214.
[48] Obituary, *New York Times*, 24 September 1976.
[49] 'James Warner Bellah on Writing for Money,' *New York Times Book Review*, 7 July 1940.
[50] Bellah, 'Massacre,' *Saturday Evening Post*, 22 February 1947, 18–18,140–46.
[51] Bellah, 'Mission With No Record,' *Saturday Evening Post*, 27 September 1947. 30–31, 138, 140, 142, 144.
[52] Bellah, 'Big Hunt,' *Saturday Evening Post*, 6 December 1947, 22–3, 199, 201, 202.
[53] James Warner Bellah, 'War Party,' *Saturday Evening Post*, 19 June 1948, 22–3, 104, 107, 109–10.
[54] Agee, *Agee on Film*, 309. And Thompson, 'McLaglen,' 587.
[55] Davis, *John Ford: Hollywood's Old Master*, 204.
[56] Sarris, '*You Ain't Heard Nothin' Yet*,' 208.
[57] See Poague, 'All I Can See is the Flags,' 8–25.
[58] Quoted in Eyman, *Print the Legend*, 331.
[59] Quoted in Ibid., 331–2.
[60] Slotkin, *Gunfighter Nation*, 335.
[61] James Warner Bellah, 'She Wore a Yellow Ribbon (First Detailed Treatment) Screenplay,' unpublished screenplay (photocopy), 1, John Ford Manuscripts, Lilly Library, Indiana University, Bloomington, Indiana.
[62] For a gender-sensitive approach that the gruff Ford might have scoffed at, see Leighninger, Jr. 'The Western as Male Soap Opera: John Ford's *Rio Grande*,' 135–8.
[63] Ferguson, *Empire*, 368–70. Quoted in Ferguson, *Colossus*, 4.
[64] See Allen, 'G. A. Henty & the Vision of Empire. Available from newcriterion.com/archive (26 October 2003); INTERNET.
[65] Lipsky, *Absolutely American*, 56. Emphasis in the original.

References

Agee, James. *Agee on Film: Criticism and Comment on the Movies*, with an introduction by David Denby, series editor, Martin Scorsese. New York: Modern Library, 2002, originally published 1959.
Allen, Brooke. 'G. A. Henty & the Vision of Empire,' *The New Criterion* 20, no. 8 (April 2002): 1–7.
Anderson, Lindsay. *About John Ford*. New York: McGraw-Hill Book Company, 1983.
Baxter, John. 'John Ford.' In *The St. James Film Directors Encyclopedia*, edited by Andrew Sarris. Detroit: Visible Ink Press, 1998.
Bellah, James Warner. 'She Wore a Yellow Ribbon (First Detailed Treatment) Screenplay.' Unpublished screenplay (photocopy). John Ford Manuscripts, Lilly Library, Indiana University, Bloomington, Indiana.
Bogdanovich, Peter. *John Ford*. Berkeley: University of California Press, 1978.
Bosley, Crowther. 'Review of *She Wore a Yellow Ribbon*.' In *The New York Times Guide to the Best 1,000 Movies Ever Made: Vincent Canby, Janet Maslin and the Film Critics of the New York Times*, edited by Peter M. Nichols. New York: Three Rivers Press, 1999.
Brauer, Ralph. 'The Fractured Eye: Myth and History in the Westerns of John Ford and Sam Peckinpah.' *Film and History* 7, no. 4 (1977): 73–84.
Buscombe, Edward. 'Painting the Legend: Frederic Remington and the Western.' In *John Ford Made Westerns: Filming the Legend in the Sound Era*, edited by Gaylyn Studlar and Matthew Berstein. Bloomington and Indianapolis: Indiana University Press, 2001.
Countryman, Edward. 'Westerns in United States History.' *History Today* 33, no. 3 (March 1983).
Davis, Ronald L. *John Ford: Hollywood's Old Master*. Norman, Oklahoma and London: University of Oklahoma Press, 1995.
Degle, Joan. 'Linear Patterns and Ethnic Encounters in Ford Westerns.' In *John Ford Made Westerns: Filming the Legend in the Sound Era*, edited by Gaylyn Studler and Matthew Bernstein, 102–31. Bloomington and Indianapolis: University of Illinois Press, 2001.
Deutelbaum, Marshall. 'The Narrative Structure of *She Wore a Yellow Ribbon*.' *Cinema Journal* XIX, no. I (Fall 1979): 60–70.
Dipple Brian W., ed. *Remington & Russell*. Austin, Texas: University of Texas Press, 1982.
Donald L. Davis. *John Ford: Hollywood's Old Master*. The Oklahoma Western Biographies, edited by Richard W. Etulain. Norman and London: University of Oklahoma Press, 1995.
Eastman, John. *Retakes: Behind the Scenes of 500 Classic Movies*. New York: Ballantine Books, 1989.
Evans, Alun. *Brassey's Guide to War Films*. Washington, DC: Brassey's, 2000.
Eyman, Scott. *Print the Legend: The Life and Times of John Ford*, Johns Hopkins Paperbacks, 2000 ed. Baltimore, Maryland: Simon & Schuster, 1999.
Ferguson, Niall. *Collossus: The Price of American Empire*. New York: The Penguin Press, 2002.
Ferguson, Niall. *Empire: The Rise and Demise of Britain's World Order and the Lesson for World Power*. New York: Basic Books, 2003.
Ford, Dan. *Pappy: The Life of John Ford*. Englewood Cliffs, New Jersey: Prentice-Hall, 1979.
Fraser, George MacDonald. *The Hollywood History of the World: From One Million B.C. to Apocalypse Now*. New York: Beech Tree Books, William Morrow, 1988.
Gallagher, Ted. 'John Ford's Indians.' *Film Comment* 29, no. 5 (September–October 1993): 68–72.
Hassrick, Peter H. *Frederic Remington: Paintings, Drawings, and Sculpture in the Amon Carter Museum and the Sid Richardson Foundation Collections*, New Concise N. A. L. Edition. New York: Harry N. Abrams, 1975.
Heffernan, Jeanne. '"Poised between Savagery and Civilization": Forging Political Communities in Ford's Westerns.' *Perspectives on Political Science* 28, no. 3 (Summer 1999): 147–51.
Horan, James D. *The Life and Art of Charles Schreyvogle: Painter-Historian of the Indian-Fighting Army of the American West*. New York: Crown Publisher, 1969.
Leighninger, Jr., Robert D. 'The Western as Male Soap Opera: John Ford's *Rio Grande*.' *The Journal of Men's Studies* 6, no. 2 (Winter 1998): 135–8.
Lipsky, David. *Absolutely American: Four Years at West Point*. Boston: Houghton Miffin, 2003.

McBride, Joseph. *Searching for John Ford: A Life*. New York: St. Martin's Press, 1999.

Nolly, Ken. 'Printing the Legend in the Age of MX: Reconsidering Ford's Military Trilogy.' *Film Quartelry* 14, no. 2 (1986): 82–8.

O'Brien, Geoffery. *Castaways of the Image Planet*. New York: Counterpoint Books, 2002.

Poague, Leland. '"All I Can See is the Flags": *Fort Apache* and the Visibility of History.' *Cinema Journal* 27, no. 2 (Winter 1988): 8–25.

Prater, Jeffery. 'John Ford's Cavalry Trilogy.' Ph.D. diss., US Army Command and General Staff College, Leavenworth, Kansas, 1989.

Prater, Jeffery. 'John Ford's Cavalry Trilogy: Myth or Reality?' M.A. Thesis, US Army Command and General Staff College, Leavenworth, KA, 1989.

Remington, Frederic. *Crooked Trails*. New York and London: Harper & Brothers, 1899; reprint, Scituate: Digital Scanning, 2001.

Sarris, Andrew. *'You Ain't Heard Nothin' Yet': The American Talking Film – History and Memory, 1927–1949*. New York: Oxford University Press, 1998.

Sarris, Andrew. *The John Ford Movie Mystery*. Bloomington and London: Indiana University Press, 1975.

Slotkin, Richard. *Gunfighter Nation: The Myth of the Frontier in Twentieth-century America*. New York: Athenaeum, 1992.

Thomas Doherty. *Projections of War: Hollywood, American Culture, and World War II*. New York: Columbia University Press, 1993.

Thompson, David. *The New Biographical Dictionary of Film*, 4th ed. New York: Alfred A. Knopf, 2002.

Utley, Robert M. *Frontier Regulars: The United States Army and the Indian, 1866–1891*. New York: MacMillan Publishing Co., 1973.

Wagner, Dave, and Buhle, Paul. *Radical Hollywood: The Untold Story Behind America's Favorite Movies*. New York: The New Press, 2002.

Westerbrook, Max. 'The Night John Wayne Danced with Shirley Temple.' *Western American Literature* 25, no.2 (1990), 157–69.

Notes on Contributors

Joseph G. Dawson III is professor of history at Texas A&M University, College Station, Texas. His research interests address the American military, including the army, navy, and Marine Corps, especially during the nineteenth century. His publications include *Army Generals and Reconstruction: Louisiana, 1862–1877* (1982) and *Doniphan's Epic March* (1999).

Brian Holden Reid is professor of American history and military institutions and Head of the Department of War Studies at King's College London. Since 1993 he has been a member of the Council of the Society for Army Historical Research and served as chairman 1998–2004. His books include *The Origins of the American Civil War* (1996) and *Robert E. Lee: Icon for a Nation* (2005).

Martin A. Novelli is Dean of Humanities, Fine Arts, and Media Studies at Ocean County College in Toms River, New Jersey. He has taught and written on the Vietnam War, the politics and culture of the 1960s, and western film and literature.

Glenn Robins is assistant professor of history and director of the honors program at Georgia Southwestern State University. He is currently editing for publication the Civil War prison diary of Sergeant Lyle Adair, 111th United States Colored Infantry. His *The Bishop of the Old South: The Ministry and Civil War Career of Leonidas Polk* is forthcoming with Mercer University Press.

William B. Skelton is professor emeritus of history at the University of Wisconsin-Stevens Point, where he taught from 1969 to 2002. His book, *An American Profession of Arms: The Army Officer Corps, 1784–1861* (1992), received a Distinguished Book Award from the Society for Military History. He is currently working on a study of the army's commanding generals and the issue of civilian control of the military during the nineteenth century.

Samuel J. Watson is associate professor of history at the United States Military Academy, West Point, New York, where he teaches United States history. He is the author of *Federal Diplomats: The Army Officer Corps in the Borderlands of the Early Republic* (forthcoming, University Press of Kansas, 2006).

Frank J. Wetta is Vice President of Academic Affairs at Ocean County College in Toms River, New Jersey. He is co-author with Stephen J. Curley of *Celluloid Wars: A Guide to Film and the American Experience of War* (1992).

Robert P. Wettemann, Jr. is an assistant professor of History at McMurry University in Abilene, Texas. His current research interests include civil–military relations and public history. In addition to his academic work, he serves as Director of Historical Interpretation for the Grady McWhiney Research Foundation. Based in Abilene, Texas, the Foundation owns and operates the Buffalo Gap Historic Village, The McWhiney Foundation and State House Presses, and The McWhiney Collection.

Robert Wooster is a professor of history at Texas A&M University-Corpus Christi, where he has taught since 1986. His books include *The Military and United States Indian Policy, 1865–1903* (1988); *Nelson A. Miles and the Twilight of the Frontier Army* (1993); and *The Civil War 100: A Ranking of the Most Influential People in the War Between the States* (1998).

Index

Abert, Colonel John J. 67
Adams, John Quincy 20, 21, 22, 59, 60, 61, 85
Afghanistan 10
American civil military relations 2
American Indians 35
American political traditions 15
Anderson, John 60
Apache, Fort 10
Aristocratic Elite 7
Army; standing 3
Artillery School 21, 29
Arts of peace 2
Ashanti Wars 10
Atlanta; expulsion of civil population 9

Baker, Cushing 124
Baker, Edward 121, 131
Barbour, James 20
Barney, Joshua 60
Bartlett, Harriet 36
Bartlett, William H 36
Barton, Alexander S. 42
Beard, William 90
Balkan, William W. 5, 43
Bell, Peter H. 130
Bella, James Warner 9, 169
Bellows, Barbara 144
Bissell, William H. 118, 121, 130
Bloom, John 124
Board of visitor 96
Bourke, John G. 166
Bowles, William A. 12, 121, 130
Bradbury, Malcolm 156
Breckinridge, John C. 130
Brent, J. L. 150
Britain 1, 9, 10; army 2, 3, 10, 11; USA 3, 10
British leaders; (1914) 9
Brown, Major General Jacob 3, 86, 92
Buchanan, James 69, 70, 130

Bell, Don Carlos 7
Burnett Ward B. 119
Burnside, Ambrose E. (Senator) 42, 44
Burr, Aaron 18, 90
Buncombe, Edward 168
Butler, Benjamin 68
Butler Pierce M. 119

Calhoun, John C. 3, 6, 19, 20, 21, 57, 58, 59; biographers 3
Call, Richard K. 93
Calvary Trilogy 166
Campbell, William B. 121
Carlyle, Thomas 8, 150
Cass, Lewis 6, 23, 24, 62, 63, 67
Chase, William H. 67
Cheatham, Benjamin F. 121
Civil control 16
Civil military friction 17, 25
Civil military nexus 16, 21
Civil military relations 16, 17, 22, 24, 28, 92
Civil war 6, 8, 11, 16, 29, 37, 38, 46, 47, 86
Clark, Charles 121
Clausewitz, General Karl 118
Clay, Henry 61
Cochrane, Thomas 150
Coffey, John 125
cold war 10
colonial legislation 16
commanding general 18, 19, 20, 24
Confederacy 9
Congress 7, 19, 20, 25
Conkling, Roscoe 43
constitution (USA) 16
Cook, William 60, 61
Cooper, James 67
corp of engineers 23, 59, 62, 96
Cortina, Juan 94
coup; military 3
Creek, Wilson 36

Crockett, David 64
Cromwell, Oliver(Lord Protector) 3
Crow, Jim 143, 158
Cruz, Vera 27
Cullum, George 65, 66
Cunliffe, Marcus 118
Curti, Merle 2
Curtis, Samuel R. 119, 124
Cushing, Caleb 28, 118
Custer, George A. 265

Dakin, James H. 121
Davis, Horatio 119
Davis, Jefferson 3, 4, 5, 28, 100, 119, 132
Davis, Reuben 118, 127
Dawson, Joseph G. III 7, 8
Delafield, Richard H. 101
democracy; Jacksonian 6, 7
Democratic Party *122, 123, 126, 129*
D'Eon, Chevalier 147
DeRussy,Lewis G. 117, 119
dictatorship; military 3
Dillahunty, John 60
Dix, Roger 67
Doniphan, Alexander 121, 127
Doolittle, James R. 40
Drake, James 121, 130
Drake, James P. 121
Duffy, Christopher 154

Eaton, John 62
enlightenment 9
Evarts, William M. 40

Ferry, Thomas W. 43
Fessenden, William P. 40
films 9-10
Findlay, John 60
Flintridge Cohill (Lieutenant) 170, 171
Floyd, John B. 28, 29
Ford, John 9, 10
Foreman, Ferris 118, 121
Fort, Adams 65
Fremont, John C. 94

Fuller, E. W. 150
Fuller, Sam 162

Gaines, Edmund P. 21, 67, 91, 93, 94
Garfield, James A. 45
Gates, John M. 5, 6, 36, 56
Geary, John 121, 130
general order No. 48, 67, 68
general staff bureaus 19, 20
General Survey Act (1824) 6, 56, 57, 59, 63, 66, 69, 70, 86, 96
Gilpin, William 121
Gorman, Willis A. 121
Graham, James 62
Grant, General Ulysses S. 4, 17, 36, 37, 41, 43, 44, 46, 47
Great Plains 10
Grimes, James 40
Grimsley, Marks 8
Grotius, Hugo 154
guerrilla war in Florida 24
Gulf of Mexico 45
Gwnn, Walter 60

Hackett Fisher, David 1
Halleck, Henry W. 4, 9, 30, 87, 154
Hamtramck, John F. 117, 120, 125
Hancock, Winfield Scott 43, 45
Hardin, John J. 120, 121, 127
Harney, William S. 29, 94
Harrison, William Henry 26
Hart Benton, Thomas 27, 92, 94
Haskell, William T. 120
Hassrick, Peter 168
Hawes, Albert G. 64
Hayes, Rutherford B. 7, 43, 44, 45, 46
Hays, John Coffee 120
Hazzard, Edward 60
Heintzelman, Second Lieutenant S. 55, 56
Henty, G. A. (1837; 1902) 179
Hill, D. H. 87
Holden Reid, B. 1-11
Hood, John B. 8, 9, 36, 151, 158

House of Representatives 8
Hughes, George W. 117
Hull, William 116

Irvin, Colonel William 119

Jackson, Andrew 6, 23, 61, 62, 67, 84, 89, 90, 91, 93, 94
Jackson, Henry R. 118, 121, 125
Jacksonian 81, 82, 88, 89, 90
James, William 2
Jefferson, Thomas 85, 118
Jeffrey, Francis (Canon of St Paul's) 146
Jennings Brown, Jacob 19, 20, 21
Johnson, Andrew 4, 17, 38, 40, 41, 46
Johnston, Albert Sidney 119, 131
Johnston, Joseph E. 9
Jones, Colonel Roger 23, 27, 66

Kearney, James 70
Kearney, Stephen W. 94
Kings College; London 5
Kohn, Richard H. 18
Korean war 10

Lane, James H. 121
Lane, Joseph 122
Latrobe, Benjamin 59
Lee, Robert E. 7, 8, 9, 151
Lincoln, Abraham 29, 36
Linn, Brian M. 11
Linn, Lewis F. 92
Logan, John A. 132
Long, James 90
Long, Stephen 67
lost cause 8, 9, 10
Lovell, Harrison Rousseau 40
Luttrell, John K. 42

McBride, Joseph 163
McClellan, George B. 7, 29, 148, 151, 173
McConnell, H. H. 166
McKee William R. 119
Mackenzie, Randall S. 167
McLaglen, Victor 165

McNeill, William 63, 66
Macomb, Alexander 22, 23, 24, 25, 26, 28, 30, 62, 65, 71
McPherson, James 1
Madison, James 18, 57, 84, 85
Magee, Augustus 90
Major Thursday 172
Mann, Anthony 162
Marks, Samuel 130
Marshall, Charles 8
Marshall, Humphrey 120, 121
Massarene, D. L. 177, 178
Maximillian 38, 46
Maysville Veto 6, 62, 70
Metcalfe, Thomas 60
Mexican War 4, 7, 26, 51, 71
Mexico; government in exile 37, 38
Michell, Alexander M. 119
Miles, Wilson A. 4
military affairs 23
military authority 18
military challenge to civilian authority 16
military coup d'etat 3, 16
military dictatorship 3
military education 7, 20
military functions 16
military management 22
Military Peace Establishment Act 57
military professionalism 4
Mina Xavier 91
Monroe, James 3, 19, 59, 84, 85, 94, 98
Morgan, George W. 119, 130
Mountbatten; Lord 169
Mrs. Yorke 177

Napier, Sir William 9
Naval war with France 18
Navy department 23
new military history 2
new south 9
New York volunteers 20
Newburgh conspiracy 16
Newby, Edward 121
Niagara battles 26

190 *Index*

Northern material and technological superiority 9
Novelli, Martin 9, 10
Nunnelle, S. F. 125

O'Brien, Geoffrey 168
operational military history 2
Ord, E.O.C. 39
order no. 62, 63, 68, 69
Oregon 71, 116
Ormsby, Stephen 121
Owen, Wilfred 9, 158
Owsley, William 117

Paine, Robert 126, 131
Patridge, Alden 95
Pearl Harbor 42, 46
Peckinpah, Sam 162
Penn, Arthur 162
Pennock, Alexander M. 42
Peyton, Balie 121
Pickett, George 94
Pierce, Franklin 4, 8, 28, 64, 94, 129
Pierpont, Francis H. 39
Poinsett, Joel R. 24, 25, 69
Political Party Affiliation by Region *122*
Political Party Affiliation by State *123*
Polk, James K. 26, 27, 91, 92, 93, 94, 116, 117
Pope, Joan 39
Porter, Peter B. 21, 22
Postwar Political and Military Participation *129*
Prater, Jeffery 167, 177
Pre-War Political and Military Experience *126*
Price, Sterling 121
Prussia 4, 5, *see also* Clausewitz

radical assault 7
radical republicans 7
Radicals 7
Ralls, John 121
Randolph, Thomas B. 120

Rawlins, John A. 4, 5, 41
Ray, Nicholas 162
reason and romanticism 8
reconstruction 17, 29, 36, 38, 46, 47
relief and protection of refugees 10
Remington, Frederic 9, 166, 167
report of roads and canals 58
Republicans 38, 40
revolution 17, 18; army 16
Rhode Island 65, 66
Rio Grande 10, 26, 37, 38
Ripley, Eleazar 90
Rives, Alexander 39
Rives, William 59
Roberts, William B.122 121, 127
Robins, Glen 8, 9, 10
Romero, Matias 37, 38
Root, Elihu (Secretary of War) 44
Ruff, Charles 127

Sassoon, Siegfried 9, 158
Schofield Board 41
Schofield, John M. 4, 30, 36, 39, 41, 43, 45, 46, 47
Second Seminole War 86
Secretary of War 18, 21, 26, 40
Seward, William 37
She wore a yellow ribbon 10
Sheridan, Philip H. 37, 39, 41, 177
Sherman, William T. 4, 5, 9, 36, 37, 41, 43, 44, 46, 47, 151
Sickles, David 39
Sidney Jessup, Thomas 89
Simmons, Seneca 67
Skelton, William 3, 56
Snyder, Antes 66
Southhall Freeman, Douglas 145
Spanish-American war 16, 46
standing army 3
Stanton, Edwin M. 40
Stephens, Alexander H. 9, 148, 151
Stevenson, Jonathan 121
Stevenson, Jonathan D. 117
Stockton, Thomas B.W. 117, 119

Stoneman, George 40
Stonewall, Jackson 9
Swift Joseph G. 95
Swift, William 63

Tate, Michael 5, 35, 36
Taylor, Richard 8, 9, 158
Taylor, Zachary 27, 91, 92, 93
technological superiority
  (northern material) 9
Thayer, Sylvanus 85, 95, 100
Thomas, George H. 41
Thomas, Philip 60
Thompson, David 162
Tilden, Samuel J. 43, 46
Tommy 9
topographical engineers 24, 60
Totten, Joseph G. 65
Transcontinental Treaty (1821) 91
Trimble, Isaac 60
Tunnard (Battle of Oak Hills)
  155, 156, 158
Tunnard, W. H. 8, 9
Turnbull, William 67
Tyler, John 26

United States of America (USA): Military
  Academy (Westpoint) 3, 6, 7, 17, 26,
  28, 29, 36, 44, 45, 46, 47, 57, 58, 61, 65;
  ministry officials 37
Upton, Emory 132

Values of Contemporary Urban (USA) 5
Van Buren, Martin 6, 24, 68, 69, 70, 71,
  89, 93
Vattell de, Emerich 9, 154
Ver Planck Van Antwerp 69
Vietnan War 5, 10
volunteer colonels 7, 115-41
Vroon, Peter 62

Wade, Benjamin F. 7
War Department 96

Washington, George
  (Continental Army) 16, 18, 27
Waterhouse, Richard 120
Watson, Samuel J. 6, 7
Wayne, John 163
Weatherford, William 121
Weigley, Russell E. 2, 10, 11, 56
Wellington, Duke of 3
Wells, Henry Horatio 39
West pointers 7
Wetta, Frank 9, 10
Wettemann, Robert 5, 6
Whig Party 7, 8, 26, 115, *122*, *123*, *126*,
  129
Whistler, George 66
White, Edward 63
White Geary, John 121
White, Leonard 101
Whittaker, Johnson C. 44, 45, 46
Wilkinson, James 18, 90, 116
Williams, Harry T. 7
Williams, Jonathan 95, 101
Williams, William G. 67
Wills, Garry 163, 164
Winders, Richard Bruce 115
Winfield Scott, Major General H. 4, 20,
  27, 28, 67, 86, 88, 89, 91, 92
women 2
Wood, Fernando 36
Wood, George T. 130
Wool, John 127
Wooster, Robert 4, 5, 6
World War I 9
World War II 10
Wright, Isaac 122
Wynkoop, Francis 121

Yell, Archibald 118, 120, 122
York, Kirby 173
Young, William C. 120

Zulus 10

For Product Safety Concerns and Information please contact our EU
representative GPSR@taylorandfrancis.com
Taylor & Francis Verlag GmbH, Kaufingerstraße 24, 80331 München, Germany

www.ingramcontent.com/pod-product-compliance
Lightning Source LLC
Chambersburg PA
CBHW081817300426
44116CB00014B/2391